CONSTITUTIONAL PROTECTION OF EQUALITY

Studies in Comparative Law
under the Auspices of the
Netherlands Association of Comparative Law

No. 2

CONSTITUTIONAL PROTECTION OF EQUALITY

edited by

T. KOOPMANS

Professor of Constitutional Law
University of Leyden, the Netherlands

A. W. SIJTHOFF — LEYDEN
1975

ISBN 90 286 0355 7

Printed in the Netherlands.

Se la teoria della giustizia è stata trascurata dai giuristi, non si può dire che i filosofi l'abbiano intensamente coltivata; del resto, se c'è da aspettarsi un progresso in questo campo di studi, questo dipenderà non tanto da astratte speculazioni sul concetto di giustizia, quanto dallo sviluppo degli studi di diritto comparato, che si trovano, un po' dappertutto, in istato di deplorevole arretratezza.

Norberto Bobbio
Giusnaturalismo e positivismo
giuridico (2da ed. Milano 1972).

(The theory of justice, if neglected by the jurists, cannot be said to have been intensively cultivated by the philosophers; besides, if any progress in this field of studies is to be expected, it will not so much depend upon abstract speculations on the concept of justice, as on the development of studies of comparative law, which are almost everywhere very badly in arrears.)

Table of Contents

1

T. Koopmans

Introduction

1. Comparative constitutional law presents some of the features characteristic of comparative law in general: it is usually thought to be a very important object for legal research, but practice corresponds scarcely to this theory. Literature on the necessity of doing comparative legal research has been abundant, but it was not followed by a flow of books and articles which replied to this appeal. As far as comparative constitutional law is concerned, it still lacks a firm body of doctrine.

This situation makes one wonder about the causes. True, comparative law is a difficult subject, but so are the British law of real estate and the French law of torts. The difference is, of course, that British and French lawyers can avail themselves of a strong tradition when they think and write about their municipal law: there is no need for them to develop their own *methods* of dealing with legal questions. For the lawyer, municipal law constitutes a 'system', constructed in the course of some centuries and consisting in particular of a set of highly interdependent notions, arranged and classified in such a way as to facilitate the solution of practical legal problems. Lawyers make implicitly use of this system, by fitting their views into it: they analyse and interpret some of its notions, they oppose or favour the application of a particular notion to a particular case, they sometimes rearrange classifications and they always give an appreciation of the way these operations contribute to solving legal problems.

It may be obvious that such a sophisticated basis for legal reasoning fails in comparative constitutional law. Still, literature on methods and techniques of conducting legal research in this field is scant. For a long time, the aim was more or less to describe and to compare entire constitutional systems. This approach may be useful for political scientists, who might draw conclusions from such a comparison as to how effective different constitutional systems are in transforming, for instance, political demands into legislative or administrative action. For lawyers, however, the approach is not very adequate: they feel that for them it would only result in a juxtaposition of systems, not in the kind of comparative analysis which might be of interest to them. But if entire constitutional systems seem too large and elaborate to be manageable for legal doctrine, the question arises what kind of more modest scope for comparative research could yield better results.

First of all, one could think of comparing institutions. This may seem fairly simple – one could think of comparing for example the powers and composition of the American Congress to those of British Parliament –, but the method raises many difficulties. Institutions are working within a certain constitutional framework and against a certain social background: they can hardly be examined when cut loose from their roots – which brings us back to comparing entire systems. And this is by no means the only disadvantage. When one takes, for example, such a famous institution as the French *Conseil d'Etat,* it will be clear that an institution of that kind simply doesn't exist in countries like Britain or the United States. Its judicial tasks are performed there by the ordinary courts of justice, or by special tribunals, or not at all; its advisory tasks appear to be scattered over a great many institutions and persons. The fundamental problem is, however, that the powers of the *Conseil d'Etat* are not perceived as a unity in Anglo-saxon legal thinking; they are not covered by one notion, or one set of notions, but they belong to very heterogeneous chapters of the legal encyclopedia.

When one turns to legal principles, instead of institutions, the situation is somewhat better, but the same difficulties may persist, albeit to a lesser degree. Separation of powers could serve as an example. It is considered as a fundamental principle in some constitutional systems, like those of the United States and France, but it has a different meaning and a different importance in either of the two countries; it can hardly be traced in British constitutional law, and it is squarely rejected by current Soviet doctrine and practice. One could compare, then, the meaning and the practical application of the principle in American and French law, but it would not be possible to use it as a general starting point for making comparative inquiries. The search for the counterpart of separation of powers in British constitutional law would inevitably lead to a study of the entire British system.

The same arguments apply to many other notions which serve as a shorthand for – often complicated – legal principles or legal relations. In constitutional law, we seem to think in different categories, determined by our national traditions, political doctrines and legal systems; and the categories of our thinking show hardly any correspondence. This explains why even translation of important legal expressions into other languages is more often than not a somewhat doubtful affair. There would be no English or French equivalent for such a basic notion of German constitutional law as *Rechtsstaat*. Other expressions may at first sight bear translation, in the sense that one is able to find corresponding words in the other language, but sometimes these words don't impart any meaning at all: thus, 'administrative contract' is a hollow expression in English, whereas *contrat adminis-*

tratif has a precise meaning in the context of French administrative law.

2. The present book is not a handbook of comparative constitutional law; it is part of a series of comparative legal studies and has no further purpose than making a comparative inquiry into one subject of constitutional law. Choosing a subject, however, more or less implies defining a method. A comparative study of, say, the powers of heads of State would have to be conducted in quite another way than studies of the *ultra vires* doctrine or of judicial review. Apparently, issues of methodology cannot be avoided.

For the editor of this book, the question was therefore how to select a subject of constitutional law that would be suitable for comparative study, without exposing readers and authors alike to the risk of running into difficulties concerning the method of approach. Nobody is able to compare, when the terms of the comparison have not been fixed; and it may be clear from the foregoing considerations that, in law, this simple truth is not so simple in its elaboration. On the contrary, it may well constitute one of the keys to understanding the slow development of comparative legal research.

A rudimentary theory underlies the choice of the equality issue as a theme for this book. It is founded on the belief that certain basic problems are bound to occur in any constitutional system: in kingdoms and republics, under dictatorship and under democratic government, in highly elaborate and in very plain legal systems, in Asia and in Europe, and under the Constitution of the United States as well as in an Indian tribe of 35 persons living isolated in a lost part of the Mato Grosso. I am thinking of questions which are fundamental in the sense that they involve the very essentials of constitutional law. We are accustomed to think of a constitutional system in terms of patterns of rules, institutions, powers, relations, rights and duties; but logically, certain basic choices are to be made before such a pattern can be established: some choices as to political power, particularly as far as its limits and its distribution are concerned, and as to the legal position of the population in face of this power. If this be true, lawyers could perhaps take some inspiration from the method of structural analysis, in vogue in modern linguistics: we leave out the legal 'grammar' invented and applied by native lawyers, but we discover first the basic questions which must necessarily have got an answer before any system can come into operation. In that case, the questions to be posed with regard to different legal systems should be rigorously the same, and the diverging answers will enable us to examine and to appreciate basic differences among constitutional systems. Working along these lines, we might come to a real comparison, worthy of that name, and to be able to construct a first foundation for further comparative analysis. In other terms: comparative constitutional law should first engage in examining the universals of constitutional systems.

Now my contention is that the problem of equality is one of these universals. The question whether the laws give an equal protection to all those to whom they apply, and what equal protection means, in theory and in practice, can be examined for every kind of society, whatever its further legal or political characteristics may be; and the answer to this question gives us information about basic attitudes towards the legal system, prevailing in that society.

When we turn, therefore, to equality before the laws, we seem to be sure of finding a solid basis for making comparative studies. Ours is, of course, an isolated study; but it could in the same time be a test permitting us to see if it is really feasible to meet the two requirements just mentioned: defining a legal problem of a general character, and getting answers with a high degree of relevance to the way constitutional systems are organized.

3. And here the difficulties begin already to arise.

First problem: in modern constitutional systems, equal protection of the laws is generally recognized as a fundamental principle; in the prevailing ideologies of the 20th century inequality is anathema. One should perhaps have to go back in history for finding legal structures embodying inequal treatment of citizens, according to birth, rank, wealth, profession etc. On the other hand, it is well known that our century is more struggling with equality problems than any previous period of human history; each of the great nations of the world has its own experience of that struggle. For modern industrialized countries our question is, therefore, to be slightly reframed; it should not bear on the existence or non-existence of legal principles embodying equality before the laws, but on the scope and on the implementation of these principles. Even so, however, the question retains its character of concerning a legal probleem which is, in our times and for the purpose of comparative research, a universal one. The answers will give us a kind of 'map' of the transformations the application of the equality principle shows in different constitutional frameworks.

Second problem: how to make a selection among the major constitutional systems of the world? As the pursuit of equality is very characteristic of socialism, it was tempting to include the U.S.S.R., as the oldest socialist country, whose legal developments, moreover, are well known in this part of the world. Among the 'Western' countries, two had to be chosen because of the important part the judiciary plays in developing the notion of equal protection: the United States and the Federal Republic of Germany. Their constitutions (the American constitutional amendments and art. 3 of the German *Grundgesetz*) explicitly recognize the principle of equality before the laws; under the system of judicial review, conformity of legislation to this principle is ultimately appreciated by the courts. This particular combination of an explicit constitutional guarantee of equal protection on the one hand, and a system of judicial review on the other, often had unforeseen and sometimes even revolutionizing effects. Two other countries have been included because they lack this combination. Canadian constitutional law does have judicial review, but its scope and its impact make it very dissimilar to anything displayed by German or American law. Moreover, the Canadian Bill of Rights, which embodies the equality principle, is not part of the ordinary constitution, like its American sister-document; the legal status of the Canadian Bill of Rights is in itself a legal problem. France, finally, though a country traditionally opposed to judicial review, has an important body of case law on equality as one of the 'general principles of law' which guide the controlling action of the *Conseil d'Etat.* This principle can be founded on a constitutional basis, as the French Constitution refers indirectly back to the 1789 Declaration of the Rights of Man.

Third problem: how to find a certain unity of procedure in dealing with five widely diverging constitutional systems? It is first of all necessary to describe for each national system the problems and their possible solutions as these are perceived from the perspective of that system itself; for some countries, and especially for the United States, this is already a huge task, as the subject of equal protection covers a tremendous field there. Therefore, five chapters, written by specialists, will be devoted to the five systems under consideration. In each of the five chapters, however, the description will be focused upon some central questions, and these questions will again be taken up in the concluding chapter. That chapter will then try to give a comparative analysis on the basis of the materials offered by the preceding descriptive part; it should help the reader in discovering and evaluating correspondence and difference between the legal systems under consideration. Needless to say that we expect this outline to confront the reader with some of the main issues of constitutional law.

4. In the selection of our central questions, we aimed again at universal applicability whatever the shape of the constitutional systems to be examined. In this instance, the choice proved not too difficult. Three problems can not be dissociated from the application of any principle of equality: the exact meaning of this principle, the method by which it is enforced and the kind of social problems to which it is applied.

It would have been possible to start our studies with a definition of the notion of equality before the law. In this book, we try to do it the other way round: the meaning of the notion should gradually be developed on the basis of the materials collected in the descriptive chapters. In other words: a conceptual analysis is not the starting point for our study, but one of its results, and afterwards the object of a comparative approach. We start from the assumption that all constitutional references to equality share a common core of meaning, then look to case law and to legislative and administrative practice of the different countries, in order to find out the exact limits of the differents notions. The distinctions to be discovered might tell us something about differences in perception of the role of law in the various national communities: as we assume that equality necessarily presents a problem in a society of human beings with unequal resources (intellect, property, power etc.), it is a matter of legal policy to decide what contribution the law should make to banishing unequal treatment. This policy may be decided by the legislature, by the courts, by a combination of both or by any other body, but it always has a direct bearing upon the limits of the notion of legal equality: these limits translate more or less the policy.

The second problem is of a more technical nature. It is centred on the question what citizens can do in practice to realize their claims to equal treatment. Thus it requires examination of the various methods by means of which the principle of equality tends to become a guarantee for the citizen: how it is elaborated by the courts, by the legislature, by the administration, and what kind of sanctions can be relied upon for its protection. This question is very much of a legal nature, and the answers to it will enable us to have a general idea about the legal framework in which the equality issue presents itself.

The third central subject concerns the kind of social problems which have given rise to case law or legislation on equality. It is evident that these problems will be entirely different in the five constitutional systems we propose to examine: they may regard racial relations, or discrimination of women, or treatment of foreigners, or economic unequalities. In every country, there are some main issues in the practical application of the equality principle; by determining these issues, we could arrive at some conclusions as to the relationship between legal and social problems. This does not mean that our study intends to focus upon problems of political, cultural or economic unequality as such, for these problems will almost certainly show a high degree of diversity from a legal point of view. However, in evaluating our legal materials, we could try to formulate some opinions on the connexion between the application of the equality principle and the underlying social problems. If this principle has not had any noticeable impact on well-known inequalities in a certain country, it might even be interesting to look briefly into the question why these topics have not been tackled on the basis of equality before the law.

5. I am aware that this introduction may look somewhat presumptuous; and perhaps it is. But as I said before, comparative law is still lacking a fixed method; we have more or less to invent it, and this introduction makes an effort to give at least some information on the ideas that guide the organization of our study. One of the charming things of sociologists

and political scientists is the way they explain their method of research before actually plunging into their subject. Sometimes, lawyers might do the same.

So much having been said about the choice of our subject and the method of dealing with it, we shall turn to the subject itself. We take first the countries in which the role of the judiciary in defining and interpreting the notion of equality has been paramount: the United States and the Federal Republic of Germany. Canada, with its intermediate position, serves as a bridge to the discussion of the countries without judicial review: the French Republic and the Union of Socialist Soviet Republics.

At first sight, the five countries form a queer party; but legal analysis may show how certain fundamental problems concerning relations among humans occur everywhere. After all, we should not forget that, quite apart from considerations of a more academic nature, a tiny bit of mutual comprehension may be one of the fruits of comparative legal research.

2 *Louis Lusky and Michael Botein*

The Law of Equality in the United States

CONTENTS

Introduction

The legal position of equality in the United States can best be surveyed by reviewing the work of the Supreme Court. Since World War II, the Court has become the leading exponent of the equality ideal. Its constitutional decisions reflect the extent to which the nation has moved toward elimination of disadvantages resulting from personal status, and has softened other inequalities as well. Various provisions of the Constitution have been held to guarantee equality in one way or another, and they will be referred to where pertinent in the ensuing discussion. It is suitable, however, to set forth at the outset a few of them which have played the largest part.

Equality was not a primary objective of the original Constitution. It recognized and protected slavery, which it treated as a matter within the jurisdiction of the several states; and so long as such a complete denial of personal equality was tolerated, lesser discriminations could hardly become a major concern of the federal government.

Controversy over slavery was a main cause of the Civil War. In 1865, at the end of that war, the Thirteenth Amendment was adopted. It provided:

> Neither slavery nor involuntary servitude, except as a punishment for crime whereof the party shall have been duly convicted, shall exist within the United States, or any place subject to their jurisdiction.

A number of Southern states moved quickly to impose civil disabilities on the ex-slaves, there being serious doubt whether this Amendment limited their power to do so. They enacted 'Black Codes' which limited or denied (for example) the legal capacity of Negroes to testify, to own real estate, and to engage in business. The Fourteenth Amendment, adopted in 1868, was primarily designed to prohibit such discriminations. Unlike the Thirteenth, however, it spoke in terms not limited to the problems of blacks but applicable to any discrimination by state governments; and it has proved to be the main constitutional basis for decisions on equality. Its most important provisions are the due process and equal protection clauses, contained in Section I:

> No State shall * * * deprive any person of life, liberty, or property, without due process of law; nor deny to any person within its jurisdiction the equal protection of the laws.

The due process clause has an exact counterpart in the Fifth Amendment, one of the limitations on *federal* power (known as the Bill of Rights) which was adopted in 1791, immediately after ratification of the original Constitution. There is no express limitation on federal power corresponding to the equal protection clause, however. Nevertheless, as will be seen, the Supreme Court has held that due process has an important equality component and that at least certain forms of discrimination are forbidden to the federal government as well as states.

The Fourteenth Amendment was not intended to protect voting rights, though its Section 2 contained a weak provision designed to discourage denial of the franchise to Negroes. Direct protection of Negro voting rights came in 1870 with adoption of the Fifteenth Amendment:

> The right of citizens of the United States to vote shall not be denied or abridged by the United States or by any State on account of race, color, or previous condition of servitude.

All three of these Amendments, collectively called the Civil War Amendments, were self-executing and thus called for judicial enforcement regardless of implementation by federal legislation. Each of them also included, however, a final section granting to Congress the power to enforce it by 'appropriate legislation'. These are the so-called 'enforcement clauses.'

We shall first sketch the pre-World War II period, during with the Supreme Court took little interest in equality and indeed set up major obstructions to the elimination of caste from American society. Then we shall review its massive assault on discrimination against minority groups in the thirty years just past. After that, we shall examine the Court's generalization of equality requirements beyond elimination of minority caste. Finally, we shall take note of the recently enlarged role of Congress. Recognizing that space limitations preclude a fully detailed account, we shall nevertheless endeavor to trace the main course of doctrinal development in order to illuminate the evolutionary pattern, and shall state enough of the factual background of the cases to give some sense of their societal significance.

I. *The Limited Commitment to Equality in Early Law*

For a long time the Supreme Court interpreted the Civil War Amendments quite narrowly. Its very first decision under the Fourteenth Amendment virtually nullified one part of it which could have served as a broad source of Congressional power to prohibit private as well as official discrimination. This was the 'privileges or immunities clause' which forbade the states to abridge the privileges or immunities of citizens of the United States. (The first sentence of the Amendment conferred federal citizenship on the ex-slaves – erasing the 1857 *Dred Scott* decision[1], which had held that no Negro, slave or free, could be a United States citizen – by granting such citizenship to all persons born in the United States and subject to its jurisdiction.) Had Congress been held competent to define personal privileges and immunities which the states had an affirmative duty to protect, it could have erected safeguards against various forms of private as well as official discrimination. But in the *Slaughter-House Cases* (1873)[2] the Court held that federal (as distinct from state) citizenship is attended by a narrow set of relatively unimportant privileges and immunities that cannot be expanded by statute.

In a series of later decisions the Court minimized the power of Congress under the enforcement clauses of the Fourteenth and Fifteenth Amendments – most notably in the *Civil Rights Cases* (1883)[3] which invalidated a federal statute forbidding the discrimination against Negroes by 'inns, public conveyances on land or water, theatres, and other places of public amusement.' This decision is the source of the so-called 'state action' doctrine, which declares that the Fourteenth Amendment restricts state action only; not only are its self-executing provisions inapplicable to discrimination by private persons, but its enforcement clause gives Congress no power to prohibit such discrimination.

The Court also interpreted the self-executing due process and equal protection clauses quite narrowly. It did hold that a state statute which expressly discriminates against non-whites, such as a statute making them ineligible for service on juries, is a denial of equal protection.[4] It also held that equal protection is denied by discriminatory administration of a law that speaks in impartial terms; the Court set aside the conviction of a Chinese for violating a San Francisco ordinance forbidding operation of a laundry in a wooden building without permission of a city official, because the ordinance had been enforced against hundreds of Chinese laundry operators and virtually no one else.[5] Thus, state action that was plainly predicated on the assumption that a disfavored minority group was unworthy of equal treatment was condemned. But the Court found no constitutional defect in racial segregation laws, if equal though separate facilities were provided to blacks and whites. In *Plessy* v. *Ferguson* (1896) it upheld a

Louisiana statute requiring 'equal but separate accomodations' for white and Negro railway passengers, saying:[6]

> The object of the [Fourteenth] amendment was undoubtedly to enforce the equality of the two races before the law, but in the nature of things it could not have been intended to abolish distinctions based upon color, or to enforce social, as distinguished from political equality, or a commingling of the two races upon terms unsatisfactory to either. Laws permitting, and even requiring, their separation in places where they are liable to be brought into contact do not necessarily imply the inferiority of either race to the other, and have been generally, if not universally, recognized as within the competency of the state legislatures in the exercise of their police power. The most common instance of this is connected with the establishment of separate schools for white and colored children * * *.

The single dissenter, Justice Harlan, was more sensitive to the realities. He saw that racial segregation laws are designed to perpetuate a caste system inherited from slavery days. Unlike the Court, he thought that equality of the separate facilities was not enough. In his view, the Constitution not only forbade inequality of treatment but authorized Congress to eradicate the social cleavages which provide a continuing impetus for unequal treatment by government and private persons alike. He declared:[7]

> There is no caste here. Our Constitution is color-blind, and neither knows nor tolerates classes among citizens. * * * Sixty millions of whites are in no danger from the presence here of eight millions of blacks. The destinies of the two races, in this country, are indissolubly linked together, and the interests of both require that the common government of all shall not permit the seeds of race hate to be planted under the sanction of law. What can more certainly arouse race hate, what more certainly create and perpetuate a feeling of distrust between these races, than state enactments, which, in fact, proceed on the ground that colored citizens are so inferior and degraded that they cannot be allowed to sit in public coaches occupied by white citizens? That, as all will admit, is the real meaning of such legislation as was enacted in Louisiana.

It was many years before the Court conceded the soundness of his perception and overruled the *Plessy* case.[8] Meanwhile, racial segregation laws became prevalent throughout the Southern and middle states where slavery had persisted until the Civil War, and such laws were not unknown in other states as well. Not only were common carriers and public schools segregated, but also private schools; recreation facilities such as parks, beaches and golf courses; and places of public accomodation such as hotels and restaurants.[9]

During this period the Court's efforts on behalf of equality were limited to the condemnation of provable official discrimination. It seems to have been oblivious to the fact that official discrimination reflects underlying social attitudes toward estranged minority groups, and that if government does nothing to modify these attitudes, the condemnation of particular official acts resulting from them is no more than a palliative. At the same time, moreover, the Court maintained its own jurisdictional monopoly over equality problems. Thus, on the one hand, it permitted the use of segregation laws to solidify the status of non-whites as an untouchable caste. On the other hand – under the state action doctrine – it denied the power of Congress to weaken caste barriers by prohibiting private discrimination in education, housing, employment and public accommodations.

There was one remaining avenue to relief from inequality – political action at the state level. The Fifteenth Amendment prohibited denial of the vote because of race or color; and if Negroes had been able to exercise voting power in proportion to their numbers they might, over a period of time, have been able to cause the state governments to discontinue racial segregation and forbid the more oppressive forms of private discrimination. In several different ways, however, this road to relief was blocked – particularly though not exclusively in the Southern states, where the official and private barriers to interracial contact were strongest and where potential Negro voting power was most formidable because Negroes were so numerous. The Supreme Court did invalidate one method that was used to disfranchise the Negro – the establishment of very stiff requirements for voting registration, with so-called 'grandfather' clauses exempting from those requirements persons who had been entitled to vote before 1867, *and their descendants*.[10] But other restrictive devices were held constitutional.

One such device was the literacy test. It took many forms, but a typical statute made voting registration conditional upon ability to read and write a section of the state constitution and interpret it to the satisfaction of the local registrar. The tests lent themselves to discriminatory administration by petty voting officials; and though such discrimination was theoretically unconstitutional, the would-be registrant could obtain relief only through a lawsuit that involved too much difficulty, expense and delay to be a practical remedy. Beyond this, the segregated education system – in which the separate Negro schools were rarely if ever equal in quality to the white schools, despite the nominal equality requirement of *Plessy* v. *Ferguson* – tended to hold Negro literacy to a low level, so that even a fairly administered literacy test would eliminate much of the voting power that might otherwise have been exerted to end segregation. Nevertheless the Court held literacy tests not to violate the Fifteenth Amendment.[11]

Another device was the poll tax, payment of which was a prerequisite to voting. The tax was small, often only a dollar or two, but even that was a deterrent to the very poor; and a disproportionate number of Negroes were in that category. Moreover, the tax was often made cumulative so that the right to vote depended on payment for previous years as well as the current year. The Court held it constitutional.[12]

A third device was the so-called white primary. For nearly a century after the Civil War the Republican party (the anti-slavery party of Abraham Lincoln) was virtually powerless in the deep South, and nomination as candidate of the Democratic party was tantamount to election. In those states where candidates were nominated by party elections (called 'primaries', as distinguished from the inter-party general elections), the only important election was the Democratic primary. In 1927 a Texas statute excluding Negroes from the Democratic primary was held to violate the equal protection clause.[13] A successor statute empowering the party's state executive committee to fix the qualifications of primary voters, and the Democratic committee's order for a white primary, suffered a like fate five years later.[14] In both cases the 'state action' requirement (which had been declared applicable to the Fifteenth as well as the Fourteenth Amendment) was held to be satisfied. At that point the Texas legislature abandoned all control, and the Democratic party still adhered to the white primary. In *Grovey* v. *Townsend* (1935)[15] the Supreme Court held that there was no constitutional violation because no state action was involved. Thus, the white primary remained an obstacle to Negro political power.

Reinforcing the literacy test, the poll tax and the white primary was private terrorism. The Ku Klux Klan, which became powerful shortly after the Civil War, sought to maintain white supremacy through lawless (but usually unpunished) criminal action against Negroes who were politically active or otherwise asserted their equality with whites. Congress responded with an 1870 statute making it a felony for two ore more persons to band together to intimidate a citizen with intent to hinder his exercise of a constitutional right,[16] and an 1871 statute, penalizing private conspiracies to deprive a person of the equal protection of the laws.[17] The latter provision was carried forward into the broader Civil Rights Act of 1875.[18] The Court, construing the statutes restrictively and invoking the state action requirement, repeatedly set aside convictions under these statutes and virtually denied the power of Congress to interfere with Klan violence.[19]

This brief precis reveals the extent to which inequality remained beyond the reach of law down to World War II, even for the black minority which was by far the most submerged of all the many minority groups in the United States. The Supreme Court not only failed to fulfill the promise of the Civil War Amendments, but invoked the Constitution to prevent Congress from doing so. And so long as Negro inequality remained pervasive, legal recourse against the milder discriminations suffered by other disadvantaged groups was not to be expected. Against this background, the more recent developments stand out in high relief.

II. *The New Demand for an End to Caste*

The consequences of governmental indifference to the plight of minority groups became painfully evident during World War II. After the attack on Pearl Harbor had crippled the Pacific fleet and exposed the west coast to danger of Japanese invasion, the possibility of sabotage by American residents of Japanese descent aroused military concern. Although many of them were American citizens, they had long been subjected to extensive discrimination; and at least some disaffection very probably existed. (Indeed, about five thousand of them eventually requested repatriation to Japan.) The military authorities declared that individual loyalty determinations could not be quickly made, and therefore ordered an entire group of 112,000 to be excluded from specified areas in California where they lived and worked. The hardship, visited alike upon citizen and alien, upon the loyal and the disloyal, was very great.

In 1944 the Supreme Court held the military order to be constitutional.[20] There were vigorous dissenting opinions deploring racial discrimination, but a majority was persuaded that military necessity justified the order. Yet the Court revealed deep concern at the anomaly involved in discrimination against a minority group at the very time that the nation was waging a great war in the name of liberty and equality. While insisting that military need was paramount, the Court declared that racial classification is subject to 'the most rigid scrutiny'.[21] There could no longer be any doubt that the continued existence of disaffected minorities was a grave national problem, and that the dissolution of barriers that held such minorities separate from the rest of society was a legitimate federal objective. This meant relaxation of the restrictions the Court had placed upon Congressional power, and more sensitivity to social realities by the Court itself in enforcing constitutional equality requirements.

The first significant step in that direction was taken in *Smith* v. *Allwright* (1944),[22] holding that the white primary is unconstitutional. A Negro was awarded damages for exclusion from the Democratic primary in Texas, the Court declaring that the primary is 'state action' regulated by the Fifteenth Amendment and that a federal statute providing damages for denial of a federal constitutional right can validly be applied. The contrary decision in *Grovey* v. *Townsend* (1935) was expressly overruled.

Further indication of a new determination to overthrow racial barriers came in *Shelley* v. *Kraemer* (1948).[23] The case concerned an agreement among thirty white property owners that their land would not be occupied by non-whites for the next fifty years. Such 'covenants running with the land', which are binding not only on the parties to the original agreement but also on subsequent owners of the property, are a familiar device for preserving the quality of a neighborhood, and often have no racial aspect. For example, they may provide that houses must have a minimum size or value, or must be set back a certain distance from the street. The law under which they are enforced is racially neutral, simply recognizing the power of adjoining property owners to adopt whatever mutually agreeable restrictions they please. But such covenants had been employed very widely to exclude Negroes, Jews and other unpopular minorities from many of the most desirable urban neighborhoods. The question in *Shelley* v. *Kraemer* was whether a racially restrictive covenant could be enforced against a Negro purchaser of one of the properties. It was argued that such enforcement did not violate the equal protection clause because the law itself was racially neutral, so that no discriminatory 'state action' was involved. The Court held otherwise, deciding that a court order enforcing the discriminatory *private* agreement was unconstitutional state action.

The logic of the ruling was broad enough to cover many other forms of private discrimination. For example, it would prevent the use of the law of trespass to exclude Negroes from hotels and restaurants. As it turned out, the Court never went that far, and equality of access to public accomodations had to await federal legislation. The *Shelley* decision must be explained in narrower terms, as repudiation of a particular device which had become a mainstay of neighborhood segregation.[24] Even so, it was a significant step toward the dissolution of racial barriers. Moreover, a companion case involving a racial covenant in the District of Columbia was decided the same way even though the equal protection clause was inapplicable because the District is under federal rather than state jurisdiction, so that the Fourteenth Amendment did not operate. Federal policy was held to forbid racially restrictive covenants.[25] Thus the constitutional equality requirement was extended to federal action, a position which the Court has adhered to in later decisions on discrimination against minorities.

It was in 1954 that the Court launched a full-scale offensive against isolation of the Negro minority, repudiating the 'separate but equal' doctrine of *Plessy* v. *Ferguson* in the field of public education. In *Brown* v. *Board of Education,* legally required racial segregation in the public schools was held to violate the equal protection clause.[26] Also, on the same day, such segregation in the District of Columbia was held to violate the Fifth Amendment due process clause; the Court declared that the concepts of equal protection and due process both stem from 'our American ideal of fairness' and that both of them therefore prohibit discrimination which is 'not reasonably related to any governmental objective'.[27] Both cases rest on the central proposition that inequality can result from segregation even though the separate educational facilities are equal.

This proposition involved a broadening of the previous conception of discrimination. Decisions in 1948 and 1950 had enforced the equality requirement of the 'separate but equal' doctrine with a new strictness, but had not held that segregation is itself a form of discrimination.[28] Now the Court found that the separate education of Negro children 'generates a feeling of inferiority as to their status in the community that may affect their hearts and minds in a way unlikely ever to be undone'. On this basis, the Court concluded: 'Separate educational facilities are inherently unequal'. Plainly the Court was using the term 'unequal' in a new sense. The 'inequality' prohibited by the Constitution was no longer thought limited to unequal distribution of governmental burdens and benefits, but was held to include measures perpetuating the social isolation of minority groups.

This new conception called for extensive reconsideration of existing constitutional doctrine, including the 'state action' restriction on federal power. The Court did not at once acknowledge the magnitude of the innovation, however. It elected to establish the new dimension of equality gradually, dealing with specific situations case by case. The resulting doubt and confusion, which has not yet fully abated, has led to severe aggravation of racial tensions. Negroes and other racial minorities have been exasperated by the slowness in recognition of their full acceptance into the general community, and recalcitrant whites have been angered by what has appeared to them as endless judicial pursuit of an insatiable egalitarian ideal. Hindsight suggests that it might have been wiser for the Court (a) to acknowledge explicitly that the Civil War Amendments were intended as a mandate for extirpation of racial caste by the federal government, not simply as a requirement of official even-handedness; (b) to admit the full extent of its own past responsibility for frustrating that mandate; but (c) to recognize that the social barriers which it had helped to solidify could only be dissolved over a period of time. In that way, racial integration might have been more generally understood as a defined (though not instantly attainable) objective, prescribed by the people through constitutional amendments, rather than as a product of judicial policy still being developed and therefore debatable at every step. But the Court chose a step-by-step development which it doubtless believed would encounter less public resistance. The broad position has eventually been approximated, but it has taken a long time.

The *Brown* decision itself was not only limited to the public schools, but its boldness on the substantive side was qualified by uncertainty with respect to remedy. The Court, aware that a very extensive reorganization of public education would be required in twenty-two of the fifty states, did not order immediate desegregation. Instead, after a year's delay for presentation and consideration of arguments in favor of delay, the district courts were directed to pass upon desegregation plans submitted by local school boards, and to approve plans which provided for desegregation 'with all deliberate speed'.[29] Outside the deep South, public school desegregation proceeded with some rapidity; but in the eleven states whose attempt at secession had precipitated the Civil War, the program was a failure. The elective school boards were paralyzed by adverse local opinion, and even the federal district courts were often influenced by it. By the end of 1962 only 0.4% of the black students in these eleven states had been brought into schools attended also by white children, and 2013 biracial school districts out of 2283 were still fully segregated.[30] In extreme cases, state officials openly defied the Court's interpretation of the Constitution and opposed it with the whole weight of the state's resources, including use of the militia and harassment of desegregation advocates with groundless but burdensome criminal prosecutions.[31] In one Virginia county, the public schools were closed until the Supreme Court ordered them reopened.[32] More commonly, resistance took the form of stubborn refusal to develop meaningful desegregation plans, and protracted appeals from plans eventually formulated by the federal district courts. In 1963 the Court warned that the time for 'deliberate speed' was running out,[33] and in 1968 it eventually held that delay was 'no longer tolerable'.[34]

What proved to be the decisive factor in public school desegregation, however, was Congressional action. The 1964 Civil Rights Act prohibited discrimination on the ground of race, color, or national origin by any 'program or activity receiving Federal financial assistance', and directed federal agencies to issue supporting regulations. Pursuant to this statute, the Department of Health, Education and Welfare issued regulations cutting off federal monetary grants to segregated school systems until they adopted acceptable desegregation plans. Under this pressure, general compliance with the decision in *Brown* v. *Board of Education* is at last being obtained. By 1971, at least 60.9% of black children in the South were attending schools also attended by whites.[35]

As has been indicated, however, the *Brown* opinion did not fully reveal the extent of the Court's commitment to the elimination of obstacles to interracial contact. The opinion's heavy emphasis on the importance of education, the unique role of the public schools als instruments of acculturation, and the fact that school attendance (unlike recreation and travel, for example) is compelled by law, suggested the possibility that 'separate but equal' treatment might still be permissible in other public facilities. The Court, however, summarily invalidated laws and regulations requiring segregation of facilities which the government provides or helps to finance, such as beaches, golf courses, parks, municipal buses, courtrooms and prisons.[36] (The 'deliberate speed' doctrine for public schools was not extended to other facilities.) The Court never took the trouble to explain why the *Brown* case required these results, but the breadth of its position is clear; 'it is no longer open to question', the Court declared in 1963, 'that a State may not constitutionally require segregation of public facilities'.[37]

Initially the Court evaded the delicate question whether miscegenation (racial intermarriage) can be forbidden by law, an issue which stirred feelings even deeper than those aroused by school desegregation. In 1956 it refused to decide the question, giving no comprehensible explanation for the refusal.[38] In 1964, it invalidated a statute penalizing illicit cohabitation more severely if the parties were of different races, but chose not to pass on the validity of the anti-miscegenation statute which it implemented.[39] In 1967, however, anti-miscegenation laws (which then existed in sixteen states) were declared to violate the equal protection and due process clauses.[40]

Although the distinction between official and private discrimination has not been obliterated,[41] the Court's concern for dissolution of caste barriers has led to inroads upon the state action doctrine. For one thing, the government is forbidden to encourage or facilitate private discrimination. One device employed by pro-segregation state governments to dampen pressure for racial equality was publicization of membership in organizations dedicated to promotion of Negro rights, foremost among which are the National Association for the Advancement of Colored People (NAACP) and its affiliate, the NAACP Legal Defense and Education Fund (the Defense Fund). Public disclosure of membership in such organizations exposes the members to private hostility – manifested by economic reprisals such as denial of employment and bank credit, and even by threatened or actual violence. In a series of cases the Court has struck down demands for membership information.[42] The significance of the racial element is shown by the contrasting decisions permitting compulsion to disclose membership in the Communist Party and other allegedly subversive organizations.[43]

Similar sensitivity to official encouragement of private discrimination was displayed in cases involving trespass prosecutions of Negroes for 'sit-ins' at restaurants that served whites only. Prior to the 1964 Civil Rights Act, the Court never went so far as to deny the right of a restaurant proprietor to exclude Negroes on his own initiative; nor did it hold that Negroes have a constitutional privilege to protest against such discrimination by 'sitting in', i.e., requesting service at a table or counter and refusing to leave upon demand.[44] Sit-in demonstrations took place in a number of Southern cities, as a form of civil disobedience, and criminal convictions resulted. In many cases the Court refused to intervene; but in *Lombard* v. *Louisiana* it reversed such a conviction on the ground that, within the week before the alleged offense, the local mayor and police chief had made public statements condemning sit-ins.[45] There was no proof that the proprietor was in fact influenced by the statements, which in any event did not expressly advocate refusal to serve whites and blacks together. Evidently the Court believed that the statements necessarily encouraged discrimination by promising use of the criminal law to enforce a decision by the proprietor to exclude Negroes, so that his decision resulted at least partly from state action.

The Court has also held that discrimination by the private lessee of state-owned property is state action. In *Burton* v. *Wilmington Parking Authority,*[46] a private company conducted a restaurant business in a state-owned parking garage building, under a 20-year lease which contained no provision either requiring or permitting exclusion of Negroes from the restaurant. Such exclusion by the private lessee was held to be a denial of equal protection, the Court finding that the state was involved in the restaurant operation because (a) it owned the building, (b) its adjacent garage benefited from the restaurant's proximity, and (c) the private lessee claimed that exclusion of Negroes had a favorable effect on the restaurant's profits, from which rents were paid to the state.

An even thinner governmental involvement was held to constitute state action in *Reitman* v. *Mulkey.*[47] A 1963 California statute forbidding discrimination in the sale or rental of any dwelling containing more than four apartment units, aroused great criticism. By popular referendum, the state constitution was amended the next year to provide:

> Neither the State nor any subdivision or agency thereof shall deny, limit or abridge, directly of indirectly, the right of any person, who is willing or desires to sell, lease or rent any part or all of his real property, to decline to sell, lease or rent such property to such person or persons as he, in his absolute discretion, chooses.

The effect was to nullify the 1963 statute.

It had previously been thought that the people of a state could limit the power of their legislative representatives at will; but the Court held, in effect, that state and local lawmakers must be left free to deal with racial discrimination, at least in the field of housing. The state constitutional amendment *forbidding* legislative action was held to be discriminatory state action itself. The California Supreme Court had held – evidently on the basis of judicial notice, since no evidence was introduced to support the conclusion – that the amendment in fact encouraged private discrimination; and in *Reitman* v. *Mulkey* the Court found 'no sound reason for rejecting this judgment'.

The Court has vacillated somewhat on the question whether the mere application of racially neutral laws to enforce discriminatory private decisions is state action, and therefore subject to the equal protection and due process clauses. As already noted, *Shelley* v. *Kraemer* (the 1948 restrictive covenant case) seemed to give a broad affirmative answer, but was not applied to the full extent of its logic in different factual settings. In 1957 the Court held that a testamentary trust establishing a school for 'poor white male orphans' could not be administered by the city of Philadelphia as trustee,[48] but the next year it refused to interfere after the state court had allowed the city to resign and appointed successor trustees who continued the racial discrimination.[49] In 1966 the Court rejected an effort to preserve a similar testamentary trust establishing a park in Macon, Georgia for whites only, although the state court had replaced the city with private trustees; but the decision was rested partly on the Court's assertion that the service rendered by a park is inherently 'municipal in nature', and partly on its doubt that a change of trustees would alter the public nature of a park which had been operated by the city for many years.[50] Thereupon the state court terminated the trust on the ground that its purpose had been frustrated, and decided that the park property should revert to the donor's estate. The result was that Negroes (as well as whites) were denied use of the park, but the state decision was upheld.[51] The Court said the result might be different if 'the state and not a private party [were] injecting the racially discriminatory motivation'[52] – a distinction that would be immaterial under the logic of *Shelley* v. *Kraemer*. The next year, however, the Court held that the city of Jackson, Mississippi had not acted unconstitutionally in closing its public swimming pools as soon as they had been ordered desegregated.[53]

Mention should be made of recent cases approving drastic remedies devised by the district courts to dissipate the effects of school segregation previously accomplished by law. The most controversial feature of these plans arises from the fact that neigborhoods in many cities have become exclusively or very preponderantly white or non-white, and from the further fact that it is considered desirable for children – particularly the younger ones – to attend schools near their homes. In response to the Court's directive to replace dual school systems with 'unitary' ones, a number of district courts have ordered that children be assigned to distant schools and transported back and forth by school buses, so that the racial mix in each school will approximate that in the community at large. Great resentment has been generated against 'busing' for this purpose, but the Court has held it to be a justifiable means of disestablishing previously segregated school systems.[54] The Court has not yet decided, however, whether children are to be exchanged between separate school districts when racial concentrations within the districts otherwise preclude effective integration. In 1973 it divided 4 to 4 on that question in a case from Richmond, Virginia, one Justice abstaining,[55] but the full Court is expected to consider a similar case that has arisen in Detroit, Michigan.[56]

Nor has the Court passed upon the constitutionality of so-called *'de facto* segregation'. This is the term that has been coined to describe a condition of racial concentration in particular schools which is not attributable to governmental efforts to separate the races, but results from local population patterns. It is rather an odd expression, since 'segregation' ordinarily connotes *a process* resulting in separateness rather than separateness as such. The term '*de facto* segregation' has entered current usage, however, being distinguished from '*de jure* segregation' which is brought about by public authority. In *Keyes* v. *School District* (1973),[57] where the Court found *de jure* segregation to exist in Denver, Colorado, two of the Justices declared themselves ready to provide judicial remedies against *de facto* as well as *de jure* segregation. Should the Court take that step, little if anything would remain of the state action doctrine; it would have given way to the view that the Court is omnicompetent to utilize the public schools as a means of maximizing interracial association.

As desegregation of public schools has become more and more complete, there has been a perceptible movement of white students into all-white private schools. Until now the Court has not questioned the legality of such schools, but it has forbidden governmental assistance to them or their students. They have been declared ineligible for federal tax benefits extended to other non-profit educational institutions, and a state law providing free textbooks to their students (and also to public school students) has been held unconstitutional.[58]

The foregoing review of the Court's attack on caste barriers does not touch every aspect of its effort. Enough has been shown, however, to reveal the reality and magnitude of the effort and to suggest that it has been impelled by (a) awareness of the wretched condition of socially isolated minorities in the United States, and (b) belief that no quick relief is likely to be obtained through the political process. The great majority of the cases deal with the black minority, which is much the largest and which is uniquely disadvantaged by the cultural residue of slavery; but equality requirements developed initially for the protection of Negroes apply to other socially isolated minorities as well. For example, in *Hernandez* v. *Texas*[59] the Court held that discrimination against persons of Mexican descent in the selection of juries violates the equal protection clause, saying: 'The Fourteenth Amendment is not directed solely against discrimination due to a "two-class theory" – that is, based upon differences between "white" and Negro'.

Thus far we have been examining decisions directly involving caste barriers. Those decisions comprise the central core of the equality movement, but do not represent its full extent. We now turn to the broader developments.

III. *Generalization of the Equality Concept*

Although the plight of Negroes has provided the primary impetus toward equality, the Court has been noticeably reluctant to acknowledge that racial minorities have special legal privileges. The Thirteenth and Fifteenth Amendments, which make specific reference to race and to the slavery background, might have been thought to justify the treatment of racial equality as a separate and distinct constitutional objective; but the Court has mainly relied on the Fourteenth, which applies to 'any person'. It has erected a structure of rules having the quality of universally applicable natural law principles, pervasively applicable to governmental action whether or not *racial* equality is involved.

A. Promotion of Equality through Extension of General Liberties

One feature of this approach has been the extension of other constitutional rights, such as freedom of expression, to cover cases arising from racial discrimination problems. For example, *NAACP* v. *Button* (1963)[60] held invalid a 1956 Virginia statute designed to curb the NAACP and the Defense Fund. The practice of those organizations was (and is) to encourage the bringing of desegregation suits by aggrieved individuals, to provide them with lawyers, and to pay all litigation expense. This amounts to solicitation of legal business and stirring up litigation, both of which activities are often criticized as unethical conduct for lawyers. Establishment and enforcement of ethical standards for the legal and other professions is traditionally within state power, and the Virginia statute purported merely to tighten the ethical restrictions. But it was part of a well-advertised statutory program of 'massive resistance' to desegregation, and was plainly intended to suffocate effective demand for Negro equality in Virginia. The Court did not rest decision on that ground, however. Instead, it characterized litigation of the type handled by the NAACP as 'a form of political expression' which Virginia could not suppress, and declared that 'association for litigation may be the most effective form of political association'. The opinion continued:

> Because our disposition is rested on the First Amendment as absorbed in the Fourteenth, we do not reach the considerations of race or racial discrimination which are the predicate of petitioner's challenge under the Equal Protection Clause. That the petitioner happens to be engaged in activities and expression on behalf of the rights of Negro children to equal opportunity is constitutionally irrelevant to the ground of our decision.

This enlargement of freedom of expression has given the *Button* case precedential effect beyond the racial discrimination field. For example, the Court now strictly limits state interference with labor unions' control of their members' personal injury cases.[61] In the name of free speech and association, it thus overrides state disapproval of lay intermediaries between attorney and client – hardly a matter of obvious federal concern – and recognizes a 'basic right to group legal action'.[62]

There has been a similar development in the law of defamation, which until 1964 was entirely within the realm of state tort law. In 1960 the New York *Times* carried a paid advertisement appealing for funds to support the cause of Negro students and Negro voting rights. The advertisement included ten paragraphs purporting to describe hardships inflicted on Negroes by 'Southern violators'. Two of the paragraphs included partly inaccurate statements about actions of the police in Montgomery, Alabama. The city Commissioner of Public Affairs sued the *Times* for libel, alleging a slur on his performance of official duty. A state court jury awarded $500,000 in damages although there was no evidence of pecuniary injury – as settled state law authorized it to do. The Supreme Court had previously declared that the constitutional freedom of speech and press does not apply to libelous utterances;[63] but it was clear that the danger of huge damage awards at the hands of hostile Southern juries would cripple the drive for equal rights legislation, by deterring the press from publicizing Negro grievances. (Particularly in the case of daily newspapers, time pressure prevents complete verification of all reports; and even if they are in fact true, the defendant may not be able to prove their truth – a burden that the common law imposes on defendants.) In *New York Times Co.* v. *Sullivan*[64] the Court reversed the $500,000 judgment, not as a hindrance to black equality but on broader grounds. It laid down a new constitutional rule that defamatory statements about the official conduct of public officials are not actionable unless the defendant knows they are false or is recklessly indifferent to their truth or falsity. The rule's coverage has been broadened in later cases, and its application has by no means been limited to situations involving probable hostility on the part of juries and state court judges.[65]

Another case in which the Court preferred to expand freedom of expression for everyone rather than acknowledge special Negro rights was *Edwards* v. *South Carolina* (1963).[66] Twelve years before, *Feiner* v. *New York*[67] had held that a street speaker can constitutionally be ordered to desist by a policeman who senses imminent violence because of the audience's hostility, and can be punished for disorderly conduct if he disobeys. The *Edwards* case involved a noisy anti-segregation demonstration by Negro students, on the grounds of the state capitol in South Carolina. A large crowd of white onlookers gathered; and it was probably true, as the dissenting Justice said, that there was a real danger of 'almost spontaneous combustion'. The local City Manager ordered the demonstrators to disperse in fifteen minutes, and 187 of them who refused were arrested. The Supreme Court reversed their convictions for breach of the peace. The opinion did not rely on the fact that, in a racial confrontation in the deep South, on-the-spot police evaluation of the danger of violence is less likely to be dispassionately impartial than was the determination of the New York policeman who silenced Feiner. Instead, the Court rested its decision on general freedom of speech grounds that have since provided broad shelter to anti-war demonstrators and other dissenting groups.[68]

In all probability the plight of Negroes also played a part in convincing the Court that the criminal process should be surrounded with new constitutional safeguards for persons suspected or accused of crime. Of the thousands of criminal cases brought to the Court in the past quarter-century, many if not most involved black defendants complaining of coerced confessions, unlawful searches, denial of counsel, double jeopardy, and other such abuses. Perhaps the disproportionate number of black defendants resulted from racial discrimination, perhaps from the higher incidence of crime in this socially handicapped group, perhaps from both. Whatever the reason, it was clear that the criminal process was a particularly important element in the relationship between blacks and society at large, and that abuses had dangerous potential for increase of racial tension. Awareness of this fact may well have helped induce the Court to institute the sweeping reforms of recent years, during which most of the safeguards contained in the Fourth, Fifth, Sixth and Eighth Amendments – originally adopted as restrictions on the federal government alone[69] – have been extended to state prosecutions,[70] and new safeguards of fairness and privacy have been ordered for federal and state prosecutions alike.[71] In most cases the Court has made no reference to the significance of race; but it seems to have been decisive in *Furman* v. *Georgia* (1972),[72] which held that the death penalty as then administered violated the constitutional prohibition against 'cruel and unusual punishments'. The vote was five to four. Of the five Justices in the majority, only two declared the death penalty unconstitutional *per se*. Its discriminatory aspect was decisive for Justice Douglas, one of the other three. Pointing to the disproportionate number of Negroes who had been executed, he declared it ' "cruel and unusual" to apply the death penalty – or any other penalty – selectively to minorities whose numbers are few, who are outcasts of society, and who are unpopular'.[73]

B. Promotion of Equality through Stricter Standards

The Court's awareness of racial inequality has not only made its mark on the law of freedom of expression and on the criminal process. Reluctance to assign special legal status to racial minorities has also led to generalization of the law of equality itself. Equality doctrine now extends well beyond caste problems, and narrowly restricts governmental classification in a number of other fields.

1. The doctrinal framework

The Constitution has long been understood to require some degree of consistency in governmental action. A typical formulation is that 'cities, states and the Federal Government must exercise their powers so as not to discriminate between their inhabitants except upon some reasonable differentiation fairly related to the object of regulation'.[74] This is called the 'rational relationship' test because it requires a rational connection between the discrimination and some legitimate governmental objective. In practice it has been a highly permissive one. Except where the discrimination has plainly been motivated by hostility to a socially isolated minority and not by a purpose to serve the needs of the public at large, judicial doubts have been resolved in favor of validity. In a 1935 case the Court said:[75]

> It is a salutary principle of judicial decision, long emphasized and followed by this Court, that the burden of establishing the unconstitutionality of a statute rests on him who assails it, and that courts may not declare a legislative discrimination invalid unless, viewed in the light of facts made known or generally assumed, it is of such a character as to preclude the assumption that the classification rests upon some rational basis within the knowledge and experience of the legislators. A statutory discrimination will not be set aside as the denial of equal protection of the laws if any state of facts reasonably may be conceived to justify it.

In that case a state statute allowing a longer time for suits on claims against out-of-state insurance companies than against local ones was upheld, the Court saying that the legislature *might* have thought there was a difference in the time claimants needed to prepare for litigation – though the statute did not say so.

This permissive judicial approach reflected recognition that nearly all legislation involves classification of one kind or another, that classifications often result from expedient compromise rather than logical principle, that articulation of a coherent legislative purpose is frequently impossible because different legislators have had different reasons for approving the result reached, and that the difficult business of assembling legislative majorities would be paralyzed by a requirement of rigid consistency. Moreover, the electorate has ultimate power to bring about the repeal or improvement of statutes which deviate too far from the ideal of equality, and the availability of a political remedy lessens the Court's responsibility.

In some cases, however, the Court has applied a stricter standard. It has invalidated discriminations even though they might be rationally related to a permissible objective, unless a 'compelling governmental interest' could be demonstrated. Occasionally, as in the *Korematsu* case involving relocation of Japanese-Americans for military reasons, the compelling governmental interest test has been satisfied and the discrimination upheld.[76] The test is a severe one, however, and its application usually results in a declaration of unconstitutionality.

Initially the stricter test was applied rather sporadically and on a particularistic basis. For example, *Skinner* v. *Oklahoma* (1942)[77] invalidated a state statute providing for sterilization of habitual criminals (persons convicted of three 'felonies involving moral turpitude') because embezzlement, tax violations, and other so-called white-collar crimes were excepted from its operation. The rational relationship test would probably have led to a contrary result, since the legislature *might* have had a basis for believing that criminal tendencies are more inheritable for some crimes than for others. The Court, however, held that 'strict scrutiny' was required because procreation is 'one of the basic civil rights of man'. That would have been more understandable as a reason for denying all legislative power to sterilize criminals than for an abnormally strict *equality* requirement. In any event, there was no indication that the category of 'basic civil rights' might be a broad one; the Court emphasized the special dangers of sterilization, and referred obliquely to Hitler's genocide efforts as showing the potential enormity of the deprivation.

For more than twenty years the Court maintained its deferential attitude toward the legislative judgment with respect to classification, except for racial classification which it treated as inherently 'suspect'.[78] As it said in the 1964 interracial cohabitation case:[79]

> Normally, the widest discretion is allowed the legislative judgment in determining whether to attack some, rather than all, of the manifestations of the evil aimed at; and normally that judgment is given the benefit of every conceivable circumstance which might suffice to characterize the classification as reasonable rather than arbitrary and invidious. * * * But we deal here with a classification based upon the race of the participants, which must be viewed in light of the historical fact that the central purpose of the Fourteenth Amendment was to eliminate racial discrimination emanating from official sources in the States. This strong policy renders racial classifications 'constitutionally suspect', * * * subject to the 'most rigid scrutiny' * * * and 'in most circumstances irrelevant' to any constitutionally acceptable legislative purpose * * *.
>
> * * * That a general evil will be partially corrected may at times, and without more, serve to justify the limited application of a criminal law; but legislative discretion to employ the piecemeal approach stops short of permitting a State to narrow statutory coverage to focus on a racial group. Such classifications bear a far heavier burden of justification.

Then, in a series of non-racial cases involving the right to vote, the stricter standard was applied because of the basic importance of the elective franchise.[80] And in 1968 the Court invalidated a state statute allowing legitimate but not illegitimate children to recover damages for their mother's wrongful death, describing 'the intimate, familial relationship between a child and his own mother' as a basic civil right.[81] The Court was taking a more expansive view of its authority to strike down classifications which it considered inhumane or unwise.

Shapiro v. *Thompson* (1969)[82] crystallized a broad rationalizing principle. The case involved welfare (poor-relief) laws in Connecticut, Pennsylvania and the District of Columbia. Each state has its own welfare law and fixes its own scale of payments and eligibility requirements, but must conform to federal standards in order to receive large federal grants which cover most of the cost. In the District of Columbia, welfare payments are dispensed by the federal government directly. The question was whether the two states and the District could require newly arrived residents to wait a year before receiving payments for dependent children and for disability. The Court held that the equal protection clause forbade the two states, and the Fifth Amendment due process clause forbade the District, to discriminate between old and new residents in this way.

First, the Court declared that the waiting-period could not be justified as a means of discouraging the entry of poor people, even if they had moved in order to obtain higher welfare payments than they had received in the states they left. Citing earlier cases holding that there is a constitutional right of unimpeded movement across state lines, the Court said that the withholding of benefits was a deterrent to the exercise of that right and was not a permissible objective. Then it dealt with four other claimed justifications: that the waiting period facilitated the planning of the welfare budget; provided an objective and easily administered test of residency; minimized the opportunity for recipients fraudulently to obtain double welfare payments by continuing on the relief rolls in the states they had left; and encouraged the new arrivals to take jobs. In rejecting these arguments on the ground that the state had other ways to accomplish these purposes which did not discourage interstate movement, the Court formulated a broad principle:[83]

> At the outset, we reject appellants' argument that a mere showing of a rational relationship between these four admittedly permissible state objectives will suffice to justify the classification. * * * The waiting-period provision denies welfare benefits to otherwise eligible applicants solely because they have recently moved into the jurisdiction. But in moving from State to State or to the District of Columbia appellees were exercising a constitutional right, and any classification which serves to penalize the exercise of that right, unless shown to be necessary to promote a *compelling* governmental interest, is unconstitutional. * * *
>
> * * * the traditional criteria do not apply in these cases. Since the classification here touches on the fundamental right of interstate movement, its constitutionality must be judged by the stricter standard of whether it promotes a *compelling* state interest.

It will be observed that the Court, in justifying application of the stricter standard, first characterized interstate movement as a 'constitutional right' and later referred to it as a 'fundamental right'. The two terms may not be coextensive; but the difference between them, if any, is unimportant because the Court exercises virtually unrestricted power (1) to coin new constitutional rights, and (2) to characterize as fundamental any 'right' (more precisely, any *interest*) which it thinks should enjoy extraordinary judicial protection. The Court, in later cases, has usually resorted to the 'fundamental right' terminology to rationalize its use of the compelling governmental interest test where *the especially important nature of the right affected* has been the basis for insistence on rigid equality; and that terminology will be used here.

This strict test has also been applied on a separate ground involving not the nature of the right affected but *the nature of the classification.* Certain classifications of persons are held to be 'suspect' and are held unconstitutional unless essential to the furtherance of a compelling (and permissible) governmental objective. As noted above, racial classifications were the first to be called suspect. As the equality concept has broadened beyond concern with caste, the category of suspect classifications has been extended.

For comprehension of the doctrinal basis of the decisions about to be reviewed, it should be understood that many of them have depended both on the nature of the right affected *and* on the nature of the classification. One commentator has written:[84]

> The interaction of these two factors can be visualized by imagining two gradients. Along the first of these gradients is a hierarchy of classifications, with those which are most invidious – suspect classifications, based on traits such as race – at the top. Along the second, arranged in ascending order of importance, are interests such as employment, education, and voting. When the classification drawn lies at the top of the first gradient, it will be subject to strict review even when the interest it affects ranks low on the second gradient – for example, the denial of a driver's license on the basis of race. As the nature of the classification becomes less invidious (descending on the first gradient) the measure will continue to elicit strict review only as it affects interests progressively more important (ascending on the second gradient). Thus, restrained review might be applied when a state disqualifies indigents by requiring a fee from all persons desiring a driver's license or a university education, whereas strict review is applied when indigents are disqualified from voting through a fee imposed for the exercise of that right.

There also appears to be an interrelationship between the nature of the right affected and the kind of governmental interest that will be held sufficiently compelling to justify its curtailment. Justice White has written:[85]

*** as the Court's assessment of the weight and value of the individual interest escalates, the less likely it is that mere administrative convenience and avoidance of hearings or investigations will be sufficient to justify what otherwise would appear to be irrational discriminations.

2. Poverty

Inequality of wealth has been a prolific source of litigation. The Court has never gone quite so far as to hold that the withholding of governmental services because of inability to pay for them is in itself enough to warrant strict review. In other words, it has not declared wealth to be an inherently suspect basis of classification. Yet it has done much to mitigate legal disadvantage resulting from poverty.

This is particularly evident in the criminal process area. The right to appointment of a defense lawyer without cost, for accused persons who are unable to pay a fee, was first declared to be necessary in all capital cases;[86] later, in alle cases where a substantial prison sentence was possible;[87] and, recently, in all cases involving the possibility of any imprisonment whatever.[88] Although there is no constitutional right of appeal, appellate review – if provided, as it is in all but the most trivial cases – must be equally available to rich and poor. Thus, if the appellant is too poor to pay for a typed transcript of the trial proceedings (for review by a higher court),[89] or a transcript of a preliminary hearing,[90] or if he cannot afford to pay a lawyer to present his appeal,[91] they must be provided without cost; and if he cannot pay a filing fee, it must be waived.[92] Many states have statutes requiring criminal defendants to reimburse the state for legal fees paid on their behalf. The Court has not yet passed upon the contention that this is an unconstitutional burden on the right to counsel, but has invalidated one such statute because the defendants were not allowed the same exemptions as other debtors.[93]

The Court has also limited the practice of imprisoning convicted persons because of their failure to pay fines, under statutes providing that unpaid fines must be 'worked off' in jail at a specified rate (typically $ 5 per day of confinement). Indigent defendants cannot be jailed for nonpayment of fines if the result will be to increase their term of incarceration beyond the maximum imprisonment otherwise authorized by the penal statute.[94] Thus, if a sentence up to five years and $10,000 is authorized, it is pointless to add a fine to a five-year prison sentence where the defendant is indigent. Applying this principle, the Court has held that inability to pay fines for traffic offenses punishable *only* by fine results in freedom from any punishment whatever[95] – an indication of the extent to which equality is exalted above other social values in criminal cases.

Less has been done to mitigate the disadvantage of poverty in private litigation. The Court did hold that due process requires the waiver of court fees for indigent plaintiffs in divorce cases, such cases being deemed to involve a unique need for access to judicial relief because marriages cannot be dissolved by agreement of the spouses;[96] but such relief has been held unavailable for other civil proceedings such as petitions in bankruptcy and appeals from administrative rulings on welfare benefits.[97] Legal assistance to the poor is available to some extent through legal services programs financed partly or wholly by public funds, but the demand outruns the supply and the equality of the service is uneven.[98]

The 1969 opinion in *Shapiro* v. *Thompson,* already referred to, contained a hint that the Court might be about to intervene freely against all inequalities in welfare programs, on the theory that the right to poor-relief is fundamental; in disapproving the one-year waiting period there involved, it remarked that such benefits are 'the very means to subsist – food, shelter, and other necessities of life'.[99] The later cases, however – all decided over the dissent of three or four Justices – have rejected unlimited judicial intervention in this area. A state law prescribing maximum benefits of $250 per month for families with dependent children was held not to violate the equal protection clause, although the effect was to reduce the payment per child in larger families.[100] A state statute scaling down benefits for dependent children to 75% of estimated need, while playing 100% of estimated need to the aged and 95% to the disabled and the blind, was also upheld; the Court held it immaterial that 87% of recipients of dependent child benefits were Negroes and Mexican-Americans, whereas the other three categories contained a smaller proportion of those minority groups, because it said the 'naked statistics' did not prove 'racial motivation'.[101] A federal statute reducing disability benefits to reflect receipts from workmen's compensation (compensation for injury in the course of employment, under compulsory insurance carried by employers) was held valid although persons receiving other kinds of disability compensation (e.g., tort damages, and insurance benefits under their own disability policies) do not have their federal benefits reduced.[102]

The one case that looks in the other direction invalidated a provision of the federal food stamp program. Under the statute, only households comprised of related persons – i.e., families – could obtain the stamps, which permit food purchases at very low prices. The decision that this was unconstitutional was influenced by the Court's belief that Congress intended to discriminate against 'hippie communes'; it said that 'a bare congressional desire to harm a politically unpopular group cannot constitute a *legitimate* governmental interest'.[103] Thus it seems that, in the field of welfare benefits, the Court is sensitive to discriminatory purpose but not to fiscal provisions which simply happen to result in inequality.

In the related field of subsidized housing, the Court has also been relatively unresponsive to complaints of discrimination. Federal loans and grants are made to state agencies for slum clearance and low-rent housing projects. In 1971 the Court upheld a California requirement that such a project be undertaken only after approval at an election conducted in the community where it was to be located. The requirement was attacked as a discrimination against the poor, the three dissenting Justices calling it 'an explicit classification on the basis of poverty – a suspect classification which demands exacting judicial scrutiny'. The Court, however, did not agree that poverty was a suspect basis of classification. It held that the will of the local majority should be respected because part of the fiscal burden would rest on the local community.[104]

The next year the Court addressed itself explicitly to the question whether housing is so fundamental as to justify a rigid equality requirement for laws affecting the rights of tenants against their landlords. It gave a negative answer to that broad question, and yet invalidated a procedural provision erecting a special financial obstacle against appeals from court orders of eviction for nonpayment of rent – which it called a 'discrimination against the poor'.[105]

The five to four decision in *San Antonio Independent School District* v. *Rodriguez*,[106] though it rejected an equal protection claim, reflects the seriousness with which wealth differentials are evaluated even in matters of general tax policy – where legislatures rather than courts have traditionally been considered supreme. In every state but Hawaii, public schools are mainly financed by local property taxes raised in the respective school districts. Since the districts vary greatly in taxable property and in school-age population, there are substantial inequalities in the property tax revenues per pupil – and, consequently, in expenditures per pupil. These inequalities are mitigated to some extent by state and federal grants, but it is not unusual for one district to spend twice as much per pupil as another.

In several states, the state constitutions have been held to forbid such inequality.[107] The Court declined to accept that position for the whole country, however. It pointed out that no correlation had been established between the wealth of a district and the wealth of its residents: a district inhabited mainly by poor people may contain valuable factories and commercial buildings which give it a high tax base, and may have few school-age children. Inhabitants of the tax-poor districts, the Court said, comprise 'a large, diverse, and amorphous class * * * [having] none of the traditional criteria of suspectness: the class is not saddled with such disabilities, or subjected to such a history of purposeful unequal treatment, or relegated to a position of such political powerlessness as to command extraordinary protection from the majoritarian political process'. Nor, the Court said, was public education a 'fundamental right'. And with unaccustomed humility, it acknowledged[108] that

> the Justices of this Court lack both the expertise and the familiarity with local problems so necessary to the making of wise decisions with respect to the raising and disposition of local revenues. * * * No scheme of taxation * * * has yet been devised which is free of all discriminatory impact. In such a complex arena in which no perfect alternatives exist, the Court does well not to impose too rigorous a standard of scrutiny lest all local fiscal schemes become subjects of criticism under the Equal Protection Clause. * * * We are unwilling to assume for ourselves a level of wisdom superior to that of legislators, scholars, and educational authorities in 50 States, especially where the alternatives proposed are only recently conceived and nowhere yet tested.

As noted above, four of the nine Justices dissented.

3. Illegitimate birth and alienage

In other fields the Court has been more confident of its superior wisdom. For example, various legal disabilities resulting from illegitimate birth have been held to violate the equal protection clause: disability to recover damages for a mother's wrongful death;[109] disability of a mother to recover damages for the wrongful death of her illegitimate child; [110] subordination of an illegitimate child's workmen's compensation claim to that of a legitimate child, for the death of their father;[111] and disability of an illegitimate child to claim financial support by his father.[112] However, a statute denying inheritance rights to illegitimate children whose father had not formally acknowledged paternity was upheld by a vote of five to four.[113]

The same policy of favoritism to regularity of sexual relations that underlay state discriminations against illegitimate children, also motivated a state statute forbidding distribution of contraceptives to unmarried persons for the prevention of pregnancy. The statute was held unconstitutional as a discrimination against unmarried persons.[114]

Several recent cases have invalidated laws discriminating on the basis of citizenship, which has now been denominated a suspect basis of classification. Declaring that 'classifications based on alienage, like those based on nationality or race * * * are inherently suspect and are therefore subject to strict judicial scrutiny whether or not a fundamental right is involved', the Court struck down (1) a Pennsylvania law providing state-funded welfare benefits only for American citizens, and (2) an Arizona law providing federally financed welfare benefits only for American citizens and aliens who had resided in the United States for fifteen years or more.[115] Later decisions invalidated laws making citizenship necessary for admission to law practice,[116] and to the state competitive civil service.[117] But the Court held that the refusal of a private company to employ aliens does not violate a federal statutory prohibition against employment discrimination on the basis of national origin, which it said was quite different from citizenship as a basis of classification.[118] It noted, without evident disapproval, the federal government's practice of employing citizens only – not explaining why aliens can be excluded from the federal but not the state competitive civil service.

4. Sex discrimination

The grosser forms of sex discrimination, such as denial of the franchise to women and the disability of married women to control their own property, have long since disappeared; but a heavy cultural residue persists. It is reflected partly in laws premised on the assumption that women are less capable than men in work involving physical strength or business acumen; partly in laws designed to give them preferential treatment, such as alimony provisions for divorcees, and special limitations on working hours; and partly in laws attributing significance to the woman's status as home-maker, such as exemptions from compulsory jury duty. A vigorous 'women's liberation' movement is pressing for ratification of a proposed Twenty-Seventh Amendment, providing:

> Equality of rights under the law shall not be abridged by the United States or by any State on account of sex.

The amendment was approved by Congress in 1972, and at this writing has received thirty of the thirty-eight state ratifications necessary for adoption. If and when it is adopted, every law and administrative practice which treats women more or less favorably than men, or in any way differently, will be at least presumptively unconstitutional. In order to allow time for the extensive statutory changes that it will require, the Amendment is not to become effective until two years after its ratification.

Meanwhile, a great many attacks on sex discrimination have been launched on the basis of present law, and they are beginning to reach the Court. In *Reed* v. *Reed,*[119] an Idaho law giving males a preference over females as administrators of decedent estates was held to violate the equal protection clause. (The father and mother of a deceased child were competing for the right to administer his estate.) In *Frontiero* v. *Richardson,*[120] the Court invalidated a federal statute enabling a male soldier to obtain increased pay by reason of marriage, without proving that his wife was in fact financially dependent on him, but granting such increase to a female soldier only upon proof that she supported her husband. Four of the Justices believed that sex should be declared a suspect basis of classification. Two others, without flatly rejecting that step, thought it should be deferred while the Twenty-Seventh Amendment was under consideration by the states:[121]

> * * * democratic institutions are weakened, and confidence in the restraint of the Court is impaired, when we appear unnecessarily to decide sensitive issues of broad social and political importance at the very time they are under consideration within the prescribed constitutional processes.

This seems to hold open the possibility that, if the Amendment does fail of ratification, the Court will then proceed to effectuate it nevertheless – by declaring sex classifications suspect, and applying the compelling governmental interest test.

Although the Court has not yet taken that step, which would create a sweeping presumption of unconstitutionality, it has made clear the depth of its concern by giving sex equality priority over freedom of the press (which it usually defends as a constitutional value second to none). In *Pittsburgh Press Co.* v. *Human Relations Commission,*[122] the Court upheld a local order prohibiting a newspaper from listing advertisements for jobs in sex-designated help-wanted columns. (The four dissenters protested the decision as a dangerous encroachment on press freedom, believing that no government 'can tell a newspaper in advance what it can print and what it cannot'.) A number of other sex equality issues are raised by cases now pending in the Court. It has agreed to decide, for example, whether a state unconstitutionally discriminates against women by establishing a program of disability benefits for sick and injured workers without including maternity benefits.[123] A lower federal court held such a California program to be invalid.

5. The political process

The extent to which the equality ideal has been generalized beyond the problem of caste is nowhere better illustrated than in cases involving the elective franchise. For a long time the Court, although recognizing the justiciability of claims that the right to vote had been illegally denied, refused to adjudicate complaints against inequality of voting power. The weight of a given vote in determining the make-up of a legislature depends on a number of factors, such as (1) whether legislative district lines are so drawn as to concentrate the strength of particular political parties in particular districts, (2) whether one legislator is elected from each district, or more than one, (3) the number of eligible voters per legislator, and (4) the percentage of eligible voters who vote. Legislative apportionment (i.e., establishment of legislative districts) has traditionally been prescribed by state constitutions and statutes. (Each state's total representation in the federal House of Representatives is prescribed by Congress on the basis of the latest decennial census, but the division of each state into congressional districts is a matter for its own legislature.) The adoption of an apportionment plan typically reflects a set of political bargains conditioned heavily by considerations of party advantage, and can rarely if ever be rationalized. Until 1962 the Court kept its hands off this process, presumably fearing that the lack of judicially manageable standards would render illusory any effort on its part to equalize voting power. As was said in a 1946 decision against passing upon the constitutionality of an Illinois statute establishing congressional districts of greatly unequal population, 'Courts ought not to enter this political thicket'.[124]

In *Baker* v. *Carr,*[125] however, the Court overcame its reluctance. One of the factors bearing on the weight of a vote – the number of eligible voters per legislator – is susceptible of objective measurement and judicial control if a rule of equality is prescribed. Inequalities in this regard had become widespread, and often quite extreme, by reason of population shifts away from rural areas (coupled with resistance by incumbent legislators to alteration of the districts from which they had been elected). For example, the 1901 Tennessee apportionment involved in *Baker* v. *Carr* resulted, sixty years later, in variations as high as 19 to 1 in the number of eligible voters per state legislator. The Court held that inequality in this regard presents a justiciable equal protection question.

The decision led to a burst of litigation on equality of voting power. Within nine months, state legislative apportionment was attacked in at least 34 states.[126] The Court soon decided, in *Reynolds* v. *Sims,*[127] that deviation from population equality is permissible only if 'incident to a rational state policy' and that very few such policies would be deemed rational. It said:

> * * * neither history alone, nor economic or other sorts of group interests, are permissible factors in attempting to justify disparities from population-based representation. * * * Arguments for allowing such deviations in order to insure effective representation for sparsely settled areas and to prevent legislative districts from becoming so large that the availability of access of citizens to their representatives is impaired are today, for the most part, unconvincing.

In practice, the 'one person, one vote' principle, as the Court chooses to call it[128] – the idea being that population inequality between districts has the same practical effect as giving some voters only a fraction of a vote – has been closely adhered to. For example, the Court invalidated a congressional apportionment in which the district populations ranged from 2.83% below average to 3.13% above it.[129] Recently, however, it has been held that the strict standard for congressional apportionment (which is based not on the equal protection clause but on an inventive interpretation of the Article I, Section 2 requirement that members of the lower house of Congress be chosen 'by the People of the several States')[130] is relaxed somewhat for state legislatures. There, a variation of 16.4% between the least and most populous districts has been held justified, and variations up to 10% have been said to require no justification.[131] Similar latitude has been permitted for local bodies such as county legislatures,[132] to which the 'one person, one vote' principle was extended in 1968.[133]

The United States Senate, of course, represents an extreme case of malapportionment. Each state elects two senators, despite tremendous differences in population. It was contended by some states that, by analogy, it should be enough for *one* house of a bicameral state legislature to be elected from districts of equal population. The Court has rejected this so-called 'federal analogy', however, and has held that neither house of a state legislature can represent political subdivision as such.[134] Nor does it matter that the people of a state have approved its legislative apportionment by popular referendum.[135]

In the matter of remedies, the federal district courts have been held to have very broad discretion. If the state legislature fails to formulate an acceptable apportionment, the district court can issue its own plan; and in doing so, it seems to have the power to disregard even harmless state law restrictions if it thinks a better plan will result. For example, the New York constitution sets a maximum of 150 on membership in the lower house of the state legislature, but the Court declined to set aside a plan calling for election of 165 members which the district court had approved.[136]

At the same time that it has been endeavoring to equalize voting power (or at least to achieve equality in the number of eligible voters per legislator, which is one of the determining factors), the Court has steadily broadened the franchise by striking down restrictions on voting eligibility. It has characterized the right to vote as fundamental and has unsparingly applied the compelling governmental interest test. The right to vote in a local school board election cannot be limited to persons who own or rent taxable property in the district, or whose children attend public school there; this was held to be an unconstitutional discrimination against a bachelor who resided with his parents at their home in the district.[137] For like reason, military personnel cannot be denied the capacity to acquire local residence for voting purposes in the place where they are stationed,[138] and residents of federal enclaves within a state are entitled to vote in state elections there.[139] In elections to pass upon proposed municipal bond issues, the franchise cannot be limited to property taxpayers but must be extended to all residents.[140] The Court held in 1969 that prisoners awaiting trial need not be provided with absentee ballots,[141] but in 1973 it held that they may nevertheless have a right to vote – which, unless absentee ballots are provided, would seem to require establishment of voting facilities in jails.[142]

The most sweeping decision on voting eligibility was *Dunn* v. *Blumstein*,[143] dealing with durational residence requirements. Nearly all states had imposed such requirements. The Court invalidated a typical Tennessee statute which made voting eligibility dependent on residence in the state for one year, and in the county for three months. There was said to be no governmental interest sufficiently compelling to warrant such curtailment of the fundamental rights of voting and interstate movement. The Court said it would not object to a requirement of registration thirty days before the election, and later cases have in fact upheld fifty-day periods.[144]

The Twenty-Fourth Amendment, adopted in 1964, forbade use of the poll tax to prevent voting in federal elections. Two years later, the Court held that the equal protection clause leads to the same result for state elections.[145] A contrary 1937 decision[146] was overruled.

The compelling governmental interest test has been applied to prevent not only discrimination in voting eligibility, but also discrimination in the eligibility of political parties and candidates for a place on the ballot. An Ohio law was held unconstitutional on two grounds: first, because it permitted established parties to retain their position on the ballot simply by obtaining 10% of the vote at the last election for state governor, while requiring other parties to obtain signatures totaling 15% of the voters cast at that election; and second, because it required submission of the signatures too long (nine months) before election.[147] In another case, heavy filing fees for candidates, ranging up to $8,900, were held to discriminate unlawfully against poor candidates and their probably poor supporters.[148]

The foregoing should be sufficient to reveal the breadth of the current equality concept, the determination with which the Court has been translating it into limitations on governmental action, and the rapidity with which the American law of equality has grown and is still growing. Until now we have concentrated attention on constitutional rules declared by the Court. To round out the picture, we now take brief note of the more important equality statutes.

IV. *Equality Legislation*

Each of the fifty states has a substantial body of statute law, and state constitutional law, touching the subject of discrimination. Some of it goes beyond federal equality requirements; on the other hand, some of it (particularly in the South) is designed to minimize their effect.[149] The latter type, as already shown, has fared badly under the equal protection clause and other provisions of the Civil War Amendments. As for the former type, generalization is quite impossible. It is mentioned, however, as a reminder that particular states often insist on more exact equality than the minimum required by federal law. For example, we have seen that several states have done more to equalize the per-pupil revenue of public school districts than the Court has held the equal protection clause to require.[150]

In the field of federal legislation, the past decade has witnessed two parallel developments. First, the broad equality provisions contained in the Civil Rights Acts of 1866, 1870, 1871 and 1875, enacted in the wake of the Civil War and then quickly emasculated (by hostile interpretation and the state action doctrine) have been revivified by new interpretations giving them greater effect. Second, Congress has enacted a series of new anti-discrimination statutes.

A. The early Civil Rights Acts

The 1866 Civil Rights Act contained a provision (now 18 U.S.C. § 242) for criminal prosecution of anyone who, 'under color of any law, * * * wilfully subjects any inhabitant of any State * * * to the deprivation of any rights, privileges, or immunities secured or protected by the Constitution or laws of the United States'. The 1870 Civil Rights Act contained a provision (now 18 U.S.C. § 241) for criminal prosecution of conspiracy 'to injure, oppress, threaten or intimidate any citizen in the free exercise or enjoyment of any right or privilege secured to him by the Constitution or laws of the United States'. These were the statutes involved in *United States* v. *Price* (1966).[151] Three Mississippi law enforcement officers and fifteen private individuals were prosecuted under both statutes. The charges were based on allegations that the defendants had killed three civil rights (Negro rights) workers, but the federal prosecutions were not for murder (which is a *state* crime). Rather, they were for 'punishing' the victims without due process of law in violation of their rights under the Fourteenth Amendment. The district court dismissed most of the charges, adopting restrictive interpretations of the federal statutes which it thought to be required by earlier Supreme Court decisions. On appeal, the Court reinstated the charges. It held that a private individual acts 'under color of law' when he is 'a wilful participant in joint activity with the State or its agents', so that § 242 applies to him. It also held – which it had refused to do fifteen years earlier[152] – that § 241 covers rights protected by the Fourteenth Amendment due process clause.

On the same day, the Court decided *United States* v. *Guest,*[153] involving a prosecution of six private individuals under § 241. They were charged with conspiracy to engage in violence and other illegal acts to deter Negroes from equal use of (1) theaters, restaurants and other places of public accommodation, (2) state and city facilities, and (3) streets and highways. The district court dismissed. For technical reasons the Supreme Court held it lacked jurisdiction of the first charge, but it reinstated the other two. It held that § 241 covers frustration of the equal protection clause, which guarantees equal enjoyment of public facilities, and also covers interference with the federal right of interstate road travel.

The Court has also broadened its interpretation of the civil provisions of the old Civil Rights Acts. The 1871 Act contained a provision (now 42 U.S.C. § 1985(3)) creating a right to damages against those who conspire 'for the purpose of depriving *** any person *** of the equal protection of the laws, or of equal privileges and immunities under the laws'. In 1951 the Court construed the statute as reaching only conspiracies under color of state law, or by private groups so large and powerful as to dominate the state government.[154] Twenty years later, in *Griffin* v. *Breckenridge,*[155] it discarded that interpretation. It upheld a damage suit by Mississippi Negroes who were allegedly beaten by two private individuals for the purpose of preventing them and other Negroes 'from seeking the equal protection of the laws and from enjoying the equal rights and immunities of citizens'. As so construed, the Court held the statute constitutional under the enforcement clause of the *Thirteenth* Amendment, and did not pass on the applicability of the Fourteenth – which would have required reconsideration of the state action doctrine. That doctrine does not apply to the Thirteenth Amendment, which abolished slavery and has been held to empower Congress to eliminate 'badges and incidents of slavery' resulting from private as well as state action.

It will be observed that expansive interpretation of the Thirteenth Amendment provides a basis for tighter restriction of private discrimination against Negroes than other minorities. The Court proceeded down this road in *Jones* v. *Alfred H. Mayer Co.,*[156] applying a provision of the 1866 Civil Rights Act (now 42 U.S.C. § 1982) which provides:

> All citizens of the United States shall have the same right, in every State and Territory, as is enjoyed by white citizens thereof to inherit, purchase, lease, sell, hold, and convey real and personal property.

In 1948 the Court had interpreted the statute as being directed against governmental action only.[157] In the 1968 *Jones* case, however, it was held to entitle a Negro couple to civil relief against a private company which, because of their race, had refused to sell them a home. The Court said the statute was designed 'to prohibit all racial discrimination, whether or not under color of law, with respect to the rights enumerated therein – including the right to purchase and lease property'. The earlier case was overruled. As so construed, the statute was upheld under the Thirteenth Amendment.

These are not the only decisions broadening federal remedies under the old Civil Rights Acts.[158] They suffice, however, to indicate the extent to which they have been revived by repudiation of earlier restrictive interpretation. They have now been strongly supplemented by new federal legislation.

B. Modern Federal Legislation

The 1964 Civil Rights Act[159] is the most comprehensive ever enacted by Congress. It created new federal rights of equal access to privately owned places of public accomodation, and to private employment. It also provided for federal assumption of the enforcement burden in major areas, notably through suits by the Attorney General for relief against many forms of official discrimination, and through cessation of federal financial assistance to discriminatory programs and activities of state and local governments. Other provisions strengthened voting rights, established administrative aids to desegregation, and created the Community Relations Service to conciliate racial controversies.

Title II, dealing with public accommodation, was the most controversial. It covers hotels, motels and other transient lodgings which have more than five rooms for rent; restaurants and other eating places; gasoline stations; and places of exhibition and entertainment such as theaters and sports arenas. It forbids 'discrimination or segregation on the ground of race, color, religion or national origin'. Because the 1883 *Civil Rights Cases*[160] had applied the state action doctrine to invalidate a similar statute, Congress laid a basis for reliance on the commerce clause (Article I, Section 8, Clause 3) which empowers it to regulate interstate and foreign commerce without regard to state action. The coverage of the statute was therefore limited to establishments having some connection with interstate or foreign 'travel, trade, commerce, transportation or communication', except that transient lodging facilities were considered to satisfy this requirement *per se*.

Within less than a year, the Court held Title II valid. A restaurant in Birmingham, Alabama, which refused to serve Negroes was held to have the requisite connection with interstate commerce because it bought meat from a local supplier which procured it from outside Alabama.[161] The Court also pointed to evidence that Negro travel had been impeded by racial discrimination in restaurants, and held that the commerce clause authorized Congress to remove the impediment. Later, it held even a much more tenuous connection with interstate or foreign commerce to be sufficient;[162] and except for private clubs, which the statute exempts, the coverage of the restaurant provisions is now recognized to be universal for all practical purposes.

On the same day, the statute was upheld as to an all-white motel in Atlanta, Georgia, 75% of whose customers were from outside the state.[163] Here too the Court based its decision on the power of Congress to eliminate hindrances to interstate Negro travel. It pointedly left open the question whether the statute could also have been sustained under the Fourteenth Amendment enforcement clause. Therefore one cannot now say whether the rule of the *Civil Rights Cases* is still good law.

The employment provisions of the 1964 Act (Title VII) cover employers of 25 or more employees in businesses affecting interstate or foreign commerce – which, in practice, means virtually all sizeable companies. Labor unions and employment agencies are also regulated. Discrimination on the ground of sex, as well as race, color, religion and national origin, is forbidden. The statute established the Equal Employment Opportunity Commission to receive complaints and refer them to state agencies having power to act on them – or, if there is no such agency, attempt conciliation itself. All else failing, the Commission authorizes suit by the aggrieved individual in federal court if it finds 'reasonable cause' to exist. Its lack of direct enforcement power, and the necessity of delay for possible conciliation, has somewhat impaired the effectiveness of Title VII. There has also been considerable controversy about the scope of statutory exemptions for 'bona fide occupational classification'[164] and for job screening by 'professionally developed ability tests'.[165]

The Voting Rights Act of 1965[166] provided the first effective remedy against discrimination in voting, though such discrimination has been illegal since adoption of the Fifteenth Amendment in 1870. The problem arose from the fact that the Constitution leaves the states in charge of administering all elections, subject to the power of Congress to alter state regulations as they effect congressional elections.[167] Hostility to Negro political activity, prevalent throughout the South, led to widespread abuses. Judicial relief was slow and expensive, and even that was limited by repeal or invalidation of most of the federal statutes on voting rights which Congress enacted shortly after the Civil War. The Civil Rights Acts of 1957, 1960 and 1964[168] strengthened federal remedies somewhat, but none of them took the essential step of displacing state control of the voting registration machinery. That step was finally taken in the 1965 Act.

The central provisions of the Act dealt with literacy tests, which had become a preferred vehicle for discrimination. The use of such tests was suspended for five years in any state or other governmental unit where less than half of the otherwise qualified voters were registered as of November 1, 1964. To prevent the substitution of other discriminatory devices, adoption of new voting regulations was forbidden unless the Attorney General or the federal district Court in the District of Columbia found that their use would not result in discrimination. Most importantly, the Act provided for appointment of federal examiners empowered to receive applications and register applicants if found qualified. These provisions were held constitutional under the enforcement clause of the Fifteenth Amendment.[169]

The main thrust of the Act was against anti-Negro discrimination in the South; but there was one provision for the benefit of Puerto Ricans, several hundred thousand of whom had migrated to New York City and, though literate in Spanish, were prevented from voting by an English literacy test. The 1965 Act prohibited enforcement of the English literacy requirement against persons who had completed the sixth grade of school in Puerto Rico (a United States territory where the language of instruction is Spanish). The Fifteenth Amendment did not apply, since the discrimination was on the basis of language rather than race, but the provision was upheld under the equal protection and enforcement clauses of the Fourteenth.[170]

The 1965 Act was continued and broadened by the Voting Rights Act Amendments of 1970,[171] where literacy tests were abolished for all elections. That statute also lowered the voting age to 18, in recognition of a claim that voting equality should be extended to young adults who were old enough to be drafted into military service. Late in 1970 the Court sustained the prohibition of literacy tests, and held the 18-year provision valid as to federal but not state elections.[172] Three months later Congress proposed the Twenty-Sixth Amendment, lowering the voting age to 18 for all elections. It took only another three months for three fourths of the states to ratify it, and render it effective.

Meanwhile, Title VIII of the Civil Rights Act of 1968[173] had significantly extended the federal law against discrimination in the sale or rental of housing. Subject to exemptions for most single-family houses and for apartment buildings containing four units or less (one unit of which is occupied by the owner), it covers all housing aided by federal financing since 1962. It goes beyond the 1866 Act, upheld in *Jones* v. *Alfred H. Mayer Co.,*[174] by prohibiting discrimination on account of religion and national origin as well as race and color; by covering discrimination in the provision of financing, brokerage, and other services and facilities in connection with the sale or rental of dwellings; by outlawing advertisements or other representations that indicate discriminatory preferences; and by empowering a federal administrative agency to assist aggrieved parties. On the other hand, the 1866 Act is broader in some respects since it is not limited to dwellings, and is not subject to the exemptions mentioned above.

Conclusion

Since World War II the ideal of a caste-free society has become a dominant objective in the law of the United States. Not only has the Supreme Court ceased its obstruction to congressional implementation of the Civil War Amendments. It has also taken the lead in publicizing and condemning the discrimination against minority groups that has so long pervaded American society. Moreover, it has generalized the concept of legally required equality beyond equal treatment of minority groups, and insists on the greatest possible equality in enjoyment of rights which it considers to be fundamental. Finally, as the recent federal statutes show, its efforts have stimulated a broad political movement which in the long run may prove to be the most solid basis of further progress toward unification of the national community.

NOTES

1. Dred Scott v. Sandford, 19 How. 393 (1857).
2. 16 Wall. 36 (1873).
3. 109 U.S. 3 (1883).
4. E.g., Strauder v. West Virginia, 100 U.S. 303 (1880).
5. Yick Wo v. Hopkins, 118 U.S. 356 (1886).
6. 163 U.S. 537, 544 (1896).
7. Id. at 559, 560.
8. See text at notes 26-36, infra.
9. See, e.g., C. Vann Woodward, The Strange Career of Jim Crow (1955), to which a useful bibliography is appended.
10. Guinn v. U.S., 238 U.S. 347 (1915); Lane v. Wilson, 307 U.S. 268 (1939).
11. Lassiter v. Northampton County Boards of Elections, 360 U.S. 45 (1959).
12. Breedlove v. Suttles, 302 U.S. 277 (1937).
13. Nixon v. Herndon, 273 U.S. 536 (1927).
14. Nixon v. Condon, 286 U.S. 73 (1932).
15. 295 U.S. 45 (1935).
16. 16 Stat. 140.
17. 17 Stat. 13.
18. 18 Stat. 335.
19. See, e.g., U.S. v. Cruikshank, 92 U.S. 542 (1875); U.S. v. Harris, 106 U.S. 629 (1882). For a review of the post-Civil War laws, and their fate, see Gressman, The Unhappy History of Civil Rights Legislation, 50 Mich. L.R. 1323 (1952); Carr, Federal Protection of Civil Rights (1947).
20. Korematsu v. U.S., 323 U.S. 214 (1944). On this and related cases, see, e.g., Rostow, The Japanese American Cases – A Disaster, 54 Yale L. J. 489 (1945); Dembitz, Racial Discrimination and the Military Judgment, 45 Colum. L. Rev. 175 (1945); Grodzins, Americans Betrayed: Politics and the Japanese Evacuation (1949).
21. 323 U.S. at 216.
22. 321 U.S. 649 (1944); see also Terry v. Adams, 345 U.S. 461 (1953).
23. 334 U.S. 1 (1948); see also Barrows v. Jackson, 346 U.S. 249 (1953).
24. Henkin, Shelley v. Kraemer: Notes for a Revised Opinion, 110 U. Pa. L. Rev. 473 (1962).
25. Hurd v. Hodge, 334 U.S. 24 (1948).

26. 347 U.S. 483 (1954).
27. Bolling v. Sharpe, 347 U.S. 497 (1954).
28. Sipuel v. Oklahoma, 332 U.S. 631 (1948); Sweatt v. Painter, 339 U.S. 629 (1950); McLaurin v. Oklahoma State Regents, 339 U.S. 637 (1950).
29. Brown v. Board of Education, 349 U.S. 294 (1955).
30. Morland, Southern Schools: Token Desegregation and Beyond, 4-6 (1963).
31. E.g., Cooper v. Aaron, 358 U.S. 1 (1958); see Lusky, Racial Discrimination and the Federal Law: A Problem in Nullification, 63 Colum. L. Rev. 1163, 1167 et seq. (1963).
32. Griffin v. County School Board, 377 U.S. 218 (1964).
33. Goss v. Board of Education, 373 U.S. 683, 689 (1963); and see Watson v. City of Memphis, 373 U.S. 526, 529-30 (1963).
34. Green v. County School Board, 391 U.S. 430 (1968).
35. Civil Rights Digest, December, 1971, p. 7.
36. E.g., Mayor and City Council of Baltimore v. Dawson, 350 U.S. 877 (1955) (beaches); Holmes v. City of Atlanta, 350 U.S. 879 (1955) (golf courses); Gayle v. Browder, 352 U.S. 903 (1956) (buses); New Orleans City Park Imp. Ass'n v. Detiege, 358 U.S. 54 (1958) (parks); Johnson v. Virginia, 373 U.S. 61 (1963) (courtrooms); Lee v. Washington, 390 U.S. 333 (1968) (prisons).
37. Johnson v. Virginia, supra note 36, at 62.
38. Naim v. Naim, 350 U.S. 891 (1955), 350 U.S. 985 (1956).
39. McLaughlin v. Florida, 379 U.S. 184 (1964).
40. Loving v. Virginia, 388 U.S. 1 (1967).
41. See, e.g., Moose Lodge v. Irvis, 407 U.S. 163 (1972) (discriminatory private club can be granted state liquor license).
42. E.g., NAACP v. Alabama, 357 U.S. 449 (1957); Bates v. Little Rock, 361 U.S. 516 (1960); Shelton v. Tucker, 364 U.S. 479 (1960); Gibson v. Florida Legislative Investigation Committee, 372 U.S. 539 (1963).
43. E.g., Barenblatt v. U.S., 360 U.S. 109 (1959); Uphaus v. Wyman, 360 U.S. 72 (1959).
44. The closest approach was Bell v. Maryland, 378 U.S. 226 (1964) where the six Justices who reached this issue divided three to three.
45. 373 U.S. 267 (1963); see also Peterson v. South Carolina, 373 U.S. 244 (1963).
46. 365 U.S. 715 (1961).
47. 387 U.S. 369 (1967).
48. Pennsylvania v. Board of Trusts, 353 U.S. 230 (1957).
49. In re Girard College Trusteeship, 391 Pa. 434, 138 A.2d 844, cert. denied 357 U.S. 270 (1958).
50. Evans v. Newton, 382 U.S. 296 (1966).
51. Evans v. Abney, 396 U.S. 435 (1970).
52. Id. at 445.
53. Palmer v. Thompson, 403 U.S. 217 (1971).
54. Swann v. Charlotte-Mecklenburg Board of Education, 402 U.S. 1 (1971); Keyes v. School District, 93 S. Ct. 2686 (1973).

55. School Board of Richmond v. State Board of Education, 412 U.S. 92 (1973).

56. Bradley v. Milliken, 484 F.2d 215 (C.A. 6, 1973).

57. 93 S. Ct. 2686 (1973).

58. Coit v. Green, 404 U.S. 997 (1971), aff'g without opinion Green v. Connally, 330 F. Supp. 1150 (D.D.C. 1971) (tax benefits); Norwood v. Harrison, 413 U.S. 455 (1973) (textbooks).

59. 347 U.S. 475 (1954).

60. 371 U.S. 415 (1963).

61. E.g., Brotherhood of Railway Trainmen v. Virginia, 377 U.S. 1 (1964); United Mine Workers v. Illinois Bar Association, 389 U.S. 217 (1967).

62. United Transportation Union v. State Bar of Michigan, 401 U.S. 576 (1971).

63. Beauharnais v. Illinois, 343 U.S. 250 (1952).

64. 376 U.S. 254 (1964).

65. E.g., Greenbelt Cooperative Publishing Ass'n v. Bresler, 398 U.S. 6 (1970); Rosenbloom v. Metromedia, Inc., 403 U.S. 29 (1971).

66. 372 U.S. 229 (1963).

67. 340 U.S. 315 (1951).

68. E.g., Bachellar v. Maryland, 397 U.S. 564 (1970); Gooding v. Wilson, 405 U.S. 518 (1972).

69. Barron v. Baltimore, 7 Pet. 243 (1833).

70. Much of the development is reviewed in Duncan v. Louisiana, 391 U.S. 145 (1968).

71. E.g., Miranda v. Arizona, 384 U.S. 436 (1966).

72. 408 U.S. 238 (1972).

73. Id. at 245.

74. Jackson, J., concurring in Railway Express Co. v. New York, 336 U.S. 106, 112 (1949).

75. Metropolitan Casualty Ins. Co. v. Brownell, 294 U.S. 580, 584 (1935) (footnote omitted).

76. Supra note 20.

77. 316 U.S. 535 (1942).

78. E.g., Kotch v. Board of River Pilot Comm'rs, 330 U.S. 552 (1947); Williamson v. Lee Optical Co., 348 U.S. 483 (1955).

79. McLaughlin v. Florida, 379 U.S. 184, 191-92, 194 (1964).

80. E.g., Carrington v. Rash, 380 U.S. 89, 96 (1965); Harper v. Virginia Board of Elections, 383 U.S. 663, 668 (1966).

81. Levy v. Louisiana, 391 U.S. 68 (1968).

82. 394 U.S. 618 (1969).

83. Id. at 634, 638 (emphasis in original).

84. Developments in the Law – Equal Protection, 82 Harv. L. Rev. 1065, 1120-21 (1969); see also Michelman, On Protecting the Poor Through the Fourteenth Amendment, 83 Harv. L. Rev. 7, 34 (1969); Sager, Tight Little Islands: Exclusionary Zoning, Equal Protection, and the Indigent, 21 Stan. L. Rev. 767, 779 (1969); Gunther, The Supreme Court, 1971 Term: Foreword: In

Search of Evolving Doctrine on a Changing Court: A Model for a Newer Equal Protection, 86 Harv. L. Rev. 1 (1972).

85. Concurring opinion in Vlandis v. Kline, 412 U.S. 441, 459 (1973); see also Marshall, J., dissenting in San Antonio Independent School Dist. v. Rodriguez, 411 U.S. 1, 98 et. seq. (1973).

86. Powell v. Alabama, 287 U.S. 45 (1932).

87. Gideon v. Wainwright, 372 U.S. 335 (1963).

88. Argersinger v. Hamlin, 407 U.S. 25 (1972).

89. Griffin v. Illinois, 351 U.S. 12 (1956).

90. Roberts v. LaVallee, 365 U.S. 708 (1967).

91. Douglas v. California, 372 U.S. 353 (1963).

92. Burns v. Ohio, 360 U.S. 252 (1959).

93. James v. Strange, 407 U.S. 128 (1972).

94. Williams v. Illinois, 399 U.S. 235 (1970).

95. Tate v. Short, 401 U.S. 395 (1971).

96. Boddie v. Connecticut, 401 U.S. 371 (1971).

97. U.S. v. Kras, 409 U.S. 434 (1973) (bankruptcy); Ortwein v. Schwab, 410 U.S. 656 (1973) (welfare appeal).

98. For analysis of current problems, see Botein, Appointed Counsel for the Indigent Civil Defendant: A Constitutional Right Without a Judicial Remedy?, 36 Brooklyn L. Rev. 368 (1970); Botein, The Constitutionality of Restrictions on Poverty Law Firms: A New York Case Study, 46 N.Y.U. L. Rev. 748 (1971).

99. 394 U.S. 618, 627 (1969).

100. Dandridge v. Williams, 397 U.S. 471 (1970).

101. Jefferson v. Hackney, 406 U.S. 535 (1972).

102. Richardson v. Belcher, 404 U.S. 78 (1971).

103. U.S. Dept. of Agriculture v. Moreno, 93 S. Ct. 2821, 2826 (1973) (emphasis in original).

104. James v. Valtierra, 402 U.S. 137 (1971).

105. Lindsey v. Normet, 405 U.S. 56 (1973).

106. 411 U.S. 1 (1973).

107. Serrano v. Priest, 5 Cal.3d 584, 487 P.2d 1241 (1971); Milliken v. Green, 389 Mich. 1, 203 N.W.2d 457 (1972); Robinson v. Cahill, 62 N.J. 473, 303 A.2d 273 (1973).

108. 411 U.S. at 41, 55 (footnote omitted).

109. Levy v. Louisiana, 391 U.S. 68 (1968).

110. Glona v. Amer. Guar. & Liab. Ins. Co., 391 U.S. 73 (1968).

111. Weber v. Aetna Cas. & Surety Co., 406 U.S. 164 (1972).

112. Gomez v. Perez, 409 U.S. 535 (1973).

113. Labine v. Vincent, 401 U.S. 532 (1971).

114. Eisenstadt v. Baird, 405 U.S. 438 (1972).

115. Graham v. Richardson, 403 U.S. 365 (1971).

116. In re Griffiths, 93 S. Ct. 2851 (1973).

117. Sugarman v. Dougall, 93 S. Ct. 2842 (1973).

118. Espinoza v. Farah Mfg. Co., 94 S. Ct. 334 (1973).

119. 404 U.S. 71 (1971).

120. 93 S. Ct. 1764 (1973).
121. Id. at 1773.
122. 413 U.S. 376 (1973).
123. N.Y. Times, Dec. 18, 1973, p. 27, col. 1.
124. Frankfurter, J., in Colegrove v. Green, 328 U.S. 549, 556 (1946).
125. 369 U.S. 186 (1962).
126. McKay, Political Thickets and Crazy Quilts: Reapportionment and Equal Protection, 61 Mich. L. Rev. 645, 706-10 (1963).
127. 377 U.S. 533 (1964).
128. The term was first used by the Court in Gray v. Sanders, 372 U.S. 368 (1963), a voting power case not involving apportionment.
129. Kirkpatrick v. Preisler, 394 U.S. 526 (1969); see also White v. Weiser, 412 U.S. 783 (1973).
130. Wesberry v. Sanders, 376 U.S. 1 (1964).
131. Mahan v. Howell, 410 U.S. 315 (1973) (16.4%); Gaffney v. Cummings, 412 U.S. 735 (1973) (under 10%); White v. Regester, 412 U.S. 755 (1973) (same).
132. Abate v. Mundt, 403 U.S. 182 (1971).
133. Avery v. Midland County, 390 U.S. 474 (1968); see also Hadley v. Junior College District, 397 U.S. 50 (1970).
134. Reynolds v. Sims, 377 U.S. 533 (1964).
135. Lucas v. 44th General Assembly, 377 U.S. 713 (1964).
136. WMCA, Inc. v. Lomenzo, 382 U.S. 4 (1965); but cf. 67th Minnesota State Senate v. Beens, 406 U.S. 187 (1972).
137. Kramer v. Union Free School Dist., 395 U.S. 621 (1969).
138. Carrington v. Rash, 380 U.S. 89 (1965).
139. Evans v. Cornman, 398 U.S. 419 (1970).
140. Cipriano v. City of Houma, 395 U.S. 701 (1969); Phoenix v. Kolodziejski, 399 U.S. 204 (1970).
141. McDonald v. Board of Election Comm'rs, 394 U.S. 802 (1969).
142. Goosby v. Osser, 409 U.S. 512 (1973).
143. 405 U.S. 330 (1972).
144. Marston v. Lewis, 410 U.S. 679 (1973); Burns v. Fortson, 410 U.S. 686 (1973).
145. Harper v. Virginia Board of Elections, 383 U.S. 663 (1966).
146. Breedlove v. Suttles, 302 U.S. 277 (1937).
147. Williams v. Rhodes, 393 U.S. 23 (1968); cf. Jenness v. Fortson, 403 U.S. 431 (1971) (milder restrictions upheld).
148. Bullock v. Carter, 405 U.S. 134 (1972).
149. See, e.g., Greenberg, Race Relations and American Law (1959).
150. Supra note 107.
151. 383 U.S. 787 (1966).
152. U.S. v. Williams, 341 U.S. 70 (1951).
153. 383 U.S. 745 (1966).
154. Collins v. Hardyman, 341 U.S. 651 (1951).
155. 403 U.S. 88 (1971).

156. 392 U.S. 409 (1968).
157. Hurd v. Hodge, 334 U.S. 24, 31 (1948).
158. See, e.g., Adickes v. Kress & Co., 398 U.S. 144 (1970); Lynch v. Household Finance Corp., 405 U.S. 538 (1972).
159. 78 Stat. 241.
160. Supra note 3.
161. Katzenbach v. McClung, 379 U.S. 294 (1964).
162. Daniel v. Paul, 395 U.S. 298 (1969).
163. Heart of Atlanta Motel v. U.S., 379 U.S. 241 (1964).
164. E.g., Phillips v. Martin Marietta Corp., 400 U.S. 542 (1971).
165. E.g., Griggs v. Duke Power Co., 401 U.S. 424 (1971).
166. 79 Stat. 437.
167. Article I, Section 4.
168. 71 Stat. 634; 74 Stat. 90; 78 Stat. 241.
169. South Carolina v. Katzenbach, 383 U.S. 301 (1966).
170. Katzenbach v. Morgan, 384 U.S. 641 (1966).
171. 84 Stat. 314.
172. Oregon v. Mitchell, 400 U.S. 112 (1970).
173. 82 Stat. 73.
174. Supra note 156.

ABBREVIATIONS

A. 2d	Atlantic Reporter, Second Series (1938-date)
Colum. L. Rev.	Columbia Law Review
F. 2d	Federal Reporter, Second Series (1924-date)
F. Supp.	Federal Supplement (1932-date)
Harv. L. Rev.	Harvard Law Review
How.	Howard (U.S. 1843-1860)
Mich. L. Rev.	Michigan Law Review
N.W. 2d	North Western Reporter, Second Series (1941-date)
N.Y.U.L. Rev.	New York University Law Review
P. 2d	Pacific Reporter, Second Series (1931-date)
Pa.	Pennsylvania State Reports
Pet.	Peters (U.S. 1828-1842)
S. Ct.	Supreme Court Reporter
Stan. L. Rev.	Stanford Law Review
Stat.	Statutes at Large
U. Pa. L. Rev.	University of Pennsylvania Law Review
U.S.	United States Supreme Court Reports
Wall.	Wallace (U.S. 1863-1874)
Yale L. J.	Yale Law Journal

3

Edward McWhinney

Equality before the Law in Canadian Constitutional Law

The Canadian constitutional system is, in its historical origins, British-derived and British in fundamental spirit and tone. This is understandable enough, considering that British political power in North America was finally established against the French by superior military power. The intellectually detached historian, free from local nationalist prejudices, might conclude that the main military-strategic factors in the expulsion of France from Canada were Frederick the Great's brilliant victories against the French in the Continental European campaigns of the Seven Years' War. Canada was, for the French, necessarily a military sideshow where they faced British forces absolutely unburdened by military commitments in Continental Europe. The British military victory in Canada was, in this sense, as Frederick the Great himself had rightly recognized, rendered largely inevitable because of the multifront (Europe, North America, India) aspect of the French participation in the Seven Years' War. The Battle of Québec of 1759, which consummated the French military defeat in Canada, was eventually juridically ratified in the Treaty of Paris of 1763, which formally ended the Seven Years' War.

British North America was, in its origins, an appendage of Empire, governed according to essentially Roman Law, pyramidal conceptions of a radiation of sovereignty downwards from the supreme Imperial authority in London; and a corresponding and reciprocal reference of ultimate legal decision-making exercises back to London for review and either confirmation or quashing. The succesful break-away of the American colonies from Great Britain in the American Revolutionary War of 1776 – and the resistance by British legal subjects (both English-speaking and French-speaking) in what is now Canada, to all the enticements and blandishments of the American colonists to join them in their defection from Great Britain, tended to reinforce and accentuate, in their North American isolation, the derived British elements in Canadian constitutional history.

Late 18th century British constitutionalism, at the time the French were defeated in North America, could hardly be called democratic or representative in any real sense. But it had, in spite of the obstinacy and obdurateness shown in dealing with the American colonial political leaders in the years immediately prior to 1776, a large element of grace and aristocratic wisdom in it – what Frederick the Great, in an era of enlightened absolutism, saw as the *Rechtsstaat* ideal. Thus victorious Britain, in the aftermath of the military defeat of French power at the Battle of Québec in 1759, did not embark on any policy of forced, compulsory 'Anglicisation' of the newly acquired territory of Québec. The 'gentlemen's understanding' that accompanied the French military surrender of 1759 included some highly pluralistic principles of government – tolerance of the special position and privileges of the French Roman Catholic Church and church hierarchy; and specific retention, as *droits acquis,* of the French civil law or *droit coutumier,* derived from the *coutumes de Paris* and as yet, of course uncodified in France itself or in Québec.

It was the High Anglican tolerance of the British Imperial political establishment, *vis-à-vis* conquered French Québec in 1759 – as opposed to the Low Protestant high-mindedness and selfrighteousness and seeming intolerance of the essentially Puritan-influenced American colonies, that explains more than anything why French Québec preferred in 1776 – and again in the British-American War of 1812 – to remain with its military conqueror and occupant, Great Britain, and not to join the newly emerging, independent United States.

The differences in constitutional traditions help explain why British North America was hardly influenced at all by the emerging American constitutional experimentation, either in the crucial early period of the 1780's when the original American Articles of Confederation were giving way to the American Constitution in the basic form that has continued to the present day; or else in the 1860's when the British Imperial decision was made to federate the remaining colonies and territories of British North America into what is now present-day Canada – a decision concretised in the present Canadian constitution, the British North America Act of 1867.

The British North America Act of 1867, unlike the American Constitution, has no formal Bill of Rights, and indeed no fundamental-style formalised constitutional guarantees, other than Section 133 which, for very limited purposes, establishes French and English as, in effect, languages that may be used officially in the Canadian federal Parliament and in Canadian federal courts, and in the Québec Provincial (state) legislature and in Québec Provincial courts; and Section 93 which guarantees continuance of the separate confessional (Roman Catholic and Protestant) schools in the Province of Québec. British Parliamentary drafting, as applied to the elaboration of constitutional charters for the dependent British Imperial colonies and dependent territories Overseas, never favoured, stylistically, the inclusion of Bills of Rights in constitutions. This intellectual attitude of mind was applied fairly consistently in the historical development of the British colonial Empire; and with only a very limited number of special exceptions being made and these only when absolutely dictated by the political ground rules (*Grundnorm*) of the particular British Empire political society concerned – see, in this regard, the British South Africa Act of 1909 devised for the then newly-created Union of South Africa which was established as a selfgoverning Dominion within the British Empire after the British military defeat of the two Dutch-descended Boer Republics in the South African War of 1899–1902 –, until the aftermath of World War II and the then widespread and rapidly ensuring liquidation of the British colonial Empire in Asia and Africa in the wave of national selfdetermination and independence movements of that post-War era.

It is not surprising, therefore, that the British North America Act of 1867 contains absolutely nothing in the way of a formal constitutional guarantee of the 'equal protection of the laws' on the basis of the celebrated principle enunciated in the American Constitution's Fourteenth Amendment. Even if the British Imperial constitution-makers of 1867 had been disposed to examine the constitutional ferment in the post-Civil War United States devoted to the elaboration of what were to become the Thirteenth, Fourteenth, and Fifteenth Amendments to the United States Constitution, (adopted, respectively, in 1865, 1868, and 1870), sentiment in favour of a constitutionally-institutionalised Equality before the Law would have been a little anachronistic for the Great Britain of that period. Disreali's Second Reform Bill, passed in 1867 in Great Britain, widening the highly restricted British electoral franchise from the land-owners and the industrialists and manufacturers (the latter the political beneficiaries of the First electoral Reform Bill of 1832), to take in the urban middle class, still left excluded from the electoral franchise, and consequently vote-less, a considerable portion of the adult population of Great Britain. The legal disabilities on Roman Catholics and other religious out-groups in Great Britain had, of course, been abolished some thirty years earlier; as had also the institution of slavery.

With what was, from the strictly racial viewpoint, a relatively homogeneous population living in Great Britain, the only areas where any significant, publicly manifest conditions of inequality existed were in those of economic opportunity and social well-being, the differences here being essentially in terms of extreme disparities in wealth dividing the one ethnic-cultural community into different classes – a privileged 'establishment' class that was drastically limited in numbers, and other classes that were more or less disadvantaged economically *vis-à-vis* the privileged upper class.

These conditions, as we say, were manifest in sociological terms; but they did not really enter into the political-constitutional dialogue until very much later, with the political rise of the Labour Party and other left-of-centre political pressure groups. As late as the end of World War II, the socially crusading Archbishop William Temple could speak of the 'indefensible inequalities of wealth and social opportunity' existing in the Great Britain of that era.

When Dicey postulates the principle of 'Equality before the Law' as part of his cardinal constitutional principle of the Rule of Law, he is simply elevating to the level of constitutional folk-lore a condition of formal juridical equality, irrespective of religious affiliations or of official (governmental) or private status of the citizen concerned, already achieved in British statute law earlier in the 19th century. Dicey's principle of Equality before the Law has nothing to say as to economic equality; and it would, of course, have quite surpassed the constitutional universe of discourse of his time to have included economic privileges or status within the ambit of his principle. The concept of Equality before the Law, in any case, so far as it is represented in Canadian constitutional law thinking in the period prior to the so-called Diefenbaker Bill of Rights of 1960, enters in the character of constitutional folk-lore in the late 19th century, by way of reception of the teachings of the venerable Dicey, who quickly became the *doyen* of British and British Empire constitutionalism, and who was universally read and studied in British and British Empire law schools right up to the period of World War II. A whole generation of post-World War II, independent Asian and African leaders were intellectually formed by Dicey, through study of his ideas at the British Inns of Court or at the ancient Universities. In Canada, Dicey's influence was more indirect, since coming second-hand through Canadian Universities and Canadian Law Societies; but is was no less pervasive.

Dicey's Rule of Law concept, with its precept of Equality before the Law, operated, as we have said, as constitutional folk-lore: the constitutional affectation, or enlightened liberalism if you wish, of judicial decision-makers and similar members of the political-legal establishment, in the highly limited or marginal number of cases coming before them in their official capacities. In the period before the adoption of the Diefenbaker Bill of Rights in 1960, the constitutional implementation of any such Dicey-derived postulate would have to be achieved, in Canada, as in England before it – lacking any formal constitutional Bill of Rights – in the interstices of ordinary non-constitutional (private law or administrative law) principles such as the principle that the courts will not enforce restrictive covenants that are 'too vaguely' formulated; or that a delegation of administrative discretion must be clearly specified as to the powers it confers.

Thus, the scattered, and temporally isolated, examples of this nature that have arisen in Canada over the years do occasionnally reflect some of the inspired ingenuity of the earlier British case law in striking down restrictions based on religion (usually the 'Jewish' religion).

In *Re Drummond Wren,* 1945,[1] a restrictive covenant contained a restriction on the resale of a house to '... Jews or persons of objectionable nationality'. The late Mr. Justice Keiller MacKay of the High Court of Ontario, a distinguished soldier and jurist in the full, Dicey-trained, 'English' constitutional tradition, in a rightly celebrated and wideranging judicial opinion that cited the United Nations Charter and the Atlantic Charter, ruled that the restrictive covenant was void as being against public policy, and also for reason of uncertainty. As Mr. Justice MacKay noted in his opinion: 'The common law courts have, by their actions over the years, obviated the need for rigid constitutional guarantees in our policy by their wise use of the doctrine of public policy as an active agent in the promotion of the public weal'.[2]

On the other hand, in *Noble* v.*Wolf and Alley,* 1948,[3] the High Court of Ontario, called on to consider a restrictive covenant restricting resale of a house to '... any person of the Jewish, Hebrew, Semitic, Negro or coloured race or blood', rejected Mr. Justice Keiller MacKay's decision of only three years earlier in *Re Drummond Wren* and upheld the restrictive covenant, Mr. Justice Schroeder commenting that 'the notion of any danger to public interests involved in the use of restrictive covenants such as the one in question seems to me fanciful and unreal'. This decision was upheld by the Ontario Court of Appeal,[4] on appeal from the Ontario High Court; but finally reversed by the Supreme Court of Canada.[5] The grounds of decision in the Supreme Court of Canada are mixed, for it is a case in which multiple judicial opinions are filed: the majority *ratio decidendi* seems to be based on a restrictive interpretation of the sort of restrictive covenants that courts will enforce - those that 'touch or concern the land', as contra-distinguished from a 'collateral' effect (per Kerwin, Taschereau, Rand, Kellock, and Fauteux, JJ.); and a court majority also held the restrictive covenant concerned to be unenforceable because of 'uncertainty' (per Rand, Kellock, Fauteux, and Estey, JJ.).

However, the courts are not quite so happy or inspired in problems of a more strictly racial character involving Canada's very tiny Negro minority.

In *Loew's Montreal Theatres Ltd.* v. *Reynolds* the Québec High Court rejected an action for damages under the Québec Civil Code (based on the *Code Napoléon*) stemming from the refusal of a theatre proprietor to sell an orchestra seat to a Negro because of his colour, the Court holding that '... the management has the right to assign particular seats to different races and classes of men and women as it sees fit'.[6] Similar decisions were rendered in *Franklin* v. *Evans*[7] (Ontario High Court rejecting an action for damages by a Negro refused service in a restaurant in London, Ontario) and *Christie* v. *York Corporation*[8] (Supreme Court of Canada rejecting an action for damages by a Negro refused sale of beer in a tavern in Québec City). In the latter case, the Court noted, in a 4 to 1 decision, that '... the general principle of the law of Québec is that of complete freedom of commerce. Any merchant is free to deal as he may choose with any individual member of the public. It is not a question of motives or reasons for deciding to deal or not to deal; he is free to do either'.[9] In *Rogers* v. *Clarence Hotel Co. Ltd.,*[10] the British Columbia Court of Appeal held the Canadian Supreme Court's *Christie* case decision as not being limited solely to the civil law of Québec but as applying also to the common law provinces (the Court thus rejecting an action by a Negro based on the refusal of service in a beer parlour).

The cases, here, are not many, of course, because the social tension issues that could have given rise to them have been numerically small; and so it seems correct to say that this particular opportunity for a judicially-based civil libertarian activism in favour of equality before the law has hardly penetrated into popular political consciousness and awareness.[11] Worse still, in the numerically larger number of cases – usually turn-of-the-century cases – involving the Asiatic groups (mainly Chinese), originally introduced as low-cost indentured labour in the Western mining industry, there is not merely not very much evidence of an affirmative judicial civil libertarian activism, but, on the contrary, a judicial insensitiveness to racial out-groups and their special problems that almost implies judicially-held policies of a quite contrary, even at times 'racialist', character.

In *Union Colliery Co. of British Columbia* v. *Bryden* (1899),[12] the Privy Council (the highest British Empire tribunal and thus, at the time, the highest Canadian court) held to be *ultra vires* the Province of British Columbia legislature, and so unconstitutional, a law forbidding the employment of 'Chinamen', whether aliens or naturalised citizens, in underground operations in mines in British Columbia. On the other hand, in *Cunningham and Attorney General of British Columbia* v. *Tomey Homma,* rendered only four years later,[13] the Privy Council upheld, as a constitutional exercise of British Columbia legislative power, a law passed by the Provincial legislature excluding naturalised Japanese (and naturalised Chinese also) from the register of voters for the Provincial elections in British Columbia. In the *Tomey Homma* case, the Privy Council explained and distinguished its earlier decision in the *Bryden* case on the score that, in pith and substance, the Provincial law in the *Bryden* case concerned, not the 'regulation of coal mines' (Provincial constitutional competence), but 'Chinese' (federal constitutional competence). On the other hand, the Supreme Court of Canada, eleven years after the *Tomey Homma* decision, upheld, by a 4 to 1 majority, a Province of Saskatchewan law penalising the employment of '. . . any white woman or girl' in any restaurant or laundry owned or managed by a Chinese, whether naturalised or not[14] - on the score that in substance the Saskatchewan Provincial law was directed to the protection of the morals of white women and girls (Provincial competence) and not Chinese (federal competence).[15]

When we come to the Diefenbaker Bill of Rights,[16] we see an attempt by a personally intellectually radical, Conservative Party leader, as Prime Minister, to reconcile – because of still-continuing constitutional exigencies –

the British bias against any formal constitutional Bill of Rights or formalised constitutional guarantees and the American model for a Bill of Rights in the constitutional Charter itself. The Diefenbaker Bill of Rights, in its actual contents, follows the best of American formulae and even goes beyond them.[17]

The Canadian Constitution - the British North America Act, 1867, - was, in its formal, legal origins, a statute of the Imperial (British) Parliament in London which, in 1867, was juridically sovereign in relation to the British Empire overseas of which Canada was, of course, part. The BNA Act of 1867 contained, within itself, no machinery for its own amendment: any subsequent constitutional amendments had to be made, therefore, by statute of the Imperial (British) Parliament. An elaborate series of constitutional conventions (customs) grew up in Canada, over the years, involving the method and degree of Canadian federal government and Provincial (state) governments' mutual consultation and cooperation required as to the substance of any proposed amendment to the BNA Act of 1867, it being established quite easily and early that the Imperial (British) government would act immediately and without qualification as to any request emanating from Canada for amendment of the BNA Act. But attempts to replace what today stands as an inelegant reminder of Canada's past juridical subordination to Great Britain, by the introduction of a self-operating, purely Canadian, constitutional amending process within the BNA Act itself, have all failed over the past forty years because of the inability to obtain agreement between the Canadian federal government and the Provincial governments over the exact character and form of the purely Canadian constitutional amending process to be adopted for the future. Prime Minister Diefenbaker, therefore, facing the practical political difficulty that he would have to go to Londen and the British Parliament if he wished to obtain a constitutional amendment directly incorporating any Bill of Rights into the BNA Act - a procedure for which, according to substantial constitutional opinion, the unanimous consent of the Provincial governments was a condition pre-requisite - concluded, (correctly I think, under the political circumstances of the late 1950's), that if he wanted a federal Bill of Rights at all it would have to be adopted by ordinary federal statute. Prime Minister Diefenbaker did try to get the best of both worlds, however, by enacting in the statutory Bill of Rights itself a form of guide to general statutory interpretation under which, unless the contrary intention were clearly expressed by the federal Parliament, 'ordinary' statutes of the federal Parliament should be construed and applied so as not to conflict with the statutory Bill of Rights. Though quite clearly incapable, as a strictly juridical matter, of derogating from the principle of the Sovereignty of Parliament and its concomitant rule that a later statute necessarily derogates from and controls any earlier statute to the extent of any inconsistency, Prime Minister Diefenbaker's strategy did give a certain extra psychological weight to the Bill of Rights, and subsequent history has tended to vindicate his political judgment on this point, allowing that the more direct political route of a direct constitutional amendment incorporating the Bill of Righs into the BNA Act was foreclosed. In the end, (as indicated by the present writer in correspondence with Prime Minister Diefenbaker, at the time), questions such as these turn not on legal logic but on social-psychological factors, going to the basic political premises of any *régime* – its extra-legal *Grundnorm.*

The Diefenbaker Bill of Rights 'declares' certain 'human rights and fundamental freedoms' to exist – 'without discrimination by reason of race, national origin, colour, religion or sex'; and it lists among such the '. . . right of the individual to equality before the law and the protection of the law' (section 1). After a period of considerable judicial disdain in which the Diefenbaker Bill of Rights was largely ignored by the judiciary or else effectively relegated to the status of ordinary legislation – it had, in fact, been adopted as ordinary legislation of the Canadian federal Parliament and not (for reason of the still-continuing political difficulties already referred to) as a formal admendment to the Canadian federal constitution – the Diefenbaker Bill of Rights was finally accepted by the Canadian Supreme Court, in 1970, in the *Drybones* case,[18] as being in some sort of special, or supereminent, constitutional category and deserving of special deference from the courts on that account: if not quite in the category of a formal constitutional amendment, it was at least beyond the status of 'ordinary' legislation.

The *Drybones* case involved the status of the Indian minority in Canada, and specifically the prosecution of an Indian, in terms of the federal Indian Act, for being 'unlawfully intoxicated off a reserve'. The *Drybones* case, in the Supreme Court of Canada, was rendered as a multi-opinion judgment, and so it is difficult to extract a single, firm principle (*ratio decidendi*) from the Court's final judgment. Even if we accept that, in its end result, the judgment's quashing of Drybones' conviction represents a vindication of the principle of equality before the law – the claimed right of an Indian 'off a reserve', of being intoxicated if he so desires quite as much as a non-Indian – difficult issues of fact finding were involved which go quite beyond the scope of the present chapter.

What is really at stake, in terms of final evaluation of any attempted application of equality before the law to the case of Indians, is an assessment of two presently competing, and in some ways polar alternative, Canadian federal policies as to Indians: the one 'paternalistic' policy that gives the Indian a certain legally privileged status while on 'reserve' but with certain corresponding disabilities purportedly designed to protect the Indians, as to their actions; and the other policy that would end this federal government 'paternalism' but throw the Indian more or less completely back on his own resources, spiritual and material. Both policies claim to be designed to further the Indian's interest; the latter one clearly corresponds to the old 'common law rights of Englishmen', celebrated by Dicey, of a formal, juridical equality before the law; where the former one claims to be a more nuanced one directed to ensuring a genuine equality for the Indian - in the concrete, as distinct from merely in the abstract.

On another plane, the widespread popular movement in the Province of Québec for national self-determination for French-Canadians, while focussed, in terms, primarily upon the 'language' issue – French as the sole 'official' and 'working' language of Québec – has also had a major underlying economic component. In 1968, the Government of Québec constituted a Royal Commission on the French Language and Language Rights in Québec;[19] the Royal Commission was composed of 5 Royal Commissioners, for four of whom French was the maternal language, with English the maternal language of the remaining member. The Commission found in its – unanimous – report[20] that French-Canadians today enjoy, in the Province of Québec in which they represent at least 80 per cent of the population, marked inferiorities, in comparison to the economically dominant, English-speaking ('Anglo-Saxon') *élite,* in terms of wealth, and annual income, and access to decision making and command posts in industry and commerce within Québec.

We quote from the Royal Commission's report: 'The following key societal facts . . . emerge from the Commission's field researches and from the facts adduced in the Commission's public hearings:
1. The historically demonstrated inferiority of the French-Canadian, on the economic plane, in Québec;
2. The essentially rather negative conception historically taken by the English-speaking economic *élite* in Québec of the French-Canadians' claims to equality of opportunity in the direction of the industrial and economic development of Québec;
. . .
6. The comparative failure of institutions of advanced learning in Québec, whether Universities or technical institutes, to develop a technologically-sophisticated, managerial skill group of sufficient numbers among the French-Canadian population, capable of entry into, and also of taking over, positions of command in the commercial and industrial decision-making *élite* in Québec, this failure existing equally on the part of French-speaking and of English-speaking advanced institutions in Québec, all of which are financially underwritten by the Government of Québec as to the substantial part of their annual operating expenses and also their special capital expenditures'.[21]

The French-Canadian drive of our times, while expressing itself symbolically in such terms as political separation and French language primary, is a movement for equality in the most substantial and concrete sense of the word, so far as it is directed towards the wide-spread and rapid redressing of the economic wealth and power (meaning, here, decision-making power) imbalance as between the French-Canadian majority in Québec and the economically more privileged 'Anglo-Saxon' minority in Québec.

> We quote again the Royal Commission's report: '...We find an added intellectual increment, in Professor Lasswell's study,[22] in his trenchant comments on the problem solving capability, or lack of capability, of 'established *élites*' in society, and on why such an 'established *élite*' may, through arrogance or sheer incompetence, allow a political situation 'to become provocative and to get out of hand'. The problem solving task, as Professor Lasswell points out, is to '...give attention to any controversial element while dissipating its symbolic inflation'; the implicit question, in a Québec context, must be why an essentially 'Anglo-Saxon' social and economic 'establishment', with all the problem solving resources available at its command, failed to read the political signals correctly, or in time, and allowed, instead, a crisis situation to develop'.[23]

It is likely, in this regard, that the key battles of Canadian constitutional law of the last quarter of the century will be directed towards achieving some greater measure of economic equality – of opportunity and also of actual possessions – in the concrete.

By comparison, the older issues of formal juridical equality will tend to remain – because of the historical accident of the still relatively uncomplicated ethnic-cultural elements in Canadian society as opposed to other more 'difficult' multi-racial societies such as the United States –, essentially secondary or even marginal questions, constituting interesting foot-notes to constitutional history but hardly, in themselves, providing major battlegrounds for the vindication of key societal values. On the other hand, their contribution to a particularist 'classical' constitutional tradition should not be ignored. The rightly celebrated Québec constitutional *cause célèbre,* the *Roncarelli* case,[24] provides a clear example of such a contribution: the Supreme Court of Canada held that, under the general principles of civil law liability in *délit,* established in the Québec Civil Code, the Provincial Premier could be held personally liable in damages for abuse of his governmental powers. Although the case is based strictly on Article 1053 of the Québec Code (equivalent to Article 1382 of the *Code Napoléon*), it is perhaps closest of all to Dicey's linking of the principle of equality before the law as part of his more general 'rule of law'-concept: namely, the placing of the governmental official, elected or otherwise, on the same plane of strict juridical equality as the ordinary private citizen.[25] The scientific-legal weight of the *Roncarelli* decision (a 6 to 3 decision), if not also its full political persuasiveness, may perhaps have been weakened by the fact that, as a public law decision that purported to base itself on the Québec Civil Code, it was rendered by the English-Canadian, common law majority of the Supreme Court of Canada over the dissents of the French-Canadian, civil law judges of the Court.

NOTES

1. (1945) O.R. 778; (1945) 4 D.L.R. 674.
2. (1945) O.R. 778, at 783.
3. (1948) O.R. 579.
4. (1949) O.R. 503.
5. (1951) 1 D.L.R. 321.
6. 30 K.B. (Québec) 459 (1919).
7. 55 O.L.R. 349 (1924).
8. (1940) 1 D.L.R. 81.
9. Per Rinfret J. (1940) 1 D.L.R. 81, at 82.
10. (1940) 3 D.L.R. 583.
11. As to judicial activism and its (limited) application in Canada, see, generally, the author's *Judicial Review* (4th ed. 1969), chapters 4, 11 and 13; *Comparative Federalism* (2nd ed. 1965), chapter 3; *Federal Constitution-making for a Multi-national World* (1966), chapter 6.
12. (1899) A.C. 580.
13. (1903) A.C. 151.
14. *Quong Hing* v. *The King*, 18 D.L.R. 121 (1914).
15. See also *Attorney General for British Columbia* v. *Attorney General for Canada,* (1924) A.C. 203 (Privy Council).
16. An Act for the Recognition and Protection of Human Rights and Fundamental Freedoms, 1960 (8-9 Eliz. II, c. 44).
17. See the author's article, The new Canadian Bill of Rights, 10 *American Journal of Comparative Law* 87 (1961).
18. *The Queen* v. *Drybones*, (1970) S.C.R. 282.
19. Commission d'enquête sur la situation de la langue française et sur les droits linguistiques au Québec (*Commission-Gendron*).
20. The Royal Commission completed its work on December 31, 1972, its report (in three volumes) being published officially in 1973, in both French and English versions.
21. *Rapport de la Commission d'enquête* (1973), volume 2, *Les droits linguistiques*, at p. 10.
22. The report refers to Harold D. Lasswell, *Elites* and *Elite* Formation, in *Rapport de la Commission d'enquête* (1973), volume 2, *Les droits linguistiques,* Appendix A (II), p. 99 et seq.
23. *Rapport de la Commission d'enquête* (1973), volume 2, *Les droits linguistiques*, at p. 60.
24. *Roncarelli* v. *Duplessis*, 16 D.L.R. (2nd) 689 (1959).
25. The *Roncarelli* decision is discussed by the author in 37 *Canadian Bar Review* 503 (1959).

ABBREVIATIONS

A.C.	Appeal Cases
D.L.R.	Dominion Law Reports
K.B.	King's Bench
O.L.R.	Ontario Law Reports
O.R.	Ontario Reports
S.C.R.	Supreme Court Reports

4

Eckart Klein

The principle of Equality and its Protection in the Federal Republic of Germany *

* Translation by H. G. Grossland LLB, solicitor, postgraduate student at the University of Exeter, England; revision by the author

I. *The Constitutional Basis*

1. The Basic Law (*Grundgesetz*)

The provisions dealing with the principle of equality in the Basic Law of the Federal Republic of Germany[1] are characterized by the fact that besides the general guarantee of equality – 'all persons shall be equal before the law' art. 3 par. 1 GG – there are particular provisions, which refer to equality in a particular respect, by reason of particular criteria. Of these the foremost are par. 2 and 3 of art. 3 GG which read 'men and women shall have equal rights' (par. 2) and 'no one may be prejudiced or favoured because of his sex, his parentage, his race, his language, his homeland and origin, his faith or his religious or political opinions' (par. 3).

Art. 6 par. 5 GG requires that illegitimate children shall by means of legislation be provided with the same opportunities for their physical and spiritual development and for acquiring a position in society as enjoyed by legitimate children.

In connection with public rights and duties the following provisions are found in art. 33 GG: 'Every German shall have in every *Land* the same political rights and duties' (par. 1); 'Every German shall be equally eligible for public office according to his aptitude, qualifications and professional achievements' (par. 2); 'Enjoyment of civil and political rights, eligibility for public office and rights acquired in the public service shall be independent of religious denomination. No one may suffer any disadvantage by reason of his adherence or non-adherence to a denomination or ideology' (par. 3).

Finally art. 38 par. 1 GG guarantees not only that election to the German *Bundestag* is direct, free and secret but also that it is universal and equal.[2]

2. Constitutions of the *Länder*

Most of the Constitutions of the *Länder* contain provisions expressing the equality principle, but they are of varying intensity and extent. It is interesting to note here the often emphasized right to equal opportunities for economic, social, intellectual and cultural development (art. 6 Berlin Constitution[3]; art. 2 Bremen Constitution[4]; art. 11 Baden-Württemberg

Constitution[5] gives, within limits, the right to education and occupational training according to capability regardless of origin and economic conditions).

In so far as the provisions of the Constitutions of the *Länder* go beyond the protection given by the Basic Law, they remain in force – subject to any contrary provision of federal law.[6] On the whole it may be said that the protection of the fundamental rights on the federal level show a unitary tendency, which is strengthened by the decisions of the Federal Constitutional Court (*Bundesverfassungsgericht*), and that this tendency has put the legal significance of the basic rights contained in the Constitutions of the *Länder* into the background.[7] As we shall see, this also applies very much to the equality principle.[8] The following discussion therefore concerns mainly the equality provisions of the Basic Law.

3. Obligations under international law

As far as the international law obligations are in question to which the Federal Republic of Germany is subject in relation to the principle of equality, a short reference is sufficient. This is justified on the ground that international law provides, neither as customary law nor as treaty law, higher standards of protection than the Basic Law. Moreover, rules of international law, regardless of origin, rank below the constitution.[9] The principles of equality enunciated in the United Nations' Universal Declaration of Human Rights, 1948 (art. 2 and 7),[10] and in the European Convention on the Protection of Human Rights and Fundamental Freedoms, 1950 (art. 14),[11] are therefore not included in the following discussion. This also applies, for example, to the prohibitions of discrimination which are contained in the Treaty establishing the European Economic Community,[12] even though they go in part beyond the corresponding guarantees of the Basic Law[13] and may even take priority over these guarantees.[14] This exclusion does not mean, however, that the resulting influences on the legal and social order based upon the principle of equality would be neglected. They simply involve different approaches from those which have developed from national constitutions, and it is not the object of this work to deal with them.

4. General outline

A survey of the constitutional guarantees of equality reveals a relatively wide set of general and specified clauses. This statement alone is however not very illuminating. Above all the degree of binding force of the (as yet undefined) equality principles for the acts of public authorities will be important, but next to it the role they play in the relations between citizens. Moreover, the search for a system into which these principles can be incorporated is relevant, both as regards their relationship to each other and that to other fundamental rights. The problem of the actual enforcement of the equality principles is central, at least from the point of view of the citizen. Besides, the discussion wil identify the areas in which the principle of equality has been able to achieve particular importance since the Basic Law entered into force, and in particular the social issues which have dominated in the legislative and judicial attitudes to the equality principle.

II. *The Principle of Equality in the Decisions of the Federal Constitutional Court*

1. Equality and judicial review

If a discussion of the protection of the principle of equality in the Basic Law proceeds from the pronouncements of the Federal Constitutional Court (and of its critics), this has two reasons. Firstly, the court is the guardian of the fundamental rights. The acts of the public authorities, whether legislative, executive or judicial, are – with a few exceptions – subject to its control whether they comply with the standards laid down in the Basic Law. Furthermore, the highly disputed question[15] caused by the ambiguous wording[16] – equality 'before' the law – in the Weimar Constitution of 1919,[17] whether this also meant equality before the legislature, has been unexpectedly quickly and clearly resolved in a positive manner under the Basic Law.[18] The Constitutional Court early decided without further discussion that also the legislature is subject to the principle of equality according to art. 1 par. 3 and art. 20 par. 3 GG.[19] As little as judicial review of legislation and the submisson of the legislature to the equality principle are logically connected,[20] so similarly it can hardly be pure coincidence that both ideas emerged in German constitutional law at the same time;[21] judicial review of legislation would just have remained a patchwork if scrutiny of legislative measures contradicting the principle of equality would have been excluded. Inversely, its inclusion must lead to a considerable strengthening of the Court's position in dealing with the legislative power; this position had the effect that excess of judicial power became possible. Anyway the question was raised that was henceforth decisive: what are the contents of the principle of equality, i.e. what interpretation will the Court – as supreme authority – give to it? One must proceed from the fact that the answer given by the Federal Constitutional Court has had in mind the above mentioned problem; criticism of the Court's decisions was inevitable, no matter which answer would have been given.

2. Art. 3 par. 1 GG and legislative power

a. The arbitrariness formula of the Federal Constitutional Court

Already in one of its first decisions the Constitutional Court[22] took the opportunity to define the general equality clause. In that case, the situation was untypical as it did not concern the unequal treatment of one citizen in relation to another; rather, the dispute concerned the reorganisation of the *Länder*. The *Land* of Baden, through its government, argued that it was receiving unequal treatment in comparison with the other *Länder* under the first Federal Reorganisation Act.[23] It was also untypical that the first basic exposition of the equality clause by the Constitutional Court, which had an influence greater than any other decision, was merely contained in an *obiter dictum*. Pronouncements that the legislature had violated art. 3 par. 1 GG had already been refused on other grounds. Obviously the Court thought it, however, important to have at hand as quickly as possible a formula for the solution of questions concerning the problem of equality which would foreseeably become more and more urgent.

According to the Constitutional Court, the equality clause does not require all (in this case: all *Länder*) to be treated equally. It merely forbids that persons or facts which are substantially equal are treated differently, but not that persons or facts which are substantially unequal shall be treated differently in relation to the existing inequality.[24] The equality clause is violated when no reasonable ground can be found for legislative differentation or non-differentation, arising from the nature of the object or from otherwise objective circumstances, that is when the regulation must be described as arbitrary.[25] On the particular facts, the Court held for the south-western area that there was a difference of objective circumstances in comparison with the rest of the country, which justified unequal treatment; thus, there was no arbitrariness on the part of the legislature.

In describing the equality clause as a prohibition of arbitrariness the Constitutional Court relied on the legal theory developed in the 1920's in relation to art. 109 of the Weimar Constitution. One of its main exponents was Gerhard Leibholz. In 1925 he defined the equality of all Germans before the law 'as the – according to the current legal opinion – not-arbitrary application of the laws addressed to the subjects of the law by the legislature and by those who enforce the laws (courts and administration)'.[26] For him, arbitrariness was present when a reasonable objectively obvious ground for the differentation or non-differentation in question could not be found.[27] Leibholz was a member of the Federal Constitutional Court from its establishment till 1971.[28] His influence on the interpretation of the equality clause as expressed by the Court has been unmistakable.

b. Legislature and the prohibition of arbitrariness

One of the most urgent tasks of the Constitutional Court was to mould the formula in which it had expressed the equality principle by applying it to the multitude of cases to be dealt with. Retrospectively, the most important aspect – and this had already been indicated in the framing of the principle as a prohibition of arbitrariness – was that the legislature was allowed wide room for action. This legislative discretion extends primarily to the choice of the circumstances which shall have the same legal consequences and therefore are to be treated equally.[29] Since these circumstances are never identical in real life, certain differences have to be continually ignored; the legislative decision is therefore in fact a choice simply of one or more distinguishing facts common to the set of circumstances. The legal consequences, also to be laid down by the legislature, are linked with these criteria.

The Court, therefore, controls legislative power only as far as it may go beyond its limits; and these limits are defined by the prohibition of arbitrariness: i.e. of taking into account facts for which there is no obvious reason to do so.[30] The decisive point in judicial review of legislation under art. 3 par. 1 GG is therefore always whether the Court can find such an obvious reason. This form of control resorts in particular to two concepts of natural justice: 'adequacy regard to the object' (*Sachgerechtigkeit*) and 'adequacy with regard to the system' (*Systemgerechtigkeit*).

The Court based its judgment of 20 May 1959, for instance, essentially on the concept of '*Sachgerechtigkeit*'.[31] The case concerned the constitutionality of a provision of the Fire Service Act of Baden-Württemberg.[32] The statute empowered the municipalities to call on all men between the ages of 18 and 60 living on their territory for payment of fire service duties. Since it was not clear from the statute for what task this contribution was required, the Court considered all possible alternative meanings and checked whether they were in accordance with art. 3 par. 1 GG. The alternative legal purposes were therefore scrutinized as to their standards of justice. If the fire service duty was understood in a purely fiscal sense, the statute would violate the equality principle, for although the levying of duties may be legitimate in return for the service rendered, it was, of course, not at all obvious that only men between 18 and 60 did benefit from the existence of the fire service. Beneficiaries are above all the houseowners, who may be female or even companies; but these persons were not liable to the duty. If, however, the duty was to be a kind of substitute payment in place of personal service, it was not reasonable to expect all men in that age group to contribute without exception, for men who are physically incapable are not subject to personal service. If the duty was to be understood as a personal tax, then it contradicted the generally recognised principles of tax law, in so far as it would be levied on a particular group; it should rather have been levied on all inhabitants of the municipality, since every person has an interest in the existence of a fire service. Thus the Court proceeded from an examination of the various possible objects of the statute and considered the question of *'Sachgerechtigkeit'* – with negative results.[33]

In a more recent decision of 22 March 1971 the reason for legislative differentation was clear.[34] Sec. 12 of the Act concerning compensation for preventive detention of innocents gave this compensation to aliens only on the basis of reciprocity. The Constitutional Court held that there was no violation of Art. 3 par. 1 GG. Although this basic right is available to all persons, thus also to aliens, the differentation within the group 'aliens', on the basis of whether their own State has given similar rights reciprocally, was *'sachgerecht'*.[35] It corresponds to the legitimate concern of a State to exercise strong pressure in this way on other States in order to promote also legal protection for its citizens outside its boundaries.

The decision, however much it tries to find its basis in the object of the statute, still reveals a defect which many judgments of the Federal Constitutional Court have.[36] In the examination it is not so much concerned with an attempt to uncover the structure of the provision made by a statute, but it rather examines whether the alleged reason for differentation is obvious or not. The criterion of *'Sachgerechtigkeit'* also loses its importance in that quite often the Court goes so far as to deny it only where the statute is quite obviously inadequate.[37] But such qualifications will not often be given to legislation.[38]

'Sachgerechtigkeit' has greater weight in connection with the object of statutes decreed by the law itself. If the legislature has decided for regulating a matter in a particular way, then the weight of the arguments in favour of an exception therefrom must correspond with the degree of deviation from the chosen principles.[39] Otherwise there is no *'Sachgerechtigkeit'*; the Court even once spoke of 'indication of arbitrariness'.[40] The result of this is a kind of reversal of the burden of argument.[41] While normally the unreasonableness of the statute must be proved to show violation of the equality principle, here obvious objective reasons must be put forward to justify deviation from the chosen basic rules. Since this was not possible, sec. 8 subs. 6 of the Business Tax Act,[42] for example, was declared null and void; it treated various types of companies (*Kapitalgesellschaften*) partly as such and partly as partnerships, and thereby contradicted the private law division into partnerships and companies which was also adopted in tax law.[43]

These last mentioned decisions point already to the second criterion used in the Constitutional Court's judgments to justify different treatment – the *'Systemgerechtigkeit'*. The Court soon applied this standard:[44] if the legislature, in considering whether to introduce proportional representation or majority representation based on a constituency system, chooses the former, it must accept that this choice implies certain requirements of fairness inherent in the system of proportional representation; it would be in principle contrary to the system to give the votes unequal weight.

In other cases this connection between *'Systemgerechtigkeit'* and respect for the equality principle is even more obvious. Thus the Court held that an amending Act did not violate art. 3 par. 1 GG, because the provision that was inserted accorded with the system, meaning and purpose of the statute being amended.[45] The argumentation of adequacy with regard to the system presupposes a certain determination and delimitation of various fields of life, for each of these is subject to a different system. Whether a provision fits into a system can only be decided in relation to that system. The equality clause cannot be used to impose assimilation of various fields of life.[46]

The logical conclusion of the Court's decisions is that legislation contrary to the system entails violation of the equality clause.[47] This consequence is, however, often reduced because the breach of the system can on its part be legalised if there are adequate reasons.[48] And in other cases the Court has attached no significance at all to contravention of the system.[49]

We may, therefore, assume that also the criterion of *'Systemgerechtigkeit'* is given only limited importance. It will be no surprise, then, that the question whether objective grounds exist for legislative differentiation is often answered without any reference to auxiliary concepts.[50] The only help in coming to a solution is then the 'guidance by the idea of justice'.[51] True, the Court goes further than this when it takes the precept of substantial justice as guideline for its decision:[52] only this can require that financial compensation for injustice suffered under the national socialist regime be paid not only to those who lost their positions under this regime, but also to those who were not allowed to take up any position in the public service. The same applies in the relation between those who took university degrees and those prevented from qualifying by reason of racial persecution.

Two judges of the Federal Constitutional Court dissented from this decision. Their opinion[53] is notable above all because it reveals the dilemma of judicial review with regard to the equality clause. This dilemma is that the criteria at the basis of judicial decisions are universally recognised, but can in individual cases be interpreted in completely different ways. Thus the dissenting vote could in its arguments rely on previous judgments of the Court, and later judgments are again going in the same direction. The minority opinion felt firstly that in examining an alleged violation of the equality principle the judge should only be guided by the idea of justice. Certain hardships are at any rate unavoidable when the legislature has to draw the line between two similar factual circumstances; there will always be situations where one must say that here the requirements of the statute have just about been fulfilled and there they have just failed to be so fulfilled. In this connection reference is made to otherwise completely undisputed case law, according to which it is not the Constitutional Court's duty to decide whether a different regulation from that made by the legislature would be more suitable or reasonable or just, or would correspond more to the requirement of equal treatment.[54] This formula, in which the Court's restraint in relation to the legislature is made very clear,[55] also proves that the Court does not identify justice and prohibition of arbitrariness;[56] arbitrariness would thus appear rather as unacceptable injustice. From the point of view of this case law the compensation judgments of the Court[57] are obviously exceptions to the rule; and their rationale is disputed by the dissenting judges.

Equally, the minority opinion that legislative freedom is greater in connection with statutes which accord or permit certain acts, than with encroachments on freedom and property, has often been put forward by the Court.[58] Accordingly it is recognised that the legislature has a large freedom to generalise and standardise in order to meet the multifarious circumstances of life, if the statute grants benefits or rights, but not if it imposes burdens.[59] Further the Court regularly allows the legislature a 'generous margin of error'[60] when the statutory provisions concern very complex topics not easily fathomed; therefore there is no arbitrariness where the legislative prognosis proves wrong in the course of events.[61]

According to the minority opinion, art. 3 par. 1 GG therefore requires the legislature, as far as statutes making grants are concerned (like those providing compensation) only to avoid differentiations and privileges that are obviously not objective.[62] Otherwise the Court would substitute its own appreciation of justice for that of the legislature.[63]

As the criteria which the Court applies in deciding whether legislative acts are arbitrary or not, seem liable to subjective assessment all attempts to objectify the application of Art. 3 par. 1 GG are to be welcomed. One way towards which the Court has already taken, is to take even the notion of arbitrariness in an objective sense; that is to say, it is sufficient (and necessary) to show the actual and unequivocal[64] non-suitability of the provision in relation to the situation to be regulated.[65] Subjective interpretations of arbitrariness by the legislature which do not appear objectively in the statute are not sufficient; on this assumption the adoption by the legislature of a bill proposed by an interest group cannot be objected to. Whether the equality principle has been violated depends on the objective contents of the statute, not on the way it was adopted.[66] To discover the contents, however, the mere wording is not conclusive. If the wording avoids unequal treatment but the effect in practical application is an inequality not objectively justifiable, then a violation of the equality principle exists. Accordingly, tax provisions were declared unconstitutional, which although formulated in an abstract manner, nevertheless produced in fact a situation where the tax reduction for contributions to political parties grew in proportion to the size of the contribution, thus favouring the parties whose program could attract the wealthier contributors.[67] Another path to objective standards is that the Court – bound as it to the GG (art. 1 par. 3 and art. 20 par. 3) – makes use not of its own appreciation in determining the notion of arbitrariness, but of the objective system of values which is the foundation of the whole GG and in particular of the basic rights.[68]

Finally we ought to consider whether the prohibition from treating equal things unequally corresponds to a prohibition from treating unequal things equally,[69] i.e. whether there can also be a 'lack of differentiation contrary to equality'.[70] This question is constantly answered in the affirmative by the Court's decisions. It is not necessary that different things be treated differently in all circumstances;[71] an obligation to take always account of all dissimilar factual circumstances would have the odd result of hindering unification of law in many fields.[72] Differentiation is however a constitutional obligation when factual differences are so important that there are no objective grounds for their being treated the same in law; in that case, lack of differentiation would be arbitrary.[73] Thus the prohibition of unequal treatment of art. 3 par. 1 GG is subject to the same conditions as the prohibition against equal treatment arising from that rule.[74]

It is notable that where equal facts allow statutory differentiation, the Constitutional Court subjects the differentiation to scrutiny as to its compliance with art. 3 par. 1 GG; it therefore requires differentiation which is just with regard to its object.[75] One can conclude from this and from the previously mentioned points that the equality principle has a role to play in the relationship of the similar to the dissimilar as much as in that of the similar to the similar and of the dissimilar to the dissimilar.

c. Criticism of the jurisprudence

The most frequent criticism of the Constitutional Court's decisions on the equality principle by legal authors is that the Court created an empty formula with its notion of arbitrariness; it missed the opportunity to develop definite criteria by which it could be clearly ascertained whether a legislative rule was contrary to art. 3 par. 1.[76] As the concept of 'reasonable ground' cannot be rationalised,[77] the Court in applying art. 3 par. 1 was not making a subsumption but an evaluation,[78] which led to giving the general equality principle ideological contents.[79] In establishing uncertain criteria in the interpretation of the Constitution, it is alleged, the Court overtaxed the strength of judicial power in a democratic and parliamentary system.[80] The Court also failed to recognise that the general equality principle is not intelligible of itself but that it is rather dependent on extraneous standards.[81] These considerations led some scholars to advocate 'radical dismissal of the general equality principle'.[82] They recommend instead complete reliance on the specific equality clauses, that are defined more precisely, as well as on other basic principles to be gleaned from the GG.[83] Other scholars understand art. 3 par. 1 GG in such a way that it provides for a procedure for the search of grounds for the intended differentiation: the differentiation should be positively supported, and a negative test that arbitrariness does exist should not be sufficient.[84]

However, the interpretation of the general equality principle as a prohibition of arbitrariness has also received support. In this connection Günter Dürig has pointed to art. 1 par. 1 GG: 'The dignity of man shall be inviolable'. Unequal (or equal) treatment resulting from lack of a sensible reason i.e. from arbitrariness, would put the person concerned at the mercy of state activity or inactivity and would thus make him the object of the events.[85] Even Hans Zacher, despite many reservations, has pointed out that the adoption of the suggestion made in legal literature would imply renouncing any attempt to realize the general equality principle;[86] for this principle could not be fully compensated for by reliance on the specific equality clauses and on other constitutional rules.[87] And the related question, if after all historical experiences the legislature should retain the last word on whether a provision violates the general equality principle, does not lend itself to a simple answer.[88]

In my opinion the critical point in the jurisprudence of the Constitutional Court on the general equality principle is that the Court is not consistent in using criteria which are supposed to determine whether objective reasons exist for differentiation or non-differentiation. Exemplary judgments like that on the Baden-Württemberg fire service duties, are rare.[89] However, evaluations by the courts are almost inevitable, especially in the exercise of judicial review of legislation. The Court could not escape from this dilemma if it merely obtained the standards for its decisions from the specific equality clauses. At the heart of this problem lies the fundamental question whether judicial review in general is meaningful and compatible with the legal system; but this question cannot be examined further here.[90] A good measure of judicial self-restraint could, however, take account of these considerations. There are distinct moves towards this attitude in the very field of the Court's decisions on the general equality principle.[91]

3. Art. 3 par. 1 GG and the executive

In contrast to the position regarding the legislature it is no problem of principle to apply the general equality clause to the institutions that put the laws into effect, i.e. the executive and the judicature. In this field the realisation of the equality principle has a long tradition. However, one can question how the principle is applied in its details. As regards the executive art. 3 par. 1 GG has particular significance in two respects.

a. Art. 3 par. 1 GG as a restraint on discretion

The administration is certainly not always fully bound, i.e. it is not so governed by legal rules that its only task is merely to execute them. On the contrary, the administration is given large room for decision whether and how to make use of its legal powers.[92] But even in this area of expediency, of discretion, the administration is not entirely free. It is undisputed that the equality principle forbids the administration, also in the area of its discretion, 'every arbitrary act or omission, i.e. one which is not justified by objective differences';[93] the Constitutional Court puts administrative discretion explicitly under the imperative requirements of the equality principle, which is for the executive and judiciary also defined as a prohibition of arbitrariness.[94] The other courts have followed,[95] and also legal doctrine has recognised that the equality principle is part of the discretion doctrine.[96]

The arbitrariness of the administration arises either out of a non-objective motive or of a non-objective purpose; conclusive here is naturally not the actual intention of the administrative authority, but the motive which can be objectively established.[97] In this connection reference should be made to what the Court once called the 'stronger tie' of the administration to the equality principle, in comparison with the legislature: the administration must omit or undertake such differentiations in its acts as the legislature has or has not made. The reasons of the authority and its intended goal must remain within the framework set by the law, whereas the legislature is only bound by the Constitution itself.[98] Without doubt it is easier, therefore, to objectify in the determination of the authority's arbitrariness. This point of view, on the other hand, obviously does not apply where the administration performs something without a statutory basis: in that case, no concretisation of the equality principle through legal consideration is intended. It is significant, however, that the equality principle plays a particularly important role in practice here, especially in the administration of subsidies, although this field is not governed by the principle that executive action requires a statutory basis.

b. Self-binding action of the administration

It goes beyond mere restriction of administrative discretion by the equality principle when – on the basis of art. 3 par. 1 GG[100] – it is generally recognised that the administration binds itself by the consistent exercise of its discretion in similar cases; the discretionary decision then acquires normative force.[101] The freedom given to the administration to exercise its discretion in choosing for itself the differentiation system,[102] involves this system being binding.[103] This means that the administration cannot treat an individual case contrary to its usual practice in similar cases. In this connection the so-called administrative guidelines have a role to play: they are issued by superior administrative authorities and intend to produce a uniform practice. The self-binding effect does not occur simply because of the guidelines, but only as a result of the uniform way of dealing with the situations covered by the guidelines.[104] Art. 3 par. 1 GG also implies that the administration will treat equally corresponding cases that are to be decided at the same time.[105] This means that, apart from the duty of equal treatment, there is an individual right for respect of the similarity of various situations but this right only involves obtaining certain administrative decision when every other decision should be defective;[106] this will occur often in such cases. Part of legal literature goes further;[107] it affords a substantial right for objective legal equality and thus abandons the traditional place of the equality principle in the theory of administrative discretion. But even in traditional theory it is clear that with regard to self-binding action of the administration, the equality principle has taken a positive form, contrasting with its negative meaning of simply a prohibition of arbitrariness.[108]

The principle of self-binding action of the administration is not without limits. The administration would be unduly restricted if it were never allowed to depart from its previous practice: naturally this is only possible if it then gives the same treatment to similar circumstances again.[109]

A further check arises from the fact that only a lawful practice is conducive to this self-binding effect. Nobody can invoke art. 3 GG to require that his case be treated in the same way as others where the solution violated the law; likewise, the administration need not tolerate illegal behaviour because no action was taken in similar previous cases.[110] This principle that art. 3 GG does not give a right for a repetition of an illegality is usually covered by the formula 'no equality in illegality'. The Federal Constitutional Court has embraced this formula: if A is given a permission illegally, then it does not give rise to a claim by B to receive similar treatment; and criminal proceedings against A are not inadmissible if no action was taken against B who committed the same breach of law.[111]

This principle generally recognised until now has recently come under attack. Otto Bachof had already warned that the phrase should not be misunderstood as giving freedom for arbitrariness.[112] Two decisions of the Baden-Württemberg *Verwaltungsgerichtshof* (Administrative Court) have now turned from it somewhat. When a *Land* is obliged to levy charges and does not do so generally but only in specific cases, then the formal validity of the statute cannot assert its legal realisation against the principle of equal treatment; especially not when the intended aim of the legislature is not so important that non-application of the statute would undermine the legal order. As a result, the isolated cases of levying charges are seen as inconsistent with art. 3 par. 1 GG.[113] The second decision annulled an otherwise legal decision to pull down a weekend house, on the ground that the same authority permitted the enlargement of the neighbouring house in violation of the law shortly afterwards.[114] In legal doctrine, only Volkmar Götz welcomed this tendency.[115] While he is also of the opinion that the administration should not hold on to its breach of law for future cases, nevertheless this reversal should not be carried out to the detriment of the individual citizen; otherwise the right to equal application of the law would be reduced to the right to correct application of the law.

We admit that administrative actions of the type just mentioned are unsatisfactory; but the views in question presuppose a content in art. 3 par. 1 GG which must first be proved, namely that one can demand equal treatment in injustice. As it is unlikely that a norm in a legal order which is based on the principle of legality would produce a result in violation of the law, then the burden of proof rests with those supporting the contrary. As long as such a content is not disclosed, one can proceed from the assumption that the equality principle only allows a right for treatment according to the objective legal situation.[116]

c. Executive acts as non-legal acts

We take the act of mercy which is exercised by executive organs as an example of acts which do not belong to the category of acts of law and are therefore non-legal acts. Then there is no possibility to measure the act of mercy against the Constitution, especially against art. 3; therefore all possibility of judicial control falls away too. The Constitutional Court held this indeed in a case concerning refusal of mercy, but it treated revocation of mercy differently.[117]

We conclude this paragraph by noting that in relation to the executive the equality principle draws as a rule only the outer limits within which the administration can exercise its discretion. In this respect, the case law of the Constitutional Court on art. 3 took its inspiration from the administrative courts, which are primarily competent to control executive action.

4. Art. 3 par. 1 GG and judicial power

As State institutions the courts are also bound by the fundamental rights in general and by the equality clause in particular. Thus, in individual cases, also judicial acts can violate art. 3 GG.

However, a breach of art. 3 GG is not already present if the court misapplies simply the law or if judicial proceedings contain mistakes;[118] similarly the equality principle is not violated when different courts have different punishment practices, by applying different penal sanctions, interpret the law differently or depart from their previous decisions.[119] Art. 3 GG is however violated when the same court applies criminal law differently to different persons: 'The criminal court is according to art. 3 GG solely obliged to come to a decision without respect of persons and to sentence without making arbitrary distinctions'.[120] Misapplication of the law is not the only condition for a breach of the equality clause, for the latter presupposes mistakes which defy a reasonable assessment of the fundamental idea of the GG; in such a case, one can only conclude that the decision rests on non-objective considerations.[121] However, it is not sufficient if an alternative interpretation other than that made by the court can be found which would possibly be more compatible with the equality principle.[122]

In accordance with these principles the Constitutional Court held that it was not unconstitutional that the Federal Revenue Court (*Bundesfinanzhof*) answered the same legal question in two different ways when it arose at two different occasions. True, the Revenue Court was thus violating ordinary law, but this did not have any effect at the constitutional level.[123] On the other hand the BVG has often annulled judicial decisions based on interpretations which misunderstood the direct effect of art. 3 par. 1 on ordinary legislation.[124]

5. The specific equality clauses

Beside the general equality clause (art. 3 par. 1 GG) there are specific expressions of the equality principle[125] which are important because they provide more concrete standards than the general principle in the areas they cover; they therefore serve the purpose of the general principle in the field of legislation and of application of the law.

a. Art. 3 par. 2 GG (equality of men and women)

The provision that men and women have equal rights is not merely a principle of policy to be materialised by legislation: it provides indeed a right which is directly enforceable in law.[126] It is comprehensive in its application and effects every area of law.[127] The political question whether difference of sex can form a relevant ground for legal differentiation has been answered in the negative by the Constitution itself. Interpretations bringing some relativety into this prohibition by saying that art. 3 par. 2 GG does not require equality but only equivalence, are to be rejected.[128] A Constitution, which recognises human dignity as its supreme principle, would contradict itself, if it were to regard equivalence of human beings as not automatically admitted: art. 3 par. 2 GG would then be only declaratory.

Art. 3 par. 2 GG concretises the general equality clause. In contrast to art. 3 par. 1 GG which leaves the legislature wide scope for discretion,[129] art. 3 par. 2 GG draws strict limits.[130] Obvious objective reasons which justify differentiation under the general equality clause, cannot justify differentiations under art. 3 par. 2 GG.[131] The different legal treatment of men and women is only allowed when the biological or functional distinctions of sex are so decisive in the circumstances to be regulated, that common elements can no longer be perceived at all, or at any rate are fading.[132] Conventional and traditional views about the functions of men and women are, however, no suitable basis for differentiations; [133] this has been apparent, in particular, with regard to the relationship of men and women in marriage and family, which receive special protection from the State (art. 6 par. 1 GG).[134]

A few examples will elucidate these statements. The Federal Constitutional Court held that there is a breach of art. 3 par. 2 GG where the legislature has appraised the wife's commercial activities as destructive of marriage and therefore treated the profits of it unfavourably for the purpose of tax.[135] On the other hand, a provision regulating working hours differently for men and women is in accordance with art. 3 par. 2, because the biological peculiarity of women has to be protected in the field of employment.[136] Likewise, the provision formerly in force that the father had responsibility for the support of an illegitimate child prior to the mother was consistent with art. 3 par. 2. This was justified by the functional difference between the father and the mother of an illegitimate child in case of absence of a family; the mother is then responsible for personal care, which is on par with financial support, but the father can only fulfil his obligations towards the child in an equivalent way by payments for its support.[137] Consequently there is a breach of art. 3 par. 2 if the father of an illegitimate child not living with its mother has to provide the whole cost of the living: for in this situation the mother is relieved of her duty and the differentiation between father and mother is no longer based on the different functions of the parents as a result of the lack of a family but only on sex.[138] Other decisions of the Court also show that the rule of equality is not just aimed at the woman's legal position, but is also intended to prevent differentiations to the detriment of men; thus a widower for example cannot be placed in a worse position regarding maintenance and insurance than a widow.[139]

The Constitutional Court, it can generally be said, has taken into account the apodictic rule of the equality of men and women in an active manner. It has made clear that differences of sex are immaterial for constitutional purposes.[140] The remaining possibilities for differentiation were used sparingly.[141] Meanwhile, it appears from the tendency of legal development that the denial of legal relevance to difference of sex is still more categorical than required by the Court's decisions.[142]

b. Art. 3 par. 3 GG (prohibition of discrimination on the grounds of race, language etc.)

Art. 3 par. 3 GG has a concretising function in relation to the prohibition of arbitrariness (art. 3 par. 1 GG) in the same way as art. 3 par. 2 GG. It declares that for all areas of law[143] a more favourable or unfavourable treatment[144] on grounds of sex, ancestry, race, language, homeland or origin, faith or religious or political convictions would be arbitrary; to this extent art. 3 par. 3 contains absolute prohibitions of differentiations.[145] Art. 3 par. 3 is to be understood in the light of the historical situation confronting the framers of the Constitution in 1948 and 1949, after the end of Hitler's dictatorship and the national socialist racial and religious policies. At the same time it should aim at preventing unfavourable treatment of homeless Germans after their mass expulsion from the occupied Eastern territories of Germany.[146]

The individual features of art. 3 par. 3 have been analysed by courts and legal doctrine. There is considerable agreement that the prohibition of differentiation on grounds of sex adds nothing to the contents of art. 3 par. 2;[147] logically art. 3 par. 2 has precedence. 'Ancestry' means the natural biological relationship of a person with his forefathers, 'homeland' the geographical background and 'origin' his social and class background.[148] The reference to 'language' is intended to protect national minorities.[149] The remaining features require no explanation.

Art. 3 par. 3 is only violated when favourable of unfavourable treatment results exclusively from one of the grounds named in it. In other words there should be a causal link between the existence of one of the features listed in art. 3 par. 3 and the unfavourable treatment.[150] This was more or less the Court's argument when it decided in 1952 that the Emergency Admission Act,[151] allowing Germans from the Soviet Occupied Zone to be precluded from staying in the Federal Republic of Germany, did not violate art. 3 par. 3: the prohibition did not rely on the 'homeland' of the Germans in question but on the threat to the social and economic situation within the Federal Republic.[152] Nor is there discrimination on grounds of 'homeland' or 'origin' when a German from the Soviet Occupied Zone, who in accordance with the law in force there has attained majority on reaching 18, keeps this status after his flight to the Federal Republic; the reason for this special treatment of the young man in relation to those of the same age in the Federal Republic is not the place he comes from, but the fact that on his 18th birthday he was subject to a foreign legal system.[153]

However, the Court held that a 1941 decree of the national socialist regime providing for compulsory revocation of German nationality for Jews was *ab initio* null and void because it violated art. 3 par. 3. The loss of nationality was here solely occasioned by 'race'.[154]

It should be mentioned that nationality is not one of the grounds named in art. 3 par. 3. Thus foreign nationality can be the reason for differentiation, provided it does not go as far as arbitrariness (art. 3 par. 1 GG). In all these cases, however, the foreigner will also claim discrimination on the ground of homeland, language, race etc. This is the kind of unavoidable overlap one should put up with. Art. 3 par. 3 can only be applied when it is established that the reason for the different treatment is not his quality of foreigner, but his language or race.[155]

The Constitutional Court derived a special kind of restriction from art. 3 par. 3, as far as the differentiation on the ground of political views is concerned. As the Federal Republic conceives itself as a democracy willing to defend itself,[156] the Constitution cannot be read so as to allow the rights protected therein to be used for destroying or impairing the basic order of freedom and democracy[157] by actual fighting.[158]

c. Art. 6 par. 5 GG (illegitimate children)

Proceeding from the recognition that illegitimate children on the whole meet with worse conditions of life than legitimate children,[159] the Constitution charged the legislature to provide that children shall not be prejudiced by their illegitimate birth and that the law shall give them the same opportunities as legitimate children, in short that they escape social discrimination.[160] The Court considers art. 6 par. 5 as an expression of the general equality clause.[161] However, one should not conclude from this conception that it would be necessary to transfer the existing rules of law governing legitimate children schematically to illegitimate children.[162] Because of the dissimilar factual starting-point the legislature will often choose other ways to obtain the constitutional goal, which may include more favourable treatment of illegitimate children. For this reason a provision which is attacked for violation of art. 6 par. 5 must always be examined in the context of the legal position of illegitimate children as a whole:[163] only a total comparison will disclose whether the constitutional task[164] has been fulfilled.

Like art. 3 par. 2 and 3, also art. 6 par. 5 is a specialised provision of the general equality clause.[165] But, unlike them, art. 6 par. 5 is not strictly a differentiation prohibition, but it rather empowers the legislator to differentiate as much as necessary to reach the constitutional goal of changing social attitudes towards illegitimate children.[166]

d. Art. 33 par. 1-3 GG (civic equality)

These provisions have become important in two respects. Firstly they guarantee that every German has the same civic rights and duties, regardless of his *Land* of residence. The federal structure does not affect the legal position of the individual German.

Secondly it must be stressed that art. 33 par. 2 GG does not give rise to a claim to hold public office. What this provision together with art. 33 par. 3 GG does say is that it would be contrary to the principle of equality to set requirements other than professional aptitude and qualifications[167] for the holding of public office. Turning down an applicant on the ground of his religious or political views is forbidden.[168]

e. Art. 38 par. 1 GG (electoral equality)

The close connection between the equality clause and democratic government is primarily expressed in the provision for electoral equality.[169] The Constitutional Court regards it as an application of the general equality clause.[170] It works both in the active sense and in the passive sense.[171] Each person must be explicitly able to exercise his right to vote in the same way as others,[172] because only the equal valuation of all citizens at the polls is compatible with the democratic postulates of the Basic Law.[173]

6. The relationship of the specific equality clauses to the general equality clause

As already indicated the specific equality clauses are a concretisation of the general clause. The Constitutional Court, however, concludes from this approach by doubtful methods that the general clause is again superimposed on the specific clauses in borderline cases.[174] This has been elaborated in particular in regard to the relationship between art. 38 and art. 3 par. 1 GG. So, for example, the Court has recognised the admissibility of barrier clauses; that is that under the system of proportional representation a party must have a certain minimum number of votes (5%) before it can share in the attribution of seats in Parliament.[175] As a result votes that have been cast for a party that did not reach the minimum, are unequally treated, because they are wasted. The Court's view is that the electoral system is particularly intended by the Basic Law to ensure stable political majorities; in this way the general equality clause preserves its regulatory and superior meaning for the strict normal electoral equality.[176]

The Court used similar considerations with regard to the relation between art. 3 par. 2 and 3, and art. 3 par. 1 GG. The above-mentioned exceptions to the equality principle (differentiation is possible if biological or functional differences are relevant) are methodically justified by the limits the general clause itself traces to its concretisations.[177]

The argument is not satisfactory. Historical development of the penetration of the equality principle shows already that the struggle to remove privileges was carried out and won by means of specific clauses before the general equality clause was even elaborated. For this reason, one cannot accept that the general clause and the specific clauses have a mother-daughter relationship.[178] And one should add that the argument that *leges speciales* could be kept in check by a *lex generalis*, is inadmissible from the point of view of legal interpretation. The results achieved by the Court – throughout reasonable as they are – can be attained in a way which gives much less scope for dispute; thus the admissibility of differentiation between men and women on the basis of biological or functional differences can be substantiated in all important cases without reference to the general clause, by deriving the permission for differentiation from other provisions.[179] Art. 12(a) GG, for example, provides for compulsory military service for men only; art. 6 par. 4 GG places mothers under the particular protection of the State and thus justifies the existence of rules protecting mothers which are not available to men – nor for that matter to women without children.[180] A further norm of differentiation is the principle of the 'welfare state' (*Sozialstaat*). Here unequal treatment is always founded directly on the provisions of the Constitution.

7. The equality clause as a right to an equal share in State performances

The equality clause was until recently regarded as a defence against the State, just like the other basic rights (*status negativus*).[181] A radical change has occurred in this approach through the growing dependence of the individual on the modern State from an economic and social point of view. Many see freedom secured only if the basic rights are also understood as the real basis for claims to State performances (*status positivus*).[182] In this study we should therefore look into the role played by art. 3 GG in this discussion.

Legal writers have already accepted for some time that the principle of equality before the law is a guarantee of the existence of a claim to an equal share in State performances.[183] Until recently the courts followed only hesitantly.[184] However, in this area, too, the equality principle is increasingly regarded as an equality of opportunity. If for example State intervention distorts competition and thus infringes the principle of equality of opportunity, this infringement will result in a claim by the person affected to be placed on an equal footing with the person for whose benefit competition was distorted. This means as a rule that the victim should also get a subsidy. Art. 3 GG, therefore, manifests itself as the direct basis for an action.[185]

Recently the Constitutional Court made another step in this direction. Because of the congestion in the universities not all students wanting to study can be admitted (*numerus clausus*). According to the Court's decision the creation of educational establishments by the State, together with the equality principle in conjunction with the constitutionally protected freedom of profession (art. 12 GG) and the principle of the welfare state, result in claims for admission to those establishments. The Court did not, however, decide whether the basic rights also provided the legislature with the task of making enough places available.[186] This cautiousness clearly illustrates the dilemma produced by the change from a negative defensive right to positive claims to an equal share. Such claims to State performances require more detailed legislative definition; they are, therefore, also dependent on the will of the legislature and beyond that on the State's financial resourses. Thus they actually conflict with the principle enunciated in art. 1 par. 3 GG that the basic rights are directly binding law for all State powers. Anyway one will have to be very careful in deducing from the general equality clause a duty to act on the legislature.[187] The decision shows that the interpretation of the basic rights as rights to State action does not necessarily lead to more freedom and more equality.

The Court's exposition does, however, clearly show that it is willing to allot to the equality clause an important role in shaping and realising the principle of the welfare state.[188] One can hardly avoid the conclusion that the radical egalitarian factors inherent in the equality clause have shifted from political equality to social equality.

8. The equality clause in the relationship of individuals to each other

A quite different but very general problem with regard to basic rights is whether they apply exclusively to the relationship of the individual to the State or whether they also have importance in the legal relationships of one citizen to another (the so-called 'third party effect of the basic rights'). This question is of consequence above all in labour law, but also everywhere where social forces are active in areas where the State is not.

An example will demonstrate this idea. The Federal Labour Court (*Bundesarbeitsgericht*) was required to decide as early as 1954 whether it was admissible to dismiss an employee without notice for circulating election propaganda on behalf of the German Communist Party (KPD) during working hours. The Labour Court proceeded from the assumption that the discrimination prohibition of art. 3 par. 3 GG granted the individual a particular legal status with direct effect even in his relation to fellow beneficiaries. True, the dismissal was in fact held to be lawful as the petitioner was deemed not to be dismissed simply because he belonged to the KPD but because he had gravely endangered the peace of the firm by his continuous political agitation.[189]

This concept of direct effect of the basic rights in private law relationships is not shared for the most part by legal doctrine or by other court decisions. They are trying a different way. Proceeding from the view that the basic rights are not just individual rights but also constitute an objective system of values, they endow the basic rights with a weaker effect on citizens' relationships *inter se*. The gateways are here the general notions of private law such as 'public order' and 'good faith', which are interpreted in the light of the constitutional choice of fundamental values.[190]

Anyway as regards the equality clause, it must be borne in mind that its unlimited adoption into private law relationships would restrict the private autonomy of the individual too much and at every step.[191] The prohibition of any arbitrary act on the part of a private citizen does not correspond with the general prohibition of arbitrariness, because the State is not assured freedom of action while the individual is (art. 2 GG). Therefore, it does not follow that there should be no arbitrariness in private relationships.[192]

The real question is, therefore, whether private arbitrariness oversteps the limits which protect our peaceably living together in society. But these limits are traced by the general provisions of private law. With their help satisfactory solutions for individual cases can be found, which are also coloured by the historical experiences of Germany – as, for example, laid down in art. 3 par. 3 GG itself. Accordingly, one must consider as contrary to public order a contractual provision by which the purchaser of a house undertakes not to sell it in his turn to a coloured or Jewish person. On the other hand, it will hardly be treated as contrary to public order if a father disinherits his son in his will because of the son's political views.[193] Definite conclusions in this problem cannot be given. With the growth of new social problems new answers are also to be found.

III. *Realisation of the Equality Principle by the Legislature*

The equality principle needs realisation by the legislature in many spheres.[194] The prohibition of arbitrariness under art. 3 par. 1 GG and the stricter specific equality clauses present only the legal minimum; the legislature can go beyond. The following few examples will show how the legislature has carried out its activities in relation to these minimum requirements as well as in relation to wider conceptions of equality.

1. Parliament's reaction to the judgments of the Federal Constitutional Court

Art. 3 par. 2 GG secures equality of men and women. From the day the Basic Law came into force, this command was binding on newly-created rules.[195] For the adaptation of previous law a transitional period expiring on 31st March, 1953, was allowed for (art. 117 GG). After this day the old provisions of the Civil Code (BGB),[196] according to which the father was the first to have parental power (i.e. he was responsible for personal care of the child, administered its property and was its statutory representative), were no longer in force; the mother was accorded parental power only as a substitute, if the father was dead or factually incapable of acting. Not earlier than in 1957 the family law provisions were made to conform with the legal position prevalent since 1953,[197] by which parental power was to be exercised by both. If father and mother should disagree, however, the father would have the final power of decision, in which he would have to take account of the mother's opinion.

Amongst judiciary and legal authors opinions were divided whether these provisions conformed with art. 3 par. 2 GG.[198] The supporters argued primarily that they were in the interests of the family and the children, as these were best served if one spouse had the final say in case of disagreement.[199]

On the other hand, the Constitutional Court decided that the legislature did not go far enough with its attempts to accord with the new constitutional requirements.[200] The Court did not share the concern that the unity of the family would be threatened if, in the last resort, one spouse did not decide alone. The strict rule of the equality of men and women was to apply above all in the legal relationships of father and mother to their children. The equality rule was important in the very situation of disagreement between the parents.

The legislature has not replaced the provision concerning the final power of decision of the father which, by this judgment, was held null and void. Thus the present position is that in case of actual disagreement between the spouses it is possible to bring the matter before the guardianship court for a definitive decision.[201] Such cases do not arise often; the present situation has proved itself despite the fears that had been expressed.

Another example concerns the legislative realisation of the task set out in art. 6 par. 5 GG. This provision has been interpreted by the Constitutional Court as an instruction to the legislature without any time limit, to make a new and comprehensive body of rules regarding the legal position of illegitimate children.[202]

Until 1969 the legislature did not comply, and the old provisions continued to place the illegitimate child in a worse position in many respects (e.g. maintenance and succession) than legitimate children. In January 1969, however, the Court decided that–although the Basic Law laid down no time scale for the completion of the task – the legislature could not avoid its duty for as long as it chose. The Court, therefore, set Parliament a deadline at the end of the then current legislative period (autumn 1969): if no new statement of the law had been produced by then, art. 6 par. 5 GG would have to be put into effect directly by the courts.[203]

However, it did not come to this. Within the period (in August 1969), Parliament passed a law on the legal position of illegitimate children.[204] The new statute resulted in the disappearance, *inter alia,* of discriminating provisions such as the one which said that a father had no family relation to his illegitimate child. Otherwise in the fields of family law and the law of succession legitimate and illegitimate children are still by no means subject to the same provisions. In connection with the unequal treatment and to a certain extent the better treatment of illegitimate children attempts are being made to correct inequalities of substance.[205] Actual disadvantaging is eschewed nowadays. However, the Court did not have any occasion as yet to pronounce on the new provisions.

2. Independent activity by Parliament directed at the equality principle

The legislature's own concept of the equality principle has been articulated in a variety of legal fields.

a. Marriage and family law

The Federal Government's draft statute to reform marriage and family law[206] is aimed at realising the equality of women. For this purpose, the following proposals have been made.

Until now sec. 1355 BGB provides that the surname of the wife and the children is that of the man. If the wife wishes to preserve her maiden name she has the right to add it to her husband's surname. The Federal Government's view is that according to present-day understanding of the equality principle this provision is contrary to the Constitution.[207] The judiciary, for the major part, holds a different view, but in legal doctrine it is a controversial question.[208] The Constitutional Court left the question open.[209]

The draft goes also beyond the existing legal situation in providing for amendment of sec. 1356 BGB which provides that basically the wife runs the household. According to the proposals, the provision should merely say that the running of the household by the spouse – whether husband or wife – should be classed as a full contribution to the family's keep.[210]

The suggested redrafting of divorce law will also take account of changing social and economic conditions, in particular as they effect the wife's position. With the change from the principle of matrimonial offence to the breakdown principle as a basis for divorce, the divorced wife will often be obliged to find a job; only in exceptional circumstances (need to look after children; illness etc.) will there be no such obligation.[211]

This suggested law will hit hard the wife without profession or trade.

b. Nationality

According to sec. 6 of the Nationality and Citizenship Act, 1913[212] – which is still applicable –, a foreign woman married to a German had a right to naturalisation. There was no corresponding right for a foreign man marrying a German woman. This was amended by the Act of 8 September, 1969,[213] which aimed at putting men and women on an equal footing as regards nationality. Now foreign spouses whether married to German men or women have no right to naturalisation; sec. 9 stipulates simply that the scope of discretion of the competent authorities is reduced, in contrast to the decision on the naturalisation of other foreigners.

It is also doubted whether a further provision of the Nationality Act accords with art. 3 par. 2 GG.[214] Sec. 4 subs. 1 of the Nationality Act provides that only a German father can transmit German nationality to his legitimate children, but not a German mother. The Federal Administrative

Court (*Bundesverwaltungsgericht*)[215] considers this provision to be unconstitutional and now the Federal Constitutional Court must consider the question. The other view is that nationality is an objective status which does not give rise to any enforceable rights of the parents.[216] The Federal Government's view on the matter is that the provision is outdated; it is working towards a new provision on the basis of the equality of the sexes. One can, therefore, predict that regardless of which way the constitutional court decides, the legislature will anyhow be presented with amendments to the Nationality Act in the near future.[216a]

c. Criminal law

In 1957 the Constitutional Court decided that it was not contrary to art. 3 par. 2 GG for male homosexuality alone to be punished.[217] The biological differences between the sexes dominated the factual situation so completely that comparable factors had to be neglected. The correctness of this interpretation has been contested.[218] In 1969 it was enacted that ordinary male homosexuality was no longer a criminal offence.[219] While this may be partly due to changed views on the punishability of this offence, nevertheless in effect it took into account the criticism levied against the Court's decision and it does lead to an extension of the equal treatment for men and women.[220]

d. Law of aliens

According to the Basic Law several basic rights are constitutionally guaranteed only to Germans.

Above all the rights of assembly and of association (arts. 8 and 9 GG) come into this category. But besides, the legislature has given the right to all foreign nationals to take part in meetings and to form associations. The foreigners are simply subject to negligibly stricter requirements than Germans.[221] They are almost treated the same.

e. Structure of enterprise

Important problems which have already been discussed in relation to the applicability of the basic rights as between individuals *inter se,* [222] have been solved by legislative action. Thus sec. 75 of the Act on the Structure of Enterprise[223] provides that all discriminatory treatment of persons in an enterprise[224] on the ground of ancestry, religion, nationality, origin, political or trade union activity, or sex is prohibited; even the passive and active right of election to industrial councils is given to employees of foreign nationality under the new Act.

f. The socio-economic field

The legislature is particularly active in its attempts to establish actual social equality. This occurs naturally above all in the socio-economic field and usually by granting the needy a claim in law for financial support.[225] Examples are the Act on Apartment Building,[226] the second Act on Acquisition of Assets[227] and the Federal Social Aid Act.[228] Similar reasons underly the abolition by the *Land* legislatures of University fees and the establishment of the principle of free schooling (motto: equal educational opportunities for all).

IV. *Analysis of Legislation and Case Law on the Equality Principle with regard to underlying Social Problems*

An examination of the history of the equality principle shows how its function changed with succeeding epochs.[229] In the 19th century equality largely meant political equality; thus the Paulskirche Constitution (1848-49) was concerned with the abolition of class differences (nobility) and the abolition of privileges of all kinds (tax, military service). The watchword of equality before the law was to become the vehicle for the desired spiritual and national unity.[230] The equality clause was understood at the same time as having important functions of control and publicity[231] – the demand for trial by jury in criminal proceedings, the duty of law enforcement organs to prosecute every offence without exceptions,[232] public pronouncement of sentences; all this expressed the distrust against the State which was suspected of treating Lord A differently from Mr. B. At least as long as there was no equal universal suffrage (e.g. the three classes franchise in Prussia), the emphasis lay on the implementation of political equality. Even the Weimar Constitution was so coloured (art. 109 par. 3). As this development came to a certain conclusion with the civic equality of women, the strength of the equality clause as a method of acquiring political emancipation retreated into the background, but simultaneously new strength emerged. The development of the industrial society[233] created new problems. Growing production, constantly increasing demand for labour, international economic interdependence, regional integration, rising expectations and more reliance on the State and its performances almost led of themselves to a levelling of legal subjects in the economic and social area. Differentiation on the basis of sex is no longer rational when men and women are enrolled into the production process indiscriminately. The struggle for equal treatment takes place, if at all, in relation to employment; all other matters, and maybe even this one, seem settled. The courts, seized of the question of violation of art. 3 par. 2 GG are clearing up rearguard actions and providing for adjustment to a development which is basically already complete.

Even differentiation on the basis of nationality is only sustained to a limited extent in a society of production which employs millions of foreign workers. This is particularly so in the economic sector; however, there is already repeated discussion whether to give foreigners greater opportunity to participate in political activities. This question is, however, not in the foreground yet; essential is the fulfilment of expectations of State performances which are so characteristic of modern industrial society, and at the same time a stabilising force in it. Social benefits, social security and economic prosperity all are expected of the State; what is more obvious than that the equality clause should automatically acquire a distributive role? The consequence is an increasing social homogeneity unimaginable in past times.[234] Unless all indications are deceptive we are standing in the middle of a new phase of new radicalism of the equality clause, this time in the socio-economic field.

1. Political equality

In the field of civic and political liberties the equality clause lost most of its former explosive force. The absence of racial or national minorities has no doubt favoured this development.[235] The extension of active and passive voting rights to constantly larger sections of the population continues without struggles and with the blessing of all parties.[236]

Solely of importance in this connection is the Federal Constitutional Court's jurisprudence on the equal opportunity of political parties. The Court recognises rightly a close connection with the principle of the equal franchise; this results from the role of these parties in the process of forming the political opinion of the people in a modern party system.[237] Consequently the principle of equality of opportunity in the electoral process has been extended to election preliminaries and to election propaganda.[238] In electioneering especially the equal treatment of the political parties by the State is an indispensable precondition for free elections. It is, therefore, inadmissible to grant only some parties but not all transmission time on radio and television (these are public institutions), or only to refund some but not all parties part of their election expences.[239] However, a duty to assist weak political groups cannot be read into the precept of equality of opportunity. The award of time on the radio or the refund of a lump sum for election expenses is determined *inter alia* by the political significance of the party, the number of representatives it has in Parliament and its success in the previous election.[240]

2. Equality in marriage and the family

One of the main influences of the equality principle has materialised in the field of marriage and family. This resulted partly from the actualisation of art. 6 par. 5 GG by courts and legislature,[241] partly from the precept of the equality of sexes in art. 3 par. 2 GG. Many examples have already been given above.[242] Here reference will only be made to the Constitutional Court's decision that art. 3 par. 2 GG implies that the wife's work as housewife and mother shall be considered as maintenance of the family according to its actual value.[243] The Federal Supreme Court (*Bundesgerichtshof*) drew consequences from this idea for the interpretation of civil law norms: thus, where a third person injures the wife, the husband cannot claim damages for the loss of services rendered to him but only the wife has a claim.[244]

Many other branches of law have been drawn into the discussion regarding the equality principle. This applies to nationality law, as previously mentioned,[245] but also to private international law. In a recent important decision the Federal Constitutional Court confirmed the primacy of the fundamental rights also in the field of private international law.[246] With regard to art. 3 par. 2 GG one should, for example, have to consider whether German law can really provide that legal relationships between parents and their legitimate children shall be governed exclusively by the laws of the father's State; so far this has not been subjected to criticism.[247] The equality of the sexes has operated above all, however, in labour law and social law. This will be demonstrated once more by reference to wage equality. The Federal Labour Court (*Bundesarbeitsgericht*) and the Federal Social Court (*Bundessozialgericht*) have not been reluctant to deduce from art. 3 par. 2 GG that any wage differentiation on grounds of sex is unconstitutional. However, this does not prevent different payment for different work. Only where the same work is done can there be a demand for equal pay. Even doing the same work men may be paid more if they are more productive.[248] The remaining social question is how to achieve a situation where women are entrusted to a greater extent with top jobs; actually, men appear to be greatly preferred in this respect.[249]

3. Economic law

The equality principle has influenced economic conditions not simply in respect of the equality of the sexes. Much earlier the discussion concerned abolishing tax privileges (of the nobility); it required some time for this goal to be attained. It was only gradually recognised that the duty to pay taxes could not be assigned systematically to every citizen. The Prussian Income Tax Act 1891 gave effect to this notion by fixing a tax threshold of 900 mark.[250] Even today much of the cases on the equality principle concerns tax law; the legislature is constantly being called upon anew to realise the principle of equal taxation deduced from art. 3 par. 1 GG.[251]

A further point can be added here. The widespread equality before the law, long since attained, led in early liberal capitalism, with the help of the same rights for all, to the conclusion of transactions resulting in consolidation of the existing differences between rich and poor.[252] Today it is these very social situations that one is attempting to assimilate. This is taking place over an unusually wide front stretching from judicial control of so-called general conditions of trade[253] via legislative protection against unfair dismissal[254] right up to equal participation in management bodies and the modern discussion about business co-determination.[255] Basically behind all this stands the dynamism of the equality clause. Legislative and judicial powers conceive of it to an increasing extent as a means of realising a welfare state implying the duty of the State to equalise social differences and to create a fair social order. In this connection it is also proper to remember the new interpretation given to the fundamental rights, by which they are understood more and more as claims for performance rather than as rights of defence. The equality clause itself plays a prominent role in this development.[256]

V. *The Meaning of Equality in Constitutional Law*

1. Equality as equality before the law

Propositions on equality in constitutional law cannot be confined to the remark that all men are equal before God.[257] Such a statement would on the one hand be too profound, and on the other hand too high-handed as a legal principle. Constitutional equality can only be equality before the law.[258]

Any discourse on equality presumes that one can compare and equate. This means the necessity of several or at least two objects; things that are equal are therefore not identical.[259]

Recognition of objects as equal in the legal sense, because they can be equated, depends on values rooted in the legal consciousness of a given legal community.[260] These values, therefore, vary not only from community to community, but also from time to time, according to changes of legal appreciations within the community.

As the purpose of equality before the law can only be that the law attaches the same legal consequences to equal circumstances, and as also the preceding equating of objects can only be drawn from some of the circumstances and this equating is a value judgment, then the essential question concerns what is equal, i.e. what justifies equal treatment or differentiation as the case may be, and who makes the decision, i.e. makes the evaluation.

2. The equality principle as a prohibition of arbitrariness

The propagation and scrutiny of the relevant case law and legislation lead to an endorsement of the definition of the general equality clause as first expounded by the Federal Constitutional Court, at the beginning of its activities, and considered at the beginning of this chapter.[261] The formulation falters in its details; but if one looks to its results the definition remains constant as a prohibition of arbitrariness directed at all State powers (legislative, executive and judicial). What is to be considered as arbitrary, objectively unjustifiable, cannot be established in the abstract but only in the light of the concrete facts.[262] In this regard, it must be remembered that the prohibition of arbitrariness is in no way exclusively located in the equality principle. According to the Constitutional Court's decisions it is one of the fundamental priniples of law.[263] It must, therefore, also be treated as an element of the principle of the rule of law. If a law treats all citizens equally but is itself unjust or arbitrary, for example, a criminal law statute providing for life imprisonment for minor traffic offences, it cannot be measured against the prohibition of arbitrariness under art. 3 GG. The point of the art. 3 prohibition is that it forbids circumstances to be equated and to undertake or omit the consequential equality of treatment, unless there are obvious objective grounds present for it.

The specific equality clauses in the Basic Law have their greatest relevance in the determination of what is arbitrary. From them the values can be gleaned that constitutional law considers relevant, on the basis of which the decision to equate must be taken.[264] Their non-observance means the State's action is arbitrary. The Constitution restricts to this extent the freedom to decide what shall be treated as equal, which art. 3 par. 1 GG grants to legislature, executive and judiciary. A State measure which cannot be brought under one of the specific equality clauses can still fall foul of art. 3 par. 1, just as in the opposite case a measure may be objective and reasonable in the sense of the general equality clause and still not come up to the particular standards of one of the specific clauses. These complementary functions of the general clause and the specific clauses make it clear that the general clause does have an independent meaning itself.

Occasionally the question is raised whether the definition of the general equality clause as a prohibition of arbitrariness (in the above sense) represents an exhaustive statement of its normative content or whether it delineates only the framework in which the equality clause is liable to the Constitutional Court's investigation.[265] If one identifies the contents of the equality clause with the precept of substantive justice, then one will find in the Court's formula – that art. 3 par. 1 does not require the fairest and most suitable solution but simply forbids an arbitrary one[266] – a discrepancy between content and liability to scrutiny.

The Federal Constitutional Court has not as yet adopted a definite attitude to this debate. In my opinion it would be contradictory to the concept of the all-embracing jurisdiction of the Court in constitutional questions if it had only in part jurisdiction to pronounce upon the binding nature of a basic rights norm.[267] If one proceeds from this proposition, then the Court's view that outside the limits of arbitrariness rule givers and rule appliers have scope for discretion,[268] can only be understood as saying that the binding constitutional nature of art. 3 par. 1 GG expresses itself as a prohibition of arbitrariness and only as such. Then the equality clause does not itself require substantially just solutions. The legislature can, of course, strive for that aim and go beyond the minimum laid down by the equality clause, and by the other fundamental rights.

3. Systematic and differentiating, static and dynamic equality

The equality principle embodied in the general and specific clauses has many different aspects according to the Federal Constitutional Court's interpretation. To take first of all the specific clauses, one can detect that their predominant[269] application is the establishment of systematic (or formal) equality (*égalité*).[270] They place the 'equality of the human countenance' in the foreground and leave out of consideration other inequalities that can exist. Thus it makes no difference for the right to vote whether one is rich or poor, just as it is of no import in the appointment to the public service what one's religious beliefs are.

On the other hand in the general equality clause[271] it is evident that there is a differentiating (or substantial) notion of equality.[272] Room remains here for the consideration of inequalities in relation to the facts. The existing similarities or dissimilarities can lead on reasonable, objective and impartial grounds to equal or unequal treatment. This is the principle of fairness (equity), of '*suum cuique tribuere*'.

The history of the equality clause shows that the main-spring of its development is a systematically conceived equality which constantly will advance into new fields.[273] This tendency comes up against established social and economic inequalities. Equal rights and duties, burdens and benefits have unequal effect in differing conditions. Only when the factual inequalities have been set aside is there any sense in systematically equal treatment.

The various equality clauses provide little guidance themselves on overcoming existing social circumstances; to this extent the clauses are of a static nature.[274] Their dynamism is received from the goals set from outside. Such an exterior aim is in a large industrial society more or less necessarily the idea of the welfare state (*Sozialstaat*).[275] As a result of the connection between the equality clause and the welfare state principle there is, for the first time one could say, the chance to realise this welfare state. This must not lead to an alteration of the definition of the general equality principle as a prohibition of arbitrariness; but every measure not corresponding to the just social order required by the *Sozialstaat* aim can be characterised as arbitrary. In this context one can also understand why claims for State action are deduced from the equality principle more and more, and basically without dispute. Its change from a (pure) defence to (in addition) a right to performance is even recognised by those who otherwise are sceptical about the doctrine of participation rights.[276] The bridging function of the equality clause between a liberal Constitution based on the rule of law on the one side and the pressure applied to it by the idea of the welfare state on the other side, as explained by Ernst Forsthoff, is clear.[277] By its connection with the *Sozialstaat* idea the equality clause (this has been expected[278] and can now be detected) has doubtlessly entered into a new radical phase of its development. It is not just a question of the creation of an equal base, of equal preconditions, but also of the prolongation of social conditions thus made equal.[279]

This equalisation tendency inherent in the equality clause leads not only to a collision with liberal ideas of freedom, but it also has totally different consequences, e.g. at the federal level. Until now the Constitutional Court held constantly that a *Land* Act is not contrary to art. 3 GG just because its substance departs from the law of other *Länder*; thus the equality principle always applied only in the specific jurisdiction of a given legislature.[280] Also in this respect, however, the Court has gone new ways in the previously mentioned decision on *'numerus clausus'* in the universities. The judgment will at least put some relativity into earlier case law: when there is a question of the *Land* Parliament regulating a topic (in this case admission to universities) involving circumstances of life which by their very nature extend beyond its boundaries, then such regulation must be measured against the equality clause applicable to everyone.[281] Here the desired equality of the conditions of life affects considerably the federal structure; in the framework of the federal structure, the equality clause gets an unequivocally unitary aspect.

4. Freedom and equality

If one looks at the development just indicated, there seems to be some truth in the feeling of those who fear this levelling through rampant equalisation threatens freedom. An observer recently expressed his thoughts in an image with the words '. . . and the final result is a stew'.[282] On the basis of a Constitution involving liberal concepts and the rule of law the question does arise as to what is the relationship between freedom and equality.

The contradiction between these two principles is accepted as often as it is rejected. Adolf Arndt, for instance, sees the equality principle as the most fundamental right of freedom to be different without disadvantages being attached to it.[283] Besides, the overcoming of established legal institutions and, along with it, the dependence of social organization on history, as they are secured by the effectiveness of the equality clause, can certainly be evaluated as expressions of freedom.[284]

Certainly an intensive mutual relationship between freedom and equality cannot be denied. The inequality of master and slave means a lack of freedom for the slave; in many other fields inequality makes the effective use of freedom illusory.[285] On the other hand, it is certain that State measures directed to the realisation of equality can restrict freedom, e.g. when everyone is permitted to acquire only the same goods or when the same education is laid down for all. Carried to their logical extremes therefore, equality and freedom show undoubtedly an antinomy.

It is obvious to look for solution of this dilemma by reference to concrete constitutional provisions. Some have attempted to prove that the Basic Law proceeds from a preponderance of freedom,[286] so that the existing antagonism of the two principles has to be decided in favour of freedom. Even if one agrees, one has to admit that it does not really provide any assistance towards a solution; for the predominance of freedom would certainly not be understood so as never to tolerate restrictions on freedom in favour of equality. The only final certainty is that a constitutional order guaranteeing freedom and equality forbids the complete overpowering of one by the other – the Basic Law therefore admits of neither a rigorously applied socialism nor a limitless liberalism; it outlaws collectivism in the same way as it does every elitist ideology.

If in the final analysis the tension between freedom and equality is not capable of being resolved, then the State professing both principles still has the task of respecting both again and again. The Constitution requires that all State organs keep sight of this basic problem and in every case carefully arrive at a solution which is based on the fullest degree of consensus. Moreover, history is full of changes of social thought. The participation of everyone in the composition of State organs (right to vote) is no longer considered to be a loss of freedom for those few who alone used to exercise this right before. To this extent this example can serve as a model. Equality cannot be attained in such a way that rights of freedom are cut down but only in such a way that additional freedoms are established. In this sense Gerhard Leibholz was right when he perceived in the equality principle the standard according to which the collision of interests arising between individual freedoms can be settled.[287] Quite obviously, all these considerations do not definitely settle the balance the State must observe between the respective weights of freedom and equality; but this is not peculiar to that problem alone.

VI. *The Performance of the Equality Principle*

A. General

The question remains how the equality clause can be enforced in law. As a fundamental right it is not merely a policy statement, but it constitutes directly applicable law, giving the individual an enforceable right[288] to equal treatment in the framework of the prohibition of arbitrariness, i.e. a right to impartial State treatment. This opens up to the individual the possibility of calling on the help of the court for enforcement.[289]

The pressure proceeding from the equality clause led to notable consequences in this connection. Thus, for example, when in March 1953 the time-limit for adjustment of legislation to art. 3 par. 2 GG passed without legislative activity, the courts themselves took on the enforcement of the Basic Law's definition of equality through individual decisions.[290] Although it was originally only drafted as a programme for legislation, art. 6 par. 5 GG became a directly applicable right through the Constitutional Court's jurisprudence. Only because the legislature could formulate a new statute on illegitimate children in time, the judiciary was not able to create new law in this case.[291] This raises the whole problem of parliamentary neglect. In the beginning, the Court refused to sustain actions in law for a certain legislative behaviour;[292] later it held that the constitutional complaint[293] against legislative neglect was admissible, but only if the petitioner was actually, personally and directly affected by the neglect.[294] The main problem today consists of the formulation of the decision.[295]

The claim for impartial treatment cannot be forfeited. Art. 18 GG includes neither the general equality clause nor the specific equality clauses in those basic rights whose forfeiture can be ordered by the Federal Constitutional Court. The inequalities automatically ensuing from orders of forfeiture are of course unavoidable. The same applies when the Court forbids a political party because it is directed against the free democratic order (art. 21 GG); such a party loses its claim for equal treatment with other political parties.[296]

With the emergence of the equality clause out of the pure citizen-State relationship into the relationship between individuals *inter se* the problem arises as to how the equality principle can be made effective in that area. We should also make a brief incursion into the protection the equality clause may provide in questions of compensation and of criminal law.

B. Judicial Protection

Violations of the equality principle by State institutions can be denounced by means of the normal system of judicial protection. In this case there is always the possibility for the citizen of lodging a constitutional complaint. On closer scrutiny, one should distinguish whether the judicial protection applies against executive and judicial acts or aginst legislative acts.

1. Protection with regard to law-applying institutions

a. Executive

Art. 19 par. 4 GG assures full and effective legal protection against measures of the executive; its acts must be capable of complete investigation as to their legality in legal and factual respects.[297] Accordingly sec. 40 of the Administrative Courts Act (*Verwaltungsgerichtsordnung*)[298] provides a legal action before the administrative courts for all public law disputes not of a constitutional nature. Where the administration is 'bound', i.e. where it has no discretion, the question of violation of the equality clause does not really arise, because the disregard of the statutory provision would be illegal as such. If the unequal treatment is laid down in the statute itself, then the violation of the clause is primarily the fault of the legislature. The executive is then in breach of art. 3 GG for carrying out the statute, but this is not a proper case of arbitrary action on the administration's part. In the area of discretion, however, violations of the equality clause comprise the bulk of the errors of discretion,[299] and this is the very field where the administration's acts can be scrutinized (sec. 114 Administrative Courts Act).[300] In individual cases, particularly in connection with the equality clause, such a reduction of discretion by the courts can even mean that only an administrative decision in one sense can be free of error.[301]

As a rule administrative acts in violation of the equality principle are not void but they are illegal anyway: they should be revoked by the authority, or, if the administration does not recognise the illegality, by the administrative court upon complaint.[302] Up to the time of annulment the administrative acts are normally operative; they can, therefore, be carried out. Usually when an executive act is challenged it is suspended, which prevents the administration from putting it into effect until the court's decision is final.[303] The *ex tunc* nullity of administrative acts is only accepted when the illegality (i.e. breach of equality) is manifest, when the administrative act has so to say the error 'on its face'. This is seldom the case.[304]

Since the constitutional complaint is only a subsidiary action, executive acts cannot be attacked by it directly; first other legal remedies must be exhausted. The constitutional complaint is *'ultima ratio'* of judicial protection. Only in rare exceptional cases, in particular when the petitioner would suffer a heavy and unavoidable disadvantage by being referred to the ordinary procedures, is a constitutional complaint directly admissible.[305]

b. Judiciary

Closely connected with these last statements is the question of the application of the equality clause to the judicial branch. If art. 3 GG is violated by a court decision, then this is an actionable mistake which can be denounced on appeal, in the administrative field for example up to the Federal

Administrative Court.[306] But the Federal Constitutional Court is again the ultimate guardian of the observance of the equality clause, since constitutional complaints can also be lodged against decisions of other courts. Naturally the Court exercises restraint in doing so. Constitutional complaints against judicial decisions will only be allowed when a specific constitutional right (e.g. art. 3 GG) has been violated.[307] The investigation of other errors would give the Constitutional Court super appeal jurisdiction. The Court did probably not always escape this danger.[308]

Judicial decisions violating art. 3 GG will thus be annulled by higher courts or by the Federal Constitutional Court, respectively. In certain circumstances the matter can be referred back to the inferior court.[309] A decision will hardly ever be null and void for violation of the equality clause, but the possibility cannot be ruled out in extreme cases.[310]

2. Protection against the legislature

a. Constitutional complaint and norm control

If a person claims that a statute affecting him is contrary to the equality clause, then he can bring a constitutional complaint against it; it must be brought within one year of the coming into force of the statute.[311] After this year has elapsed or where only the execution of the statute leads to the infringement – not the promulgation of the statute itself –, then the individual cannot attack the statute directly. But he can avail himself of indirect ways to the same end. If any case comes before a court, in which the court itself considers a relevant statute (or individual provisions of it) as unconstitutional, it is obliged to suspend the proceedings and submit the decision on the constitutionality of the statute to the Federal Constitutional Court (art. 100 par. 1 GG). The individual cannot make the court submit to the Constitutional Court, but he can invite it to do so. If the court decides against submission because it does not share the view that the provision is unconstitutional, and superior courts do the same, the individual still has the possibility to contest the final judgment by means of the above-mentioned constitutional complaint against judicial decisions.

Over and above this 'concrete norm control' of art. 100 GG, the Federal Government, a *Land* Government or one-third of the members of the *Bundestag* can apply to the Federal Constitutional Court for investigation of the constitutionality of a statute – without reference to a concrete case already initiated before a court –, e.g. for alleged breach of the equality clause (art. 93 GG). However, this 'abstract norm control' is not normally to be considered as a legal protection for the benefit of the individual.

b. The decision on constitutionality

Violation of the Basic Law by statutory provisions leads, according to the Constitutional Court's jurisprudence,[312] usually to their nullity *ex tunc*. The Court has only rarely departed from this rule, namely when the retrospective effect of its decision would have had altogether too serious consequences threatening the normal functioning of the State.[313] But especially in case of statutory violation of art. 3 GG, the sanction, annulment of provisions containing unequal treatment, turned out to be not necessarily conducive to the establishment of the required equality, or only to a very limited extent.[314]

This becomes apparent through the example of legislative neglect.[315] The Constitutional Court has on many occasions had to consider cases brought by submission or by constitutional complaint, where the legislature did not extend the benefit of certain statutory rules to particular groups. The situation is different from that of wrongful advantages attributed by statute, which can simply be declared null and void by the Court without any difficulties; here, in the case of wrongful disadvantages, there are considerably greater difficulties.

The Court distinguished several situations.[316] If in an advantageous statute a group is expressly excluded from benefit, then the exclusion, if it is contrary to the equality clause, can be annulled with the result that the advantages automatically accrue to everyone.[317] Such a procedure does not help according to the Court,[318] where the statutory advantages are restricted to a particular group and it is impossible to interpret the statute in such a way as to attain an extension of the benefits. Simply out of technical reasons, the gap resulting from silence of the legislature itself cannot be declared null and void. Annulment by the Court is always excluded on grounds of substance where the legislature has various possibilities to comply with the equality clause – including the repeal of the whole favourable norm. The separation of powers requires here restraint on the part of the judiciary before the legislating freedom of Parliament.[319] The latter is indeed responsible, for example, for the realisation of the welfare state clause. Annulment by the Court of beneficial norms for violation of art. 3 GG would in certain circumstances result in great disadvantages for the beneficiaries, without helping those who had been excluded. Another topical example is sec. 4 of the Nationality Act.[320] If the Constitutional Court were to hold unconstitutional the rule that German nationality of the father alone passes to legitimate children at birth, then it is clear that annulment of this provision would not be very helpful; for there would be no criteria at all for the acquisition of nationality by birth. At the same time an extension of the rule by the Court in the sense that the mother's nationality would be passed on would be just as impossible. It is the duty of the legislature, in the first instance, to reinstate equality here. This would be theoretically possible, for example, by choosing the *'ius soli'* principle, but there are also other possibilities. The legislature must be free to make its choice. The Constitutional Court itself can only extend the norm by inclusion of non-beneficiaries or annul it, where this sanction can be considered as the only way of eliminating the constitutional violation, having regard to the coercive effect of the constitutional provision or to the other circumstances of the individual case.[321] The Constitutional Court's interpretive construction of the equality clause as not requiring the most just and suitable solution but only forbidding an arbitrary one, has thus its distinct equivalent in the law of procedure.

In all cases where according to the foregoing a norm can be declared null and void, the Court determines that the provision violates art. 3 GG and is to that extent incompatible with the Basic Law.[322] In this respect, it is irrelevant whether the conclusion arises out of proceedings based on a constitutional complaint or on norm control. The legislature at any rate is obliged by the decision to remove the unconstitutionality in whatever way it thinks appropriate. Up to this time the actual dispute is suspended.[323] The Court left the matter open whether, if the legislature does not remove the violation within a reasonable period, one must nevertheless assume the nullity of the norm.[324] The reasoning shows, however, that it rests on a concept of confidence in the legislators who in a democratic State will not evade their duties.

As appears from these considerations, the judiciary is in constant danger of becoming lawmaker in cases relating to the equality clause. This aspect leads to special cautiousness on the part of the Federal Constitutional Court in examining legislation in the light of the equality clause. Experience, however, shows that as yet the application of the equality clause to legislation did not suffer from it.

3. The protection of the equality principle between private persons *inter se*

In the relations between private persons it is also the courts, usually in the civil or labour jurisdictions, which guarantee protection against breaches of the equality clause. If one starts from the assumption of direct applicability of fundamental rights to third persons, then, for example, every violation of the prohibition against discrimination on political grounds (art. 3 par. 3 GG) is to be taken as a violation of a statutory prohibition leading to nullity of the transaction (sec. 134 BGB).[325] If one follows the dominant doctrine according to which the fundamental rights take their effect in private legal relations primarily via the general clauses of law, then the relevant question is whether on consideration of all circumstances violation of the equality clause is contrary to public order or to the principle of good faith. This would also lead to the nullity of the transaction (sec. 138, 242 and 826 BGB). The decisions of the court can in turn be examined for violation of a specific constitutional right (fundamental right) by the Federal Constitutional Court by way of the constitutional complaint.[326]

C. Compensation

In certain circumstances violation of the equality clause can lead to compensation, partly by restoration of the previous conditions, partly by financial settlement. If an administrative act which is contrary to art. 3 GG is put into effect but later annulled, a claim for redress is available in administrative law by which the consequences of the administrative act can be set aside by compensation in kind for the damage suffered.[327]

Violation of the equality clause can also be the basis for claims for damages. An example is the decision of the Federal Supreme Court in the case of unequal subsidies;[328] if an official is to be blamed for failing in his official duties he owes to the person affected, then the State must make good the consequential damage (art. 34 GG, sec. 839 BGB); to this extent restitution in kind is, of course, impossible.[329]

The Federal Supreme Court has further considered violation of art. 3 GG as a decisive criterion for distinguishing limits on ownership not giving a right to indemnity from infringement of ownership that do give rise to a duty to indemnify: 'Violation of the equality clause is a mark of expropriation'.[330] This theory of the 'special sacrifice', which affects individuals unequally from others, is disputed in every way;[331] however, the Federal Supreme Court has essentially adhered to it.[332] Thus violation of art. 3 GG in this regard also leads to an indemnity, which, however, unlike compensation, is restricted to replacement of the material loss.[333]

A special question is whether State liability attaches to so-called legislative injustice. This is usually denied with the argument that members of the legislature, while they may have official duties to the public at large, do not have a duty towards individuals who have been wronged.[334] The attempt to use the 'special sacrifice' theory in cases of unconstitutional statutes (violation of art. 3) is not convincing. There is no claim for compensation with regard to unconstitutional burdens.[335] On the contrary, application of such a statute by the authorities eliminates claims for damages because the persons who have been disadvantaged by this application were treated unconstitutionally; they are thus automatically classified as having brought a 'special sacrifice' vis-à-vis others.[336]

D. Criminal law protection

According to the law in force at the moment observance of the equality clause is not protected by criminal law. Apparent exceptions occur infrequently, e.g. sec. 107 (a) and (b) Criminal code (*Strafgesetzbuch*)[337] which provide that election falsifications are punished. This legal protection is given in order to attain legitimate and democratically irreproachable election results rather than to protect the equality of the franchise as a right of the individual citizen – though, of course, there is some connection.[338]

NOTES

1. 23.5.1945, BGBl. p. 1.
2. The same applies to elections to other legislative bodies.
3. 1.9.1950, VOBl. I p. 433.
4. 21.10.1947, GBl. p. 251.
5. 11.11.1953, GBl. p. 173.
6. Compare Arts. 31 + 142 GG. See BVerfGE 1, 264 (280 et seq.).
7. See also H. J. Ipsen 'Gleichheit', in Neumann-Nipperdey-Scheuner, 'Die Grundrechte', Vol. 2, 1954 p. 111 (125 et seq.).
8. See below section V. 3.
9. Compare Art. 25 GG and see H. Mosler, 'Das Völkerrecht in der Praxis der deutschen Gerichte', 1957, p. 43 et seq.
10. UN Doc. A/RES/217 (III).
11. BGBl. 1952 II, p. 686; UNTS Vol. 213 p. 221. Compare the decision of 23.7.1968 of the European Court of Human Rights (l'affaire relative à certaines aspects du régime linguistique de l'enseignement en Belgique) p. 34: 'les autorités nationales compétentes se trouvent souvent en face de situations ou de problèmes dont la diversité appelle des solutions juridiques différentes; certaines inégalités de droit ne tendent d'ailleurs qu'à corriger des inégalités de fait'.
12. BGBl. 1957 II, p. 766; UNTS Vol. 295 p. 23.
13. E.g., persons and corporations of private law are also included in the addressees of Art. 7; see K. Feige 'Der Gleichheitssatz im Recht der EWG', 1973 p. 58 et seq.
14. But see now BVerfGE 37, 271.
15. The theory of equality before the legislature was developed first by H. Triepel, 'Goldbilanzenverordnung und Vorzugsaktien', 1924 p. 26 et seq. and then especially by G. Leibholz, 'Die Gleichheit vor dem Gesetz', 1925, and H. Aldag, 'Die Gleichheit vor dem Gesetz in der Reichsverfassung' 1925. For an opposite view see G. Anschütz, 'Kommentar zur Reichsverfassung' 14th Ed., 1932, p. 521. For further references see G. Leibholz, 'Höchstrichterliche Rechtsprechung und Gleichheitssatz', AöR NF Vol. 19 (1930) p. 428 et seq.
16. See G. Leibholz, 'Die Gleichheit vor dem Gesetz', 2nd Ed., 1959, p. 226 et seq., and H. Ridder, 'Männer und Frauen sind gleichberechtigt', in: Festschrift für Gerhard Leibholz, 2nd Vol. 1966 p. 219.
17. RGBl. p. 1383 - Art. 109 para. 1 read 'All Germans are equal before the law'.

18. The only contrary opinion is R. Thoma, 'Ungleichheit und Gleichheit im Bonner Grundgesetz', DVBl. 1951, p. 457.

19. BVerfGE 1, 14 (52). Decision of 23.10.1951. This is the permanent jurisprudence, see BVerfGE 32, 346 (360).

20. See Leibholz, op. cit. (note 15) p. 237.

21. Compare on the one hand the pioneering decision of the Reichsgericht of 4.11.1925, RGZ 111, 320 and on the other hand the expositions of Triepel, Leibholz and Aldag, note 17 above.

22. BVerfGE 1, 14 - compare note 19 above.

23. BGBl. 1951 I, p. 283.

24. The formula was later amended to read that one should treat 'equal things equally and unequal things differently according to their special features', BVerfGE 3, 58 (135).

25. BVerfGE 1, 14 (52).

26. op. cit. (note 15), p. 87.

27. op. cit. p 237. Before this it was said, 'If no reasonable ground can be found for the criterion which is the determining factor in the norm, if the facts standardised by the legal provisions are plainly inconsistent with the legal consequences attached to them, if there is no intrinsic connection whatsoever between the regulations laid down and the purpose for which they were made, or if there is such a connection but on a completely inadequate footing, then the norm can be characterised as arbitrary, op. cit. p. 76.

28. As a member of the Second Senate of the BVerfGE Leibholz was also involved in reaching the decision; BVerfGE 1, 14 et seq.

29. Compare BVerfGE 9, 338 (349); 17, 381 (388); 23, 229 (240); 25, 371 (400). In other words the task of the legislature is to choose the aspects to be compared; BVerfGE 13, 331 (339, 347 et seq.); 23, 229 (240). See also R. Bernhardt, 'Eigenheiten und Ziele der Rechtsvergleichung im öffentlichen Recht', ZaöRV Vol. 24 (1964), p. 431 (433).

30. BVerfGE 27, 111 (127): 30, 409 (413).

31. BVergGE 9, 291 et seq.

32. GBl. 1956, p. 19.

33. BVerfGE 9, 291 (294 et seq.). See also BVerfGE 17, 1 (30 et seq.).

34. BVerfGE 30, 409 et seq.

35. RGBl. 1904, p. 321.

36. See also Hans F. Zacher, 'Soziale Gleichheit', AöR NF Vol. 93 (1968), p. 341 (352 et seq.), and E.-W. Fuss, 'Gleichheitssatz und Richtermacht', JZ 1959, p. 329 (330 et seq.). Criticism is directed not so much at the result as at the method.

37. For example BVerfGE 18, 121 (124); 23, 50 (60); 32, 157 (167).

38. By this way judicial self-restraint can be seen in the administration of the equality principle; see BVerfGE 13, 356 (363) 'The Court must show restraint with respect to the legislature'.

39. BVerfGE 13, 331 (340); 15, 313 (318).

40. BVerfGE 18, 315 (334).

41. See A. Hamann-H. Lenz. 'Das Grundgesetz für die Bundesrepublik Deutschland vom 23. Mai 1949', 3. Ed. 1970, p. 158 and A. Arndt, 'Gedanken

zum Gleichheitssatz', Festschrift für G. Leibholz, 2. Vol. 1966, p. 179 (184).

42. RGBl. 1936 I, p. 976.

43. BVerfGE 13, 331 et seq.

44. BVerfGE 1, 208 (248).

45. BVerfGE 12, 264 (273); 7, 129 (153). See also BVerfGE 9, 237 (243): 'the system of income tax law'; BVerfGE 21, 54 (64): 'the system of the law of businessmen's profits tax; BVerfGE 32, 78 (83): 'the nature of property tax'; BVerfGE 31, 119 (130) speaks generally about the justice of types of taxes.

46. BVerfGE 11, 283 (293); 9, 338 (349).

47. BVerfGE 17, 122 (130).

48. BVerfGE 32, 78 (83); 27, 58 (65).

49. BVerfGE 9, 3 (10); 12, 341 (349).

50. for example BVerfGE 18, 288 (298).

51. BVerfGE 1, 264 (276); 3, 58 (135); 23, 229 (240); 33, 171 (189).

52. BVerfGE 32, 173 (184); 18, 288 (298); 27, 297 (306). In these decisions the question was always that of compensation for national socialist injustices.

53. BVerfGE 32, 188. The possibility of giving dissenting and concurring votes exists since the Act of the 21st Dec. 1970 (BGB1. I, p. 1765).

54. BVerfGE 3, 58 (135); 3, 162 (182); 4, 143 (155): 30, 409 (419); 31, 119 (130); 32, 192.

55. See K. Hesse, 'Grundzüge des Verfassungsrechts der Bundesrepublik Deutschland', 5th Ed. 1972, p. 177 and H. v. Mangoldt-Fr. Klein, 'Das Bonner Grundgesetz', 2nd Ed., 1957, p. 200 et seq.

56. See P. Seisser, 'Das Verhältnis des allgemeinen Gleichheitssatzes (Art. 3 Abs. 1 Grundgesetz) zu besonderen Gleichheitssätzen', Würzburg Dissertation 1969, p. 44 et seq. and H. v. Mangoldt, 'Das Bonner Grundgesetz' 1st. Ed. 1953, p. 51 et seq.

57. See above note 52. This is different from the decisions of the BVerfG on the law relating to compensation for loss suffered through war; see references in G. Leibholz-H. J. Rinck, 'Grundgesetz', Kommentar an Hand der Rechtsprechung des BVerfG, 4th Ed. 1971, p. 95.

58. BVerfGE 11, 245 (253); 17, 210 (216); 28, 206 (214). For criticism of this see Franz Klein, 'Gleichheitssatz und Steuerrecht', 1966, p. 157 et seq.

59. BVerfGE 17, 1 (24); 26, 16 (31).

60. According to Zacher, op. cit. (note 36) p. 380 et seq.

61. BVerfGE 14, 288 (304); 16, 147 (186); 18, 315 (332); 33, 171 (189).

62. BVerfGE 32, 188 (191); 29, 337 (339).

63. BVerfGE 32, 188 (192) and already 3, 162 (182). See also H.-J. Rinck, 'Die höchstrichliche Rechtsprechung zum Gleichheitssatz in der Bundesrepublik, der Schweiz, Österreich, Italien, den USA und Indien', JöR NF Vol. 10 (1961) p. 269 (281).

64. See above note 37.

65. BVerfGE 4, 144 (155); 2, 266 (281). On the objectification of the concept of arbitrariness see W. Böckenförde, 'Der allgemeine Gleichheitssatz und die Aufgabe des Richters', 1957, p. 63 et seq.

66. BVerfGE 4, 7 (25).

67. BVerfGE 8, 51 (64); 21, 12 (27); 24, 300 (358).

68. The GG is not stamped with neutral standards but embraces immutable values as a result of Germany's past history. For an apparently different opinion see Hamann-Lenz, op. cit. (note 41) p. 154, and compare Th. Maunz, 'Deutsches Staatsrecht', 17th Ed. 1969, p. 131. Critical against the objective system of evaluation of the fundamental rights is E. Forsthoff, 'Zur heutigen Situation einer Verfassungslehre', Festgabe für Carl Schmitt, 1st Vol. 1968, p. 185 (190).

69. See on this note 24 above.

70. BVerfGE 23, 288 (313).

71. BVerfGE 2, 118 (119); 9, 237 (244).

72. BVerfGE 1, 264 (275).

73. BVerfGE 16, 6 (25); 19, 119 (124 et seq.).

74. See Seisser, op. cit. (note 56), p. 57 et seq. The main criticism of this jurisprudence is K. A. Bettermann, 'Rechtsgleichheit und Ermessensfreiheit', Der Staat Vol. 1 (1962), p. 79 (91), and A. Podlech, 'Gehalt und Funktionen des allgemeinen verfassungsrechtlichen Gleichheitssatzes', 1971, p. 57 et seq. According to BVerfGE 32, 199 (223 et seq.) there is no violation of the equality clause if a new regulation puts the holders of different offices on the same footing as regards salary when previously they had received different salaries. But even this 'levelling process from below' must rest on plausible grounds.

75. BVerfGE 23, 229 (240 et seq.).

76. See Hamann-Lenz, op. cit. (note 41), p. 161, and Klein, op. cit. (note 58), p. 162.

77. Zacher, op. cit. (note 36), p. 344.

78. E. Forsthoff, 'Der Staat der Industriegesellschaft', 1971, p. 136 et seq.; K. Schweiger, 'Zur Geschichte und Bewertung des Willkürverbots', in Festschrift zum 25 jährigen Bestehen des Bayerischen Verfassungsgerichtshofs, 1972, p. 55 (64).

79. Podlech, op. cit. (note 74), p. 196 et seq.

80. E. Eyermann, 'Gleichheitssatz, Wurzel des Willkürverbots?' in: Festschrift zum 25 jährigen Bestehen des Bayerischen Verfassungsgerichtshofs, 1972, p. 45 (49); Schweiger, op. cit. (note 78), p. 70; Fuss, op. cit. (note 36), p. 330.

81. H. P. Ipsen, op. cit. (note 7), p. 164; Klein, op. cit. (note 58), p. 163 and 166; Podlech, op. cit. (note 74), p. 85.

82. Fuss, op. cit. (note 36), p. 338.

83. For example Ipsen and Klein (note 81).

84. Podlech, op. cit. (note 74), p. 86 et seq., 89 et seq.

85. G. Dürig, 'Gleichheit', Staatslexikon Vol. 3, 6th Ed. 1959, column 983 (987); and reservedly K. Hesse, 'Der Gleichheitsgrundsatz im Staatsrecht' AöR Vol. 77 (1951), p. 167 (202 et seq.).

86. op. cit. (note 36), p. 344. Naturally this does not apply to the recently developed conception of Podlech (note 74).

87. For example, the differentiation according to nationality is not forbidden by the particular equality clauses. Art. 3 para 1 GG, however, prohibits differentiation on this ground in so far as it would be arbitrary; see Ipsen, op. cit. (note 81), p. 127 and 134.

88. Zacher, op. cit. (note 36), p. 344 et seq.

89. See note 31 above.

90. See 'Constitutional Review in the World Today, National reports and comparative studies', Beiträge zum ausländischen öffentlichen Recht und Völkerrecht (ed. by H. Mosler), Vol. 36, 1962.

91. See BVerfGE 22, 349 (362) and note 55 above.

92. BVerfGE 9, 137 (147).

93. See Bayerisches Verfassungsgerichtshof VGHE NF 3, 77.

94. BVerfGE 9, 137 (147); 18, 353 (363); 27, 297 (306).

95. For example BVerwGE 38, 191 (197); DöV 1972, p. 644 (646); BSGE 2, 201 (217); 9, 236; BFHE 55, 227 et seq.

96. See Leibholz, op. cit. (note 17), p. 89; Maunz, op. cit. (note 68), p. 132; Ipsen, op. cit. (note 7), p. 147.

97. Leibholz, p. 93.

98. BVerwGE 38, 191 (197), and Ipsen, p. 147. On the function of laws in the application of the equality clause see Schaumann, 'Gleichheit und Gesetzmässigkeitsprinzip', JZ 1966, p. 721 et seq.

99. According to the prevailing view the administration can grant subsidies, without statutory basis; to this extent provision for the necessary means in the budget is sufficient - see for this question Maunz-Dürig-Herzog, 'Grundgesetz, Kommentar', Art. 20, p. 57.

100. The basis of self-binding action of the administration rests also partly on the principle of good faith; this is rejected by M. Wallerath, 'Die Selbstbindung der Verwaltung', 1968, p. 52 et seq.

101. BVerwGE 2, 163 (167); 5, 79 (81); 8, 4 (10); DöV 1971, p. 316 et seq. See further E. Forsthoff, 'Lehrbuch des Verwaltungsrechts', 9th. Ed. 1966 p. 91, and Rinck, op. cit. (note 63), p. 287 et seq.

102. But Art. 3 GG must of course be observed in this connection.

103. G. Dax, 'Das Gleichbehandlungsgebot als Grundlage positiver subjektiv-öffentlicher Rechte', 1969, p. 89; Wallerath, op. cit. (note 100), p. 19. This principle of being bound is limited to administrative authorities, which together with the authority seized of the matter, are subject to the same superior authorities; see BVerfGE 21, 87 (91); Ipsen, op. cit. (note 81), and V. Götz, 'Das Grundrecht auf Rechtsanwendungsgleichheit und der verwaltungsgerichtliche Rechtsschutz', DVBl. 1968, p. 93 (97).

104. BVerwG DöV 1971, p. 316 et seq. See also F. Ossenbühl, 'Verwaltungsvorschriften und Grundgesetz', 1968, p. 530 et seq., and V. Götz, 'Recht der Wirtschaftssubventionen', 1966, p. 37, and F. Kopp, 'Verfassungsrecht und Verwaltungsverfahrensrecht', 1971, p. 171.

105. Wallerath, op. cit. (note 100), p. 139.

106. Wallerath, p. 80 et seq.; H. J. Mertens, 'Die Selbstbindung der Verwaltung auf Grund des Gleichheitssatzes', 1963, p. 77 et seq.

107. See Wallerath, p. 82, and compare the jurisprudential position, BVerwG DöV 1967, p. 424.

108. Wallerath, p. 41 et seq.; Mertens, p. 45 and 79.

109. See Rinck, op. cit. (note 63), p. 288, and Forsthoff, op. cit. (note 101), p. 91 et seq. and 238 et seq.

110. BVerwGE 5, 1 (8 et seq.); 34, 278 (283 et seq.); BSGE 7, 75 (78); 21, 199 (202). Legal writers: Dax, op. cit. (note 103), p. 87, Dürig, op. cit. (note

85), column 989, Ipsen, op. cit. (note 7), p. 148, Rinck, op. cit. (note 63), p. 288, Wallerath, op. cit. (note 100), p. 98 et seq. The bringing about of a lawful state of affairs is always a reason which justifies deviation; Mertens, op. cit. (note 106), p. 26.

111. BVerfGE 21, 245 (261); 25, 216 (228 et seq.); further the unpublished decision of 12th January 1967 - 1 BvR 289/65.

112. O. Bachof, 'Verfassungsrecht, Verwaltungsrecht, Verfahrensrecht in der Rechtsprechung des Bundesverwaltungsgerichts', Vol. 1, 3 rd Ed. 1966, p. 133.

113. VGH Baden-Württemberg, DVBl. 1972, p. 186 et seq.

114. VGH Baden-Württemberg, BaWüVBl. 1973, p. 14.

115. V. Götz, op. cit. (note 113), p. 93 et seq.; same author in DVBl. 1972, p. 188 et seq.

116. See also - in opposition to Götz - F. Ossenbühl, 'Administrative Selbstbindung durch gesetzwidrige Verwaltungsübung?', DöV, 1970, p. 264. Also Kopp, op. cit. (note 104), p. 169, and Seisser, op. cit. (note 56), p. 35 et seq.

117. BVerfGE 25, 352, and 30, 108. The question is disputed in legal literature; see K. Vogel, Federal Republic of Germany, in 'Judicial Protection against the Executive', Vol. 1, National Reports, Beiträge zum ausländischen öffentlichen Recht und Völkerrecht (ed. by Mosler), Vol. 52, 1969, p. 127 (136 et seq.) and the references contained therein.

118. BVerfGE 4, 1 (6 et seq.).

119. BVerfGE 1, 332 (345); 4, 352 (358); 19, 38 (47); 21, 87 (91); see also Ipsen, op. cit. (note 7), p. 150.

120. BVergG JZ 1952, p. 591; also Rinck, op. cit. (note 63), p. 291.

121. BVerfGE 4, 1 (7); 13, 132 (150).

122. BVerfGE 27, 175 (178), see alto note 54 above.

123. BVerfGE 4, 1 (6 et seq.).

124. For example, BVerfGE 2, 336 (340).

125. See above I. 1.

126. BVerfGE 3, 225 et seq. (239).

127. BVerfGE 15, 337 (345).

128. BVerfGE 3, 225 (240). But see on the other hand G. Beitzke 'Gleichheit von Mann und Frau', in: Neumann-Nipperdey-Scheuner, 'Die Grundrechte', 2nd Vol., 1954, p. 199 (209).

129. See note 29 above.

130. BVerfGE 21, 329 (343).

131. BVerfGE 15, 337 (343); 31, 1 (6).

132. BVerfGE 3, 225 (242); 21, 329 (343); 31, 1 (4 et seq.). On the other hand BVerfGE 15, 337 et seq. also considered the aim the legislature had when regulating the position. This view seems to have been given up.

133. See BVerfGE 15, 337 (345).

134. BVerfGE 3, 225 (242); 6, 55 (82); but also see W. Habscheid, 'Gleichberechtigung der Geschlechter', Staatslexikon, 6th Ed., Vol. 3, 1959, column 974 (975).

135. BVerfGE 6, 55 (82).

136. BVerfGE 5, 9 (12).

137. BVerfGE 11, 277 (281).

138. BVerfGE 26, 265 (274 et seq.).

139. BVerfGE 21, 329 (343); 31, 1 et seq. An unsatisfactory decision is BVerwGE 40, 17 et seq. according to which Art. 3 para. 2 GG does not prevent men being excluded from being midwives.

140. See also Podlech, op. cit. (note 74), p. 91.

141. F. Binder-Wehberg, 'Ungleichbehandlung von Mann und Frau', 1970, p. 33 et seq., investigated the grounds for differentiation developed by the BVerfGE. She comes to interesting conclusions; for instance a functional difference between men and women is only recognised when the woman has children.

142. See below II. 2 and IV.

143. BVerfGE 23, 98 (107).

144. BVerfGE 18, 38 (46).

145. See BVerfGE 3, 225 (240); 9, 124 (128). Further Maunz, op. cit. (note 68), p. 131.

146. von Mangoldt, op. cit. (note 56), p. 54.

147. von Mangoldt-Klein, op. cit. (note 55), p. 209. See also Binder-Wehberg, op. cit. (note 141), p. 23 et seq.

148. BVerfGE 5, 17 (22); 9, 124 (128).

149. Hamann-Lenz, op. cit. (note 41), p. 171.

150. This is also recognised in legal literature: see for example von Mangoldt-Klein, op. cit. (note 55), p. 212; Seisser, op. cit. (note 56), p. 105.

151. BGBl. 1950, p. 367.

152. BVerfGE 2, 266 (286).

153. BVerfGE 5, 17 (22). See also BVerfGE 3, 225 (241).

154. BVerfGE 23, 98 (106 et seq.). See on this E. Klein, 'Federal Republic of Germany, Yearbook on Human Rights for 1968', p. 122 (124).

155. See K. Döhring, 'Die allgemeine Regeln des völkerrechtlichen Fremdenrechts und das deutsche Verfassungsrecht', 1963, p. 195 et seq. For a different but devious opinion see M. Zuleeg, 'Zur staatsrechtlichen Stellung der Ausländer in der Bundesrepublik Deutschland', DöV 1973, p. 361 (363 et seq.). See also note 87 above.

156. BVerfGE 5, 85 (139).

157. See BVerfGE 2, 1 (12 et seq.).

158. BVerfGE 13, 46 (49).

159. BVerfGE 17, 280 (283).

160. BVerfGE 17, 148 (154); 24, 119 (149); 25, 167 (196).

161. BVerfGE 3, 225 (240); 8, 210 (221); 17, 280 (283); 25, 167 (173).

162. BVerfGE 26, 44 (60 et seq.).

163. BVerfGE 8, 210 (215); 17, 280 (284); 25, 167 (183, 197); 26, 44 (58).

164. For the realisation of Art. 6 para. 5 GG see below III. 1. (b).

165. See also BVerfGE 26, 265 (272).

166. See E. Stein, 'Lehrbuch des Staatsrechts', 2nd Ed. 1971, p. 234.

167. See recent decision OVG Lüneburg, DVBl. 1972, p. 962 et seq.

168. The question has recently become very topical whether members of political parties that are opposed to the Constitution but not forbidden by the BVerfG can be barred from public office by reason of their political views. On this see H. Maurer, 'Die Mitgliedschaft von Beambten in verfassungsfeindlichen Par-

teien und Organisationen', NJW 1972, p. 601.

169. R. Herzog, 'Demokratie und Gleichheit heute', DVBl. 1970, p. 713.

170. BVerfGE 1, 208 (242); 3. 383 (391); 11, 266 (271); 28, 220 (225); DöV 1973, p. 128 et seq.

171. BVerfGE 11, 351 (364).

172. BVerfGE 11, 266 (272).

173. BVerfGE 6, 84 (91); 11, 351 (360).

174. Compare the following writers: G. Leibholz, op. cit. (note 20), p. 6 et seq.; Maunz, op. cit. (note 68), p. 131; Rinck, op. cit. (note 63), p. 276 et seq.

175. BVerfGE 6, 84 (92 et seq.); 14, 121 (135); 24, 300 (341).

176. BVerfGE 1, 208 (247); 13, 243 (247).

177. See Leibholz-Rinck, op. cit. (note 57), p. 91 et seq.; for the corresponding jurisprudence of other courts see Rinck, op. cit. (note 63), p. 278.

178. According to Ridder, op. cit. (note 15), p. 225 et seq.

179. Similarly Seisser, op. cit. (note 56), p. 76 et seq.; Binder-Wehberg, op. cit. (note 141), p. 55 et seq.

180. Podlech, op. cit. (note 74), p. 92, says therefore that the laws giving protection to mothers do not affect Art. 3 para. 2 GG.

181. See Leibholz, op. cit. (note 20), p. 118; Böckenförde, op. cit. (note 65), p. 27 et seq. Also BVerfGE 1, 97 (104).

182. On the problematics of this see W. Martens and P. Häberle, 'Grundrechte im Leistungsstaat', VVDStRL 30 (1970), p. 7 et seq. and p. 43 et seq.; further R. Bernhardt, 'Wandlungen der Grundrechte', 1970, p. 10 et seq.

183. Hesse, op. cit. (note 85), p. 220.

184. See Zacher, op. cit. (note 36), p. 361.

185. BVerwG NJW 1972, p. 2325. See also H. Scholler, 'Die Interpretation des Gleichheitssatzes als Willkürverbot oder als Gebot der Chancengleichheit', 1969, p. 47 et seq.; G. Dax, op. cit. (note 103), p. 122 et seq., and R. Scholz, 'Die öffentlich-rechtliche Konkurrentenklage in der Rechtsprechung der Verwaltungs- und Zivilgerichte', Wirtschaftsrecht 1972, p. 35 (64 et seq.).

186. BVerfG DöV 1972, p. 606 et seq.

187. See H. H. Klein, 'Grundrechte im demokratischen Staat', 1972, p. 65 et seq.

188. See also O. Kimminich, JZ 1972, p. 696 (697).

189. BAGE 1, 185 (196); 4, 274 (276) and recently BAG, MDR 1973, p. 167 et seq. See also H. C. Nipperdey, 'Die Würde des Menschen', in: Neumann-Nipperdey-Scheuner, 'Die Grundrechte' Vol. 2, 1954, p. 1 (19 et seq.).

190. BVerfGE 7, 198 (205 et seq.); Maunz-Dürig-Herzog, op. cit. (note 99) Art. 1, p. 64 et seq.; Böckenförde, op. cit. (note 65), p. 18 et seq.

191. J. Schwabe, 'Die sogenannte Drittwirkung der Grundrechte', 1971, p. 149 et seq.

192. See Salzwedel, 'Gleichheitsgrundsatz und Drittwirkung', in: Festschrift für H. Jahrreis, 1964, p. 348. Of a different opinion W. Leisner, 'Grundrechte und Privatrecht', 1960, p. 359.

193. See G. Böhmer, 'Erbrecht 'in Neumann-Nipperdey-Scheuner, 'Die Grundrechte', Vol. 2, 1954, p. 401 (422).

194. Schaumann, op. cit. (note 98), p. 726.

195. BVerfGE 17, 1 (13).
196. RGBl. 1896, p. 195.
197. The Equality Act of 18th June 1957 (BGBl. I, p. 609). Between 1953 and 1957 the courts carried out the adjustment of those laws that had not been amended to comply with Art. 3 para. 2 GG; see BVerfGE 3, 225 (230) and BGHZ 39, 45 et seq.
198. See the references in BVerfGE 10, 59 (70).
199. For instance Habscheid, op cit. (note 134), column 977.
200. BVerfGE 10, 59 et seq.
201. Palandt-Lauterbach, 'Bürgerliches Gesetzbuch, Kommentar', 28th Ed. 1969, sec. 1627 note 2.
202. BVerfGE 8, 210 (216); 25, 167 (179).
203. BVerfGE 25, 167 et seq.
204. BGBl. I, p. 1243.
205. See Note 162 above.
206. Bundesrat Publication 260/73.
207. Bundesrat Publication 260/73, p. 97.
208. See Binder-Wehberg, op. cit. (note 141), p. 62 et seq.
209. BVerfGE 17, 168 (171 et seq.).
210. Bundesrat Publication 260/73, p. 99.
211. Bundesrat Publication 260/73, p. 60 et seq.
212. RGBl., p. 583.
213. BGBl. I, p. 1581.
214. For example Binder-Wehberg, op. cit. (note 141), p. 62 et seq.
215. BVerwG JZ 1972, p. 158 et seq.
216. See A. Makarov, 'Deutsches Staatsangehörigkeitsrecht', Kommentar, 2nd Ed. 1971, p. 224.
216a. In the meantime the BVerfG held that the mentioned provision of the Nationality Act is unconstitutional, BVerfGE 37, 217; also now BGBl. 1974 I, p. 3714.
217. BVerfGE 6, 389 et seq.
218. For the references see Beitzke, op. cit. (note 128), p. 216.
219. BGBl. I, p. 645.
220. In this connection one must also take account of the changing views regarding the special protection to be given to women according to the traditional views of the sexes. Several courts have considered sec. 1300 BGB to be contrary to the Constitution by reference to Art. 3 para. 2 GG. According to sec. 1300 a fiancée can, when the engagement comes to an end, claim financial compensation from her fiancé, if they have cohabited: OLG Hamburg, Zeitschrift für das gesamte Familienrecht 1972, p. 461 et. seq.; LG Kaiserslautern (unpublished). See also BVerfGE 32, 296 et seq.
221. Compare sec. 1 and 14 Act on Associations (BGBl. 1964 I, p. 593); sec. 1 Act on Assemblies (BGBl. 1953 I, p. 684).
222. See above II. 8.
223. BGBl. 1972 I, p. 13.
224. There is no provision to regulate the appointment of workers by the employers; see Binder-Wehberg, op. cit. (note 141), p. 75 et seq.

225. See above II. 7.
226. BGBl. 1953 I, p. 1047.
227. BGBl. 1965 I, p. 585. Active policies on the acquisition of assets and wealth are given very great importance in this connection.
228. BGBl. 1969 I, p. 1688.
229. See Hesse, op. cit. (note 85), p. 169; Ipsen, op. cit. (note 81), p. 115 et seq.
230. A. Erler, 'Alle Menschen sind vor dem Gesetz gleich', 1967, p. 29 et seq.
231. H. Hattenhauer, 'Zwischen Hierarchie und Demokratie', 1971, p. 36.
232. In BVerfGE 20, 162 (222) the legality principle is also stated to be an expression of the principle of the equality of all persons before the law.
233. See Forsthoff, op. cit. (note 78).
234. Rinck, op. cit. (note 63), p. 293; and Ipsen, op. cit. (note 7), p. 173 et seq.
235. A national minority exists only in Schleswig-Holstein (Danish); see BVerfGE 1, 208 (257).
236. See the amendment of Art. 38 para. 2 GG (BGBl. 1970 I, p. 1161); according to this a person is entitled to vote if he is 18 years of age (the old limit was 21); and a person can stand for election if he has reached the age of majority i.e. now 18, too. Previously one could only stand at the age of 25, or later of 21.
237. BVerfGE 24, 300 (340); 1, 208 (225); 6, 273 (280); 11, 266 (273).
238. BVerfGE 1, 208 (242, 255); 3, 19 (26 et seq.); 6, 273 (280); 8, 51 (64).
239. BVerfGE 8, 51 (64 et seq.); 14, 121 (133); 20, 56 (116). See on this sec. 5 and 18-22 of the Act on Political Parties of 24th July 1967 (BGBl. I, p. 773) and VG Köln, DöV 1972, p. 356.
240. BVerfGE 24, 300 (344); DöV 1973, p. 131 et seq.
241. See above II. 5. (c) and III. 1.
242. See above II. 5 (a) and III. 1.
243. BVerfGE 17, 1 et seq.
244. BGHZ 50, 304 et seq.
245. See above III. 2, (b).
246. BVerfGE 31, 58 et seq.
247. See BGH, Zeitschrift für das gesamte Familienrecht 1971, p. 429.
248. BAG, AP. No. 16 on Art. 3 GG; BSGE 8, 164 et seq.
249. See Binder-Wehberg, op. cit. (note 141), p. 78 et seq. On the effect of Art. 3 para. 2 GG on labour law and social law see Rinck, op. cit. (note 63), p. 320 et seq.
250. Preussisches Gesetzblatt 1891, p. 175.
251. BVerfGE 6, 55 (70 et seq.); 13, 290 (298); 13, 331 (338); 26, 302 (310); see also F. Klein, 'Gleichheitssatz und Steuerrecht', 1966.
252. Hattenhauer, op. cit. (note 231), p. 35.
253. General conditions of trade are contractual agreements that are usually unfavourable to the purchaser (consumer). On these problems see W. Löwe, 'Der Stand der rechtspolitischen Diskussion um die "Algemeinen" Geschäftsbedingungen', Betriebs-Berater 1973, p. 585.

254. See the Act on the Right to Notice on Dismissal, 1969 version (BGBl. I. p. 1317); G. Schnorr, 'Die Rechtsprechung des Bundesarbeitsgerichts zum GG', JöR NF Vol. 9. (1960), p. 179 et seq.

255. See above III. 2. (e) and K. H. Biedenkopf, 'Mitbestimmung', 1972.

256. See above II. 7; further H. Kreussler, 'Der allgemeine Gleichheitssatz als Schranke für den Subventionsgesetzgeber unter besonderer Berücksichtigung von wirtschaftspolitischen Differenzierungszielen', 1972.

257. Christian religion has for a long time been satisfied with this; for the importance of this knowledge in the modern development of the equality clause see Erler, op. cit. (note 230), p. 16 et seq., and Arndt, op. cit. (note 41), p. 179.

258. Seisser, op. cit. (note 56), p. 12.

259. Hesse, op. cit. (note 85), p. 172 et seq.

260. BVerfGE 1, 208 (249) - A Constitution's equality principle is by its nature filled up with ideology. This raises the question of the rationality of law. For the different possible viewpoints on equality see Hesse, op. cit. (note 85), p. 178 et seq.

261. See above note 25. For the criticism of legal writers see II. 2, (c) above.

262. BVerfGE 17, 122 (130).

263. BVerfGE 23, 99 (106 et seq.).

264. Similar values can be extracted from other constitutional provisions e.g. Art. 6 para. 1 GG, according to which marriage and the family are under special protection of the State. They differ from the specific equality clauses however in that the values taken from them normally provide a reasonable ground for differentiation but their nonobservance does not mean necessarily that there is arbitrariness. The unconstitutionality can, of course, arise from a violation of the constitutional norm; on this problem see Podlech, op. cit. (note 74), p. 135 et seq.

265. See Hesse, op. cit. (note 55), p. 177; Seisser, op. cit. (note 56), p. 44 et seq.; Leibholz, op. cit. (note 20), p. 76 et seq.

266. See above note 54.

267. As to the results, also Podlech, op. cit. (note 74), p. 88 et seq.

268. See above note 29.

269. Art. 6. para. 5 GG is an exception to this.

270. R. Herzog, 'Allgemeine Staatslehre', 1971, p. 382; Seisser, op. cit. (note 56), p. 23 et seq.

271. And also with Art. 6 para. 5 GG.

272. See Herzog, op. cit. (note 270), p. 381 et seq.; Seisser, op. cit. (note 56), p. 23 et seq.

273. Hesse, op. cit. (note 85), p. 207 and 215.

274. Herzog, op. cit. (note 270), p. 381.

275. See above IV. In older commentaries on the GG this was not recognised; see von Mangoldt, op. cit. (note 56), p. 50 et seq.

276. Bachof, op. cit. (note 112), p. 128; H. Klein, op. cit. (note 187), p. 66.

277. Forsthoff, op. cit. (note 68), p. 189.

278. Ipsen, op. cit. (note 7), p. 174.

279. See Hesse, op. cit. (note 85), p. 208. The re-orientation of Art. 3 GG goes hand in hand with a change in function of property; see P. Badura, 'Die

soziale Schlüsselstellung des Eigentums', BayVerwBl. 1973, p. 1 et seq.

280. BVerfGE 10, 354 (371); 12, 319 (324); 17, 319 (331); 27, 175 (179); 32, 346 (360).

281. BVerfG, DöV 1972, p. 606 (612).

282. Eyermann, op. cit. (note 80), p. 45 (52) and H.-J. Birkner, 'Gleichheitssatz', Evangelisches Staatslexikon, 1966, column 699.

283. op. cit. (note 41), p. 182, 185.

284. See R. Dahrendorf, 'Über den Ursprung der Ungleichheit unter den Menschen', 1961, p. 32; O. Köhler, 'Gleichheit', Staatslexikon, Vol. 3, 6th Ed., 1959, column 989 (992 et seq.); Podlech, op. cit. (note 74), p. 185 et seq.

285. H. Krüger, 'Allgemeine Staatslehre, 1964, p. 531.

286. Dürig, op. cit. (note 85) column 985 et seq.; von Mangoldt, op. cit. (note 56), p. 50.

287. op. cit. (note 20), p. 22 et seq.

288. See Leibholz (note 20), p. 115 et seq. and 216 et seq.

289. The equality clause should not be forgotten in the field of judicial protection of rights; also persons without means must be able to defend their rights in court; this results from Art. 3 para. 1 GG in conjunction with the principle of the welfare state; BVerfGE 22, 83 (86).

290. See above III. 1.

291. See above III. 1.

292. BVerfGE 1, 97 (100); 2, 287 (291).

293. A constitutional complaint can be brought before the Federal Constitutional Court by anyone who alleges that his basic rights have been violated by a public authority (Art. 93 GG).

294. BVerfGE 6, 257; 8, 1; 18, 288.

295. See below VI. 2, (b).

296. See Ipsen, op. cit. (note 7), p. 132 et seq., 170 et seq.; further note 158 above.

297. The act of mercy is an exception, see above II. 3, (c). On judicial protection against the executive see generally Vogel, op. cit. (note 117), p. 127 et seq.

298. BGBl. 1960 I, p. 17 - in certain special circumstances a case can be brought before the ordinary courts or the social insurance courts.

299. See above II. 3, (a).

300. BVerfGE 9, 137 (147 et seq.); Rinck, op. cit. (note 63), p. 287.

301. BVerwGE 11, 95 (97); 16, 214 (218).

302. See Forsthoff, op. cit. (note 101), p. 217 et seq.

303. Sec. 80 VwGO.

304. For example see Forsthoff, op. cit. (note 101), p. 222 et seq.; Redeker-von Örtzen, 'Verwaltungsgerichtsordnung', Kommentar 4th Ed. 1971, p. 170 et seq.

305. Sec. 90 BVerfGG 1971 version (BGBl. I, p. 105).

306. See sec. 137 VwGO.

307. BVerfGE 1, 4 (5); 1, 7 (8); 3, 213 (219 et seq.); 18, 85 (92 et seq.); 30, 173 (196 et seq., 201 et seq., 219 et seq.) - See also above II. 4.

308. See J. Burmeister, 'Das Bundesverfassungsgericht als Revisionsinstanz', DVBl. 1969, p. 605.

309. Sec. 95 subs. 2 BVerfGG.

310. For the nullity of judgements see L. Rosenberg, 'Lehrbuch des deutschen Zivilprozessrechts', 8th Ed., 1960, p. 338 et seq.; K Peters, 'Strafprozessrecht', 2nd Ed., 1966, p. 449 et seq.

311. Sec. 90 and 93 BVerfGG.

312. BVerfGE 1, 14 (15); see also sec. 78, 82 and 95 BVerfGG. For the problematics see Chr. Böckenförde, 'Die sogenannte Nichtigkeit verfassungswidriger Gesetze', 1966.

313. See H. H. Klein, 'Bundesverfassungsgericht und Staatsraison', 1968, p. 11 et seq., and P. Wittig, 'Politische Rücksichten in der Rechtsprechung des Bundesverfassungsgerichts', Der Staat 1969, p. 137 et seq.

314. Zacher, op. cit. (note 36), p. 350.

315. For the details see F. Jülicher, 'Die Verfassungsbeschwerde gegen Urteile bei gesetzgeberischem Unterlassen', 1972.

316. BVerfGE 22, 349 (360 et seq.).

317. BVerfGE 6, 273 (274); 22, 163.

318. The distinction made here is attacked in legal writings on the ground that often it is only caused by unconscious formulations of the statute's text; see Jülicher, op. cit. (note 315), p. 56 et seq.

319. BVerfGE 22, 349 (362) and above note 55.

320. See above III. 2, (b).

321. BVerfGE 17, 148 (152 et seq.); 22, 163 (174 et seq.); 22, 349 (362).

322. BVerfGE 22, 349 (361); 28, 324 (361 et seq.); 31, 1 (7). See also sec. 31 BVerfGG and Jülicher, op. cit. (note 315), p. 16, who quite rightly points out, that this applies regardless of whether the statute is concerned with activities interfering with private rights or activities granting subsidies.

323. BVerfGE 15, 46 (76 et seq.); 31, 1 (8).

324. BVerfGE 6, 257 (266).

325. See BAG, MDR 1973, p. 167 et seq.; also II. 8. above.

326. For example BVerfGE 7, 198; 25, 256; 30, 173. See also VI. B. 1 (b) above and note 124.

327. See O. Bachof, 'Die verwaltungsgerichtliche Klage auf Vornahme einer Amtshandlung', 2nd Ed. 1968; and recently BVerwG DöV 1972, p. 857.

328. BGH NJW 1959, p. 1429; see also BVerwG DöV 1973, p. 317; G. Jänicke, 'Haftung des Staates für rechtswidriges Verhalten seiner Organe-Bundesrepublik Deutschland', in: 'Liability of the State for Illegal Conduct of its Organs'. Beiträge zum ausländischen öffentlichen Recht und Völkerrecht', Vol. 44 (ed. by H. Mosler), 1967, p. 69 (111 et seq.).

329. BGHZ 34, 99 (105) - very much disputed; see P. Dagtoglou, 'Kommentar zum Bonner GG', (Bonner Kommentar/Zweitbearbeitung 1970), Art. 34, p. 109 et seq.

330. BGHZ 6, 270 (280). For the relationship between Art. 14 (guarantee of property) and Art. 3 GG see also Ipsen, op. cit. (note 7), p. 130 et seq.

331. See Podlech, op. cit. (note 74), p. 144 et seq., and Forsthoff, op. cit. (nota 101), p. 301 et seq.

332. For example BGHZ 37, 44 (47). BVerfGE 21, 117 (131) left open this disputed question.

333. BGHZ 6, 270 (295): 'The indemnity to be paid where a person suffers expropriation is intended to ensure the observance of the equality principle'.

334. P. Dagtoglou, 'Ersatzpflicht des Staates bei legislativem Unrecht', 1963, p. 38 et seq.

335. Jänicke, op. cit. (note 328), p. 126, and on the other hand Dagtoglou, op. cit. (note 334), p. 58.

336. On this see BGHZ 32, 208 (211 et seq.).

337. The version of 1st September 1969 (BGBl. I, p. 1445).

338. This article has been finished in August 1973. Is was not possible to make reference to books, articles and judicial decisions, which were published later. The author, however, wants to draw the attention of the readers to the commentaries on Art. 3 GG by Günther Dürig, which have been published in Maunz-Dürig-Herzog, Grundgesetz, 4th Ed. 1974.

ABBREVIATIONS

AöR	Archiv des öffentlichen Rechts (Public Law Archives)
AP	Arbeitsrechtliche Praxis (Labour Law in Practice)
BAG	Bundesarbeitsgericht (Federal Labour Court)
BAGE	Entscheidungen des Bundesarbeitsgerichts (Decisions of the Federal Labour Court, official collection)
BayVerwBl.	Bayerische Verwaltungsblätter (Bavarian Administrative Journal)
BaWüVBl.	Baden-Württembergisches Verwaltungsblatt (Baden-Württemberg Administrative Journal)
BFH	Bundesfinanzhof (Federal Revenue Court)
BFHE	Entscheidungen des Bundesfinanzhofs (Decisions of the Federal Revenue Court, official collection)
BGB	Bürgerliches Gesetzbuch (Civil Code)
BGBl.	Bundesgesetzblatt (Federal Law Journal)
BGH	Bundesgerichtshof (Federal Supreme Court)
BGHZ	Entscheidungen des Bundesgerichtshofs (Decisions of the Federal Supreme Court, official collection)
BSGE	Entscheidungen des Bundessozialgerichts (Decisions of the Federal Social Insurance Court, official collection)
BVerfG	Bundesverfassungsgericht (Federal Constitutional Court)
BVerfGE	Entscheidungen des Bundesverfassungsgerichts (Decisions of the Federal Constitutional Court, official collection)
BVerfGG	Bundesverfassungsgerichtsgesetz (Act on the Federal Constitutional Court)
BVerwG	Bundesverwaltungsgericht (Federal Administrative Court)
BVerwGE	Entscheidungen des Bundesverwaltungsgerichts (Decisions of the Federal Administrative Court, official collection)

DöV	Die öffentliche Verwaltung (The Public Administration)
DVBl.	Deutsches Verwaltungsblatt (German Administrative Journal)
Gbl.	Gesetzblatt (Law Journal)
GG	Grundgesetz (The Basic Law)
JöR	Jahrbuch des öffentlichen Rechts der Gegenwart (Yearbook of Current Public Law)
JZ	Juristenzeitung (Lawyers Gazette)
KPD	Kommunistische Partei Deutschland (German Communist Party)
MDR	Monatschrift für Deutsches Recht (Monthly German Law Journal)
NF	Neue Folge (New Series)
NJW	Neue Juristische Wochenschrift (New Weekly Law Journal)
para.	paragraph
RGBl.	Reichsgesetzblatt (Imperial Law Journal)
RGZ	Entscheidungen des Reichsgerichts in Zivilsachen (Decisions of the Imperial Court in Civil Matters, official collection)
sec.	section
subs.	subsection
VG	Verwaltungsgericht (Administrative Court, first instance)
VGH	Verwaltungsgerichtshof (Administrative Court of Appeal)
VGHE	Entscheidungen des Bayerischen Verwaltungsgerichtshofs (Decisions of the Bavarian Administrative Court, official collection)
VOBl.	Verordnungblatt (Journal of Subordinate Legislation)
VVDStRL	Veröffentlichungen der Vereinigung Deutscher Staatsrechtslehrer (Publications of the Society of German Teachers of Public Law)
VwGO	Verwaltungsgerichtsordnung (Act on Administrative Courts)
ZaöRV	Zeitschrift für ausländisches öffentliches Recht und Völkerrecht (Foreign and International Public Law Review)

J. C. Venezia

The Protection of Equality in French Public Law*

* Translation by Miss C. Crisham, postgraduate student at the University of Exeter, England; revision by the editor

CONTENTS

I. *Introduction*

Equality is a principle in French law, whatever meaning one gives to the word 'principle' – whether one looks on equality as a primary notion or as a fundamental concept of our legal system.[1]

Proclaimed by the document which marks the beginning of the history of contemporary French public law, the Declaration of the Rights of Man and of the Citizen of 1789, the principle of equality permeates the whole of our political, administrative and civil institutions. But it was precisely the antiquity, relatively speaking, of the declaration of the principle which was to permit its contents to evolve, all the more easily because its very general character allowed its interpretation in many particular ways. Evolution is perhaps not the right word; it would be more exact to speak of a gradual building-up process. Indeed, if the structure of the French legal system is still characterised by a few areas of inequality, perhaps its most distinctive feature is the building up, one on top of another, of different 'layers' of conceptions that people have had of the meaning of equality. The most recent of these conceptions has not destroyed the oldest, which, on the contrary, will act as a support to it and will even sometimes make its influence equally well felt.

This means that any research undertaken with a view to studying in depth the significance of the principle of equality in French law, must take account of the different versions of this principle which have been considered valid at different times. Nor should it lose sight of the fact that it is sometimes very difficult to distinguish equality from other principles which seem to share a similar origin, such as the principle of neutrality, or that of impartiality.

The equality proclaimed by the authors of the Declaration of Rights is, initially, a legal equality; article 1 says: 'Men are born and remain free and equal *in law*'. This is concerned with a concept of equality which will be dealt with later, namely, the concept of equality embodied in the law itself. Let us take this to mean that the legislator has fully discharged his duty once the law is the same for everyone. These are in fact the very words of the Declaration of Rights: 'The law . . . must be the same for everyone, whether it is extending protection, or dealing out punishment' (article 6). This notion of equality in the law is only the outcome of its necessarily abstract nature. One is tempted here to quote J. J. Rousseau when he writes: 'When I say that the aim of the law is always a general one, I mean that it treats those subject to it as a single group, and people's actions in the abstract, never distinguishing an individual man or a particular action', if the author of the 'Social contract' did not go on to add: 'And so the law may very well decree that privileges shall exist, but it may not grant them to anyone'. More typical in representing the wish to only see in citizens that which is common to them all, and to abolish all individual distinctions, is the preamble to the Constitution of 3 September 1791, which is by its inspiration one of the most influential texts of French public law: 'There shall be no more nobility or peerage . . . There shall be no more sale or inheritance of public office. There shall be no more privilege for any section of the nation, nor for any individual, nor shall any exception be made to the law generally applicable to all Frenchmen'. This is to say that equality, as it was considered at the outset, is an equality of opportunity and of rights, guaranteed to individuals who are subject to a generally applicable law.

It was exactly this conception of a generally applicable law which was to be tampered with, and this happened in two different ways which are not always clearly distinguished.

The idea of a common law applicable to all individuals as though they were as easily interchangeable as pieces on a draught-board, was not left untouched for long. To take only one example, the promulgation of a commercial code in 1807 surely effected a discrimination between those persons subject to it and those falling within the jurisdiction of the ordinary civil law, a discrimination based on the failure of the traditional civil law, and especially the law of obligations, to adapt itself to the needs of commerce. This first impairment of the principle of equality would not call for special mention, were it not for the fact that it inspires a reflection regarding the very idea of equality, and in particular its relationship with the closely aligned notion of identity (i.e. absolute sameness).

From this point of view, it would seem that one does not have the right to talk of a breakdown of the principle of equality once different rules are laid down for a distinct category of legal subjects. Discriminations in the legal order will only threaten the principle of equality to the extent that they take the form of the grant to one category of privileges, the benefit of which will be refused to other categories, or, on the other hand, where there exists, to the detriment of one category of persons, an obligation which is not imposed on other categories. But one can very well imagine differentiations in a legal system which would be perfectly neutral from a point of view of equality, because they would not involve, in their overall effect, either advantages or disadvantages; for example, the special status of the law regarding employment in public office, as opposed to the general law of employment. Some of the special features of the law of public employment will favour the employer, as, for example, those which aim at ensuring the continuity of public service; others, on the other hand, will benefit the public employees in giving them guarantees of security in the pursuit of their careers. But, generally speaking, the special status of those in public employment does not amount to either special privileges or special obligations for the administration or of its agents.[2] This amounts to saying that one must be careful not to jump to the conclusion that the appearance of professional laws, including, according to the profession, distinct rules and obligations, constitutes in itself a threat to equality.

However, the idea of equality of opportunity and of rights was to be altered in a much more far-reaching fashion. It was realised that to treat dissimilar situations in the same way only amounted to respecting the outward form of equality. And so, taking up the search for genuine equality, the legislator attempted to re-establish the balance between various interests, by discriminating in the application of the rules according to the situations it was necessary to deal with, thus creating distinctions which made for as many obligations or privileges. All the efforts of tax law are directed in this way towards the search for equality in the sacrifices imposed on the taxpayers.

No doubt the wish to protect the poor against the rich, the weak against the strong, will take the form of interventions by the law which can be considered as amounting as much to restrictions on liberty as threats to equality. In the same way, no doubt, the differentiation of rules may result as much from the wish to direct the economy as from the desire to bring out social justice. But, whatever it may imply, the idea to keep in mind is that of a transition from equality in the law to that of equality *before* the law, an idea of equality which adapts itself to the existence of special systems of rules, and which requires simply that the same treatment should be reserved to persons in the same situation.

In spite of this development, the idea of equality in the law continues to play an important role in French law. Its field of operation covers all the legal disciplines, and one could say of it as Dean Savatier has said of another concept: 'Like a fiery diagonal it cuts across the whole of the law, while not allowing it to be divided'.[3] Thus the civil law, if one excludes the inequalities based on natural and unchangeable features such as age or mental condition, has set itself to progressively eliminate the inequalities left standing by the French Revolution. With regard, for example, to the legal status of married women, this progress is illustrated by the law of 18 February 1938 abolishing the legal incapacity of the married woman and the marital supremacy of the husband, but conferring at the same time, in principle, on the husband the status and function of head of the family, and the law of 22 September 1942, which brings to bear on the internal functioning of the different matrimonial regimes, the extension of the role of the woman already brought about by custom and practice. One should also consider the reform of these same matrimonial regimes effected by the law of 13 July 1965, which was entirely inspired by a demand for equality of treatment. There is also the law of 4 June 1970 on parental authority, which officially establishes the equal responsibility of husband and wife with regard to the care and education of the children. Finally, one should look at the law of 9 January 1973 on nationality which establishes the equal status of man and woman as regards the acquisition and transmission of nationality; and the law of 22 December 1972 on equal pay for men and women. With regard to illegitimate children, the law of 3 January 1972 also places beyond dispute the principle of equality between legitimate and illegitimate children, and it draws the consequences of this equalization with respect both to the personal relationship of the child with his parents, and to his rights of succession.

The development of constitutional law has been distinguished, in the same way as the civil law, by the progressive elimination of inequalities still subsisting in the nineteenth century and at the beginning of the twentieth century. It was in the name of equality that universal manhood suffrage was established in 1848, and that the right to vote was extended to women in 1944. It is the principle of equality which, at different periods in the constitutional history of France, influenced the institution of a single parliamentary chamber, or at least the institution of two chambers of unequal standing. Finally, it is this principle which explains the failure of proposals aimed at instituting a 'family vote' in France.

But the principle of equality has perhaps been affirmed in the most distinctive fashion in the field of administrative law which, taking into account the development of state intervention in the economic sector, is sometimes difficult to distinguish from commercial law. This special position of administrative law is perhaps due to the fact that, while it has been possible to establish equality in civil matters at an early stage, the application of equality in administrative law, involved as it is in the balance of competing interests, may be thwarted by the operation of other factors. In that case the administration is not in the position of an impartial arbiter; rather, it is very much involved in the matter, while its role should be to reconcile the respect for equality between subjects with the requirements of the general interest and the necessities of the public service. In this situation it is obvious that in administrative law, more than in any other field of law, the principle of equality has been, and remains, a creation in continual course of development. It has only been asserted gradually, and this has sometimes been all the more difficult because the privileges of the administration – which maintains relations of inequality with its subjects, even while equality is the ruling principle among them – have risked holding up its development.

The affirmation of the principle is therefore all the more striking in the instances when it is made. This turns particularly out to be the case when the French administrative courts – and especially the *Conseil d'Etat* as supreme administrative court – confirm the application of the principle in the absence of any applicable legislative provision. But the courts have often been forestalled in their task by the legislator. This happened, for example, with the equal eligibility of everyone for employment in the public service. The principle was explicitly laid down in article 6 of the Declaration of Rights, which makes it a direct consequence of equality before the law; it formed the inspiration for the basic rules on recruitment into public employment, and in particular for the general adoption of the procedure of public entrance examinations by article 29 of the statute of 19 October 1946, the general statute of public servants, corroborated on this point by the rules at present in force.[4] The principle is also at the root of many other provisions of the statute (assessment, promotion etc.).

In the same way, the principle of equality of treatment with regard to public burdens (*égalité devant les charges publiques*) which also inspired the traditional rules on expropriation or requisition of property, has prompted the legislator to make provision for the reparation of all kinds of war damage. The fiscal law takes its inspiration entirely from the principle of equality in the payment of taxes, with, needless to say, endless problems posed for the legislator in the practical application of this principle. It is, once again, the same principle which is the basis of our legislation regarding recruitment to the armed forces.

It would, however, be a mistake to believe that the principle of equality only appears in that part of administrative law regulating relations between the administration and its subjects. It has also been the inspiration of many practices in administative law of a constitutional kind. To cite only one example, the uniform character of the organisation of our local communities – departments and communes – surely gives an illustration of the principle of equality transposed from the individual to the organisational level; and can the failure of attempts to differentiate the organisation of local administration be explained otherwise than by a profound attachment to this very principle?

Even if there are many texts which have strongly asserted the principle of equality in the field of administrative law, the role of the administrative judge remains nonetheless an essential one. It is his role, in the first place, when confronted with a rule formulated by the legislature, or by the executive in the exercise of its rule-giving power, to ensure its application in an egalitarian fashion. The administration may not make distinctions where the rule does not do so. Its decisions in individual cases, its behaviour towards those subject to it, may not go against the general nature of the solutions established in the texts. Looked at in this way, equality before the law, and subordination of a particular decision to a general rule, amount to the same thing.[5]

But with regard to rules formulated by administrative authorities, the role of the judge goes far beyond this. He does not limit himself to verifying whether the particular decision taken in respect of an individual subject is in conformity with the general rule. He also ensures that the rule itself, when stated by an administrative authority, is in conformity with the principle of equality; he takes care that it does not introduce unlawful distinctions between subjects, even in those areas which the legislator would not have chosen to submit to the control of the principle of equality – principle which the judge considers as a general principle of French law, applicable even in the absence of any legislative provision to that effect. It may even be the case that no legislative rule intervenes between a principle of which the judge intends to ensure the respect, and the administrative action, for example an individual decision. In this case, it will no longer be a question of ensuring observation of equality in front of the rule laid down by the legislature, or by the executive in the exercise of its rule-giving power; nor will it be a question of declaring whether or not the administrative authority was acting lawfully in making distinctions in the application of the rule. The judge will simply have to decide whether, in the absence of any rule laid down by the legislature or the administration, the latter may lawfully refuse to one man what it grants to another. Even if the situation of fact posed in this problem is easy to grasp, the problem itself is nonetheless, as will be seen, quite difficult to resolve.

In whatever terms the problem of equality is posed, one concludes in advance that it is the conception which the judge makes of the meaning and extent of the principle which will be central to the debate (III). I shall precede that study by an examination of the field of application of the principle (II). I shall follow on from that with a reflection on the legal channels open to the subject to obtain the respect of the principle (IV).

II. *The Field of Application of the Principle of Equality*

The delimitation of the scope of the principle of equality raises three series of problems.

First of all, there have been numerous applications of the principle; it underlies so many jurisprudential constructions that it is often applied without any express reference being made to it. This was the case, for example, when an administrative court annulled for misuse of power (*détournement de pouvoir*) a decision which clearly amounted to a violation of the principle of equality.[6]

Secondly, it is often difficult to distinguish the principle of equality from other principles or rules: from the principle of trade union freedom, for instance. When the *Conseil d'Etat* annulled a decision reserving the exclusive right to engage workers on the workyards of the 1937 Exhibition to a particular trade union, on the ground that the decision misinterpreted the principle of trade union freedom, it was clearly also penalizing a breach of the principle of equality.[7] When, in the *Barel* decision, the *Conseil d'Etat* stated that it was not possible, 'without disregarding the principle of the equal access of all Frenchmen to public offices and employment, to turn down a candidate on the grounds exclusively of his political opinions', it penalized also an infringement of the freedom of opinion.[8] Similarly, when the same court struck down as illegal an increase in electricity charges which was applied in a uniform way to all supplies of electricity consumed as from a certain date, but which would, because the meter readings were spread over a period of time, lead to a situation in which certain consumers of supplies consumed prior to its entry into force would have to pay for these supplies at the new rate, it penalized at the same time a breach of the principle of equality and an infringement of the principle of non-retroactivity.[9]

If, finally, we add that the forms which the principle of equality can take are so varied that they often overlap one on another, one will realize how arbitrary is an attempt to determine the field of application of the principle of equality and to classify the different manifestations of it.

One can, however, attempt to arrange these manifestations by distinguishing equality before statutes and regulations, equality before the public service and equality of treatment before public burdens, which implies equality with regard to the share of public expenditure which citizens are called upon to bear.

A. Equality before Statutes and Regulations

The principle of equality before statutes and regulations was, apparently, of all the general principles of law, one of the first to be expressly affirmed by the case-law of the *Conseil d'Etat*.[10] By virtue of this principle, citizens finding themselves in the same situation with regard to laws of general application, must receive identical treatment from the administration. The operation of this principle rules out the institution of favourable treatment for the benefit of certain individuals resulting either from tacit permission on the part of the agents of the administration,[11] or from an individual decision which deviates from the general rule.[12] In this context the principle of equality before the law operates in conjunction with the rule of *'tu patere legem quem fecisti'*, according to which an administrative authority is bound by its own regulations, and with the principle of subordination of individual decisions to general rules.

The principle of the equality of citizens before statutes and regulations also forbids any arbitrary discrimination between individuals or categories of individuals in the application of a general rule. Thus, a government decree relating to studies at the Faculty of Medicine in Paris which created a discrimination of a geographical nature harmful to the interests of students registered at that Faculty, failed to take proper account of the principle of equality which ought to govern the treatment of all candidates for a university degree.[13]

The possibility for the administration to create discriminations will arise either in the case where no legislative text has expressly affirmed the principle of equality, or where the principle has been affirmed by a legislative or constitutional text, but in such vague terms that the administration in applying it will apparently dispose of a discretionary power. Such is the case with regard to the principle of equal elegibility for public employment which, as article 6 of the Declaration of 1789 bears out, appears to be a corollary of the principle of equality before statutes and regulations: 'All citizens, being equal in the eyes of the law, are also eligible on an equal basis to all honours, positions and offices without any distinction between them other than their own virtues and talents'. That principle of equal admissibility has made it possible for the administrative courts to penalize discrimination which amounted also to infringements of the liberty of conscience;[14] but the most striking illustration of the operation of the principle can be seen in the case-law relating to the admission of women to public employment.

This subject offers a good example of case-law and statute-law working together to achieve their end: from the decision in the case of *Demoiselle Bobard* in 1936, in which the *Conseil d'Etat* held that as regards the admissibility of women capacity, rather than incapacity, is the rule; through the decision in the case of the *Syndicat national autonome du cadre d'administration générale des colonies* of 1956, in which, re-inforcing its earlier case-law, the *Conseil d'Etat* held that the government may not make any exception from the principle of equality of the sexes but in cases where the nature of the job or the conditions of employment require it, and then only under the control of the courts; and through the provisions of the preamble to the Constitution of 1946 to the Statute of Public Employment.[15]

B. Equality before the Public Service

In the same way it could be said of the principle of equality before the public service that it appears in many respects like an extension of equality before the law, the law in question being that which governs the public service. This principle has been the object of an evolution in case-law which has developed in two directions. On the one hand, the courts have given a general bearing to rules laid down in texts on certain individual public services. On the other hand, the courts have progressively extended the field of application of the principle, so that, where it originally covered the users of the service, it has since been applied to the employees of the service, with the result that the principle of equality in the functioning of the service has replaced the original rule of equality as between the users of the service.

In its decision in the case of the *Chambre syndicale des propriétaires marseillais* of 1928, the *Conseil d'Etat* stated that in the absence of any organic legislation applicable to the public service in question, that is to say, in the absence of one of those fragmentary dispositions which oblige the services they govern to assure equal treatment to all their users, the principle of equality as between the users constitutes one of the conditions for the legality of the statute of the public service.[16] The court went a step further in its decision in the *Veyre* case of 1936, where it stated that even in the case of those public services governed by organic legislation, the rule of equality of treatment prevails even outside the cases expressly provided for in the texts.[17]

At the end of this first evolution in case-law, the administrative courts thus consider the principle of equality as between users an imperative rule of law, of very general application, to which no exception may be made other than by express legislative provision.

Extended in this way, the principle will be applicable as much to administrative services as to those of an industrial or commercial nature. It will govern at one and the same time both the charges and the benefits of the service; consequently, the administration is not allowed to lessen the obligation of one particular citizen to contribute to these expenses, unless some element in the situation of the citizen thus favoured can justify this measure; but by the same token, the principle ensures an equal status as users to all those who fulfil the conditions laid down in the texts for the admission to the benefits of the service. It was natural that, already widened in this way, the principle of equality before the public service should still be enlarged to cover the employees of the service. This extension was realized by the decision *Société des Concerts du Conservatoire* of 1951, in which the *Conseil d'Etat* alludes to 'the equality which governs the functioning of the public service'[18] – a formula which enabled it to further extend the application of the principle in the case of the *Chambre syndicale des médecins de la Seine* where it invoked 'the equality of citizens before the public administration'.[19]

To the principle of equality in the functioning of the public service can be connected the equality which governs the use of public property by members of the public. All citizens have equal access to those areas of public property assigned to the general use. Numerous decisions confirm that every member of the public has the right to use the areas of public property as long as the use conforms to the purpose of the assignment and does not exclude the rights of others. Passage along a street and access to a public monument must be open to all members of the public equally.[20]

The principle of equality does not only apply to the use of public property, but also to the duties which may accompany it. Thus, as far as enjoyment of public property is concerned which by its nature precludes enjoyment by others (such as parking), it may be subject to a tax, but this tax should be identical for all enjoyments of the same kind. As far back as 1928 the *Conseil d'Etat* in the *Laurens* case established that a parking charge, if it is to be lawful, 'must cover all activities of the same nature indiscriminately'; the municipal council could not 'without infringing the statute of 5 April 1884, submit only a certain category of vehicles to a parking charge and thus create inequalities of treatment for enjoyments of the same kind'.

With the application of the principle of equality as to the charges which may accompany enjoyment of public property, we come already to the third main manifestation of the equality principle, namely, equality of treatment with regard to public burdens.

C. Equality of Treatment before Public Burdens

Although the principle of equality of treatment with regard to public burdens originates from article 13 of the Declaration of 1789 which provides that 'for the maintenance of a police force and for the expenses of administration a common contribution is essential: it should be divided on an equal basis among all citizens according to their means', it appears to have been affirmed by the courts only late in time. It was not, in fact, until 1944 that an administrative court explicitly stated in the decision *Sieur Fays* that 'the principle of equality with respect to public burdens does not rule out the creation of special duties on particular categories of activities or occupations'.[21] It is, however, permissible to suppose that the administrative courts had applied the principle before, but that they employed different terms to express it: 'the principle of fiscal equality'; 'the principle of equality before the burdens of a public service'; 'the principle of equality before taxation'.[22]

The expression 'public burdens' is, in fact, very wide, and includes not only taxes as such but also the whole body of obligations to which individuals may be subjected in the public interest. In the opinion of part of the authors, which is indeed supported by many court decisions, even damage caused by public authorities would amount to a 'burden' occasioned in the general interest. The effect of this view would be to imply the entire law of liability of the administration in the principle of equality with respect to public burdens; according to this view, the reparation of damage would amount to nothing more than the restoration of the victim to the situation of equality which he enjoyed before the special obligation was imposed on him as a result of the fault of the administration, or of the risk to which it had exposed him. Without going so far as to give quite such a wide field of application to the principle of equality with respect to public burdens, one has to admit that in litigation involving liability of the administration a number of situations may arise where a lawful decision of the administration, which therefore cannot be attacked as faulty, may be held to engage liability of the administration when it has caused special or unusual damage; the responsibility of the administration in such cases can only be based on the principle of equality in front of public burdens. Examples of such instances are: the refusal to carry out a judicial sentence;[23] pressure exercised on a corporation by the State in order to persuade it to transfer its business to a workers' cooperative.[24] But the principle of equality has not only been established in the area of administrative liability: where requisition of property is concerned, the administrative courts ensure that sacrifices demanded of one category of citizens do not create unfair distinctions.[25]

Although it is simply an implementation of the principle of equality with regard to public burdens, the principle of equality before taxation deserves separate consideration because of its wide field of application. When called upon to settle individual issues concerning the application of fiscal law, the administrative courts will strike down those decisions which permit facilities to one taxpayer which they refuse to others, outside the cases provided for in the legislative texts. They will annul exemption from payment of a tax that is accorded to a third party, if the exemption is systematically applied and has a general character.[26] Similarly, the courts would consider that for the administration to refrain from applying a statute or regulation in force to individual citizens would amount to a fault engaging its liability.[27]

The judge's task is more difficult when he has to decide on the legality of fiscal rules devised not by the legislator but by an authority dependent on the executive. However, the decisions of the courts have always severely penalized inequalities and unjustifiable discriminations both with regard to the calculation of dues for services rendered and to the charges made for public services. Of course, the requirements of the principle are not absolute, and case-law has allowed the existence of discriminations which are justified by differences in the situations of members of the public with regard to the public service in question,[28] or which are based on differences as to the cost or quality of the service rendered.[29] At all events, with the exception of such particular cases, the courts have very positively affirmed the obligatory character of the principle.[30]

This review of the field of application of the principle of equality leaves two questions unanswered. Firstly: is there no penumbra of doubt in the application of the principle? In other words, is the principle of equality really a principle of general application, or do there exist cases in which no recourse can be had to the rule of equality? Secondly: in cases where the administrative courts do rely on the principle of equality, how is this principle applied? Answering these questions implies enquiring into the meaning and significance of the equality principle.

III. *Meaning and Significance of the Equality Principle*

It would be a mistake to believe that equality, being a principle of general application, could govern the sum total of legal situations; neither should one think that the principle, when it can be effectively applied, is applied in a uniform manner. An overall examination of administrative case-law and of its development seems to show that it can be arranged in such a way as to cover two kinds of situation.

In certain cases, the principle of equality can be invoked, but in applying it the court is to take account of the wishes of the legislator, or of the authority issuing the regulation, by differentiating the application of the rule in accordance with the situations which it is intended to govern; this necessity ultimately conduces the courts to define the notion of 'justifiable privilege'. In other cases, however, it seems that recourse to equality by applicants can find no outlet at the level of litigation; this is so because they come up against the existence of an administrative prerogative. Just as in the first series of cases the courts are forced to limit themselves to contesting unjustifiable discriminations, so in this second series they can do no more than ensure that the prerogative of the administration is not exercised in an arbitrary fashion.

This process of transition from equality to privilege, and then from privilege to prerogative, has taken place mainly in the area of litigation on economic problems, but it also occurred in the context of general administrative proceedings. Accordingly, we shall trace the development of this two-fold process within these two areas.

A. From Equality to Privilege

Two preliminary remarks ought to be made with respect to the protection of the equality principle by the courts.

In the first place, if the principle is to be effectively invoked, the inequality complained of by the applicants must derive from the provisions of the disputed administrative decision themselves, and not from circumstances outside the activity of the administration. Thus, breaches of equality between citizens are lawful if they are the necessary consequence of a legislative provision. It is important to notice, however, that the *Conseil d'Etat* strictly interprets legislation which provides for such infringements (except where they are effected in pursuance of an economic interest) – as it showed in the *Darmon* case of 1944 relating to racist legislation enacted during the German occupation.[31]

Secondly, the administrative courts penalize inequality in law, not that which exists in fact. Forbidden inequality is that inequality which is embodied in a rule issued by an administrative authority, or in its behaviour; it is not the inequality which results from the application of the same rule to different situations of fact. The *Conseil d'Etat* established this very clearly in a decision of 1950, *Société des Ciments français*;[32] it held that, in fixing a single price for the same product, without taking into account the different working conditions of the manufacturers, the administration did not infringe the principle of equality of treatment which it ought to observe towards all producers of the same category.

But, it may be argued, if in applying a general measure in the same way to everyone as the philosophy of 1789 requires, and in refusing to take account of the particular circumstances of those to whom it is addressed, the administration does not create inequality between business corporations because of their different working conditions, it should, surely, if it wishes to respect more than just the outward form of equality, discriminate in the application of the measure in accordance with the different situations which it is meant to govern. Following the legislator, the administration and the courts reached this conclusion; and so the transition was made from the principle that the law must be the same for everyone, to the rule that persons placed in the same situation should be submitted to the same body of rules.

To this first limitation of the principle of equality the courts were to add a second: that even if limited in this way to persons in identical situations, the principle of equality may be disregarded if the derogations from it are justified by considerations of general interest.

It is within these two limits that the principle of equality operates in general administrative litigation; the scope reserved for it is sometimes rather narrow (a). But its field of operation is particularly restricted where differentiation in the application of rules is pushed to extremes and the notion of the general interest is extended to excess, as is the case in litigation on economic problems (b).

a. In the opinion of the administrative courts, it is quite possible for the administrative authorities to institute different treatment for distinct categories of citizens or activities without infringing the principle of equality. The *Conseil d'Etat* frequently affirmed this: 'The principle of equality only applies as between citizens placed in an identical situation';[33] 'As a general rule, the administration is bound to accord equal treatment to persons engaged in the same activity, but it is nonetheless empowered to make distinctions when a particular situation justifies it'.[34]

In other words, the administration is perfectly entitled to take account of the different situations of fact in which citizens may find themselves; the principle of equality is duly respected if the same treatment is reserved for persons in situations which are comparable from a point of view of the public service or of the regulations in question. Thus a municipal council could lawfully decide not to prolong a water supply pipe to a hamlet far from the town, since the inhabitants of the hamlet were not in the same situation of fact as those of the town.[35] In the same way, the administration of Posts and Telephones could lawfully impose a higher subscription rate on telephone subscribers who refused to pay the annual charge for a telephone directory, and in doing so created a special demand on the equipment and functioning of the information service.[36] Again, an administrative court held that the price of medical analyses should not vary according to the rank of the laboratory managers, but that they may be different for doctors of medical biology and other doctors of medicine, since these categories of practitioners exercise their profession in different conditions.[37]

These cases establish beyond question that the rule of equality of treatment does not rule out the introduction of discriminations between categories of persons placed in different situations. However, this statement leaves unresolved the problem of how to recognise the existence of identical situations, and how to discover the limits beyond which they cease to exist. It would be pointless to pretend that the administrative judge, in the enquiry into levels of sameness and difference in which he must engage, is provided with a just and accurate instrument of measurement. But he is at least aided by a certain number of guidelines, which vary according to the kind of equality he is seeking to protect.

With regard to equality before statutes and regulations, the courts specify that it is 'with respect to the regulation of the market', or 'with regard to the provisions in question', that discriminatory treatment may be justified by a difference of situation.[38] With regard to the rule of equality before the public service, the assessment of different situations is made 'according to the public service concerned'; more specifically, case-law permits the existence of discriminations when these are justified by differences in the situation of citizens with respect to the public service in question, or when the discriminations are based on differences bearing on the cost or quality of the service rendered. Thus, the level of a charge imposed on an industrial corporation for a refining station depends on the volume of its consumption of water and the level of pollution of the water it carries off; consequently, it was held that a mayor had introduced an unjustifiable discrimination between the factories of the commune, when he operated a distinction based not on one or other of these considerations, but on the number of workers employed by the corporation.[39]

To this first limitation on the operation of the rule of equality in general administrative proceedings, which amounts to the possibility for the administration to differentiate in the application of a rule according to the situation, is to be added a second one, derived from the qualification brought about by the general interest.

The courts, even when most emphatically affirming the principle of equality, are careful to reserve the primacy of the general interest, which may authorise derogations from the principle. As soon as the discrimination operated by the administration is necessary for 'purposes of the general interest', 'the special requirements of the public service', or for 'a public interest', it is justified in the eyes of the administrative courts. In litigation concerning public employment, for example, the courts admit that civil servants in the same legal situation have the right to respect of the principle of equality of treatment, unless the interest of the service does, in exceptional cases, justify derogations from that principle.[40] It does not therefore appear possible to assert, as is sometimes done, that the *Conseil d'Etat* only examines whether discriminations are justified by the general interest, where inequalities created in the application of economic legislation and regulation are concerned. But it remains true that in the traditional areas of State intervention, it is exceptional for infringements of the principle of equality to be justified, not by differences of situation, but by considerations of general interest. Thus, in a decision of 1972, *Dame le Marre*, the *Conseil d'Etat* considered that the equality of treatment to which employees of a same group of personnel are entitled, prevents the creation of discriminatory rules disadvantageous to some of them, at least where 'exceptional circumstances' did not justify these rules in the interest of the service.[41]

In general terms, it could be said that in the traditional areas of State intervention the administrative courts show great severity where the principle of equality is concerned, with the exception only of the compromises mentioned.

Two indications only of this severity need be mentioned.[42] Firstly, the precision of judicial control where the principle of equality is enshrined by a statute or legislative text. With regard, for example, to equal eligibility of both sexes, without discrimination, to public employment, derogations from the principle in specified areas of employment are not possible, unless the nature of the employment makes the presence of women, or possibly men, really incompatible with the public interest. No margin of appreciation, no discretionary power whatsoever, is left to the administration. Secondly, the principle of equality is applied by the courts even when there is no express provision to that effect. The administrative courts have, on number of occasions, annulled administrative decisions which infringed the principle, basing their judgments on constitutional principles, on the principles of declarations of rights, or on general principles of law, even though they were not required to do so by any legislative text, and even where the decisions in question were taken by the administration by virtue of its autonomous power to issue regulations.

b. On the other hand, however, the administrative courts show constraint, even embarrassment, when called upon to apply the principle of equality in the area of economic interventionism by the State. This state of affairs is essentially due to the fact that in economic matters a multiplication of categories has occurred, as well as a further development of the reservation derived from the general interest. The excessive differentiation which takes place in the application of rules in economic matters can be explained by reference to the aims pursued by the State and by the subject matter of the intervention; it is, in any case, made possible by the extent of the powers conferred on the administration.

The law concerning State interventions is, by its nature, the law of inequality, of discrimination and preferential treatment, since the very object of interventionism is to favour certain persons or activities at the expense of an infringement of equality. As the intervention of the State in the economy is considered indispensable in order to ensure a balance between competing interests and to establish an equality of fact, differentiation between categories becomes the avenue that rule makers necessarily must choose. Moreover, economic interventionism has a subject matter which is bound to be based on a series of discriminations; as Mr. Rivero writes: 'The participation of individuals in economic affairs is entirely based on contract, that is to say, on the voluntary and independent agreement of two persons to regulate, as they see fit, the relationship which they create between them. The contract is, in essence, discriminatory; it grants to one person what it refuses to another. This scheme of things does not change when the public authorities begin to take part in it'.[43]

Finally, differentiation in the application of a rule, or the taking into consideration of particular circumstances, can also be explained by the extent of the powers accorded to the administration in economic affairs. In the area, for example, of legislation concerning prices, laws of 1945 give the administration extraordinarily wide powers, so that simple ministerial decisions can decree the 'freezing' of all prices at a given point in time, and can also authorize exceptions for one category or another of products.

This being so, the importance of the powers of the administration permit a wide view of the differences of situation concerned, and discrimination can easily be created. The administrative courts have recognised this: 'Even while it is admitted that these provisions have infringed the principle of equality of treatment between the persons concerned, their aim is to ensure the regular functioning of measures accessory to the legislation on prices, and they are therefore justified in law'.[44] The multiplication of categories confronts the administrative courts with a difficult problem, which is to decide which discriminations are lawful, and which are not, or to decide which infringements of equality are endurable in law, and which are less so. Consideration of this problem led the court in one case to decide that it is lawful to set special rules for the vendors of a particular agricultural product, but not to make further distinctions within this group between the producers and the wholesalers of the product. As it has been put: 'It is difficult to tell at what point in this process a further differentiation of the categories to which the rule applies will amount to an infringement of equality'.[45]

This is not to say that the courts refuse to annul decisions creating discriminations which the powers of the administration are insufficient to authorize, even on a very wide interpretation. These powers meet with a first limitation in cases where an administrative measure clearly goes beyond the field of application of the legislation on which it is based; for even where the administration is given the widest of powers, its decision must still correspond to the actual object of the legislation granting it the powers. Thus, in case of a scheme for adjustment of prices to a common level by means of equalisation levies, it was held that the scheme may impose unequal levies on those concerned, but that it may not be applied to an enterprise 'which, having ceased production, no longer puts on the market the products whose prices are the object of the equalisation scheme'.[46] Moreover, even if the administration disposes of very wide powers, it cannot 'derogate by individual measures from general rules which have been previously established';[47] nor may it create a discrimination to take account of an individual situation which has nothing exceptional other than the fact of its being the only one of its kind, rather than its having a specific character with respect to the obligations in question.[48]

The arbitrary treatment which may thus result from the possibility for the administration to differentiate in the application of a rule, without the courts disposing of a criterion to enable them to establish its lawfulness with certainty, is aggravated by the development in economic matters of the reservation derived from the general interest. In a number of cases the *Conseil d'Etat* admitted that measures taken for the regulation of the economy may lawfully create discriminations to the benefit or detriment of categories of enterprises, or even of certain enterprises singled out individually, where these discriminations were required for the general interest,[49] or where they were based on considerations 'of general order' or 'of general interest', which 'it was the function of the administration to take into account for the purpose of the application of legislation'.[50]

In the same way as the multiplication of categories, the development of the reservation of the general interest in economic affairs poses difficult problems for the courts. In the first place, it is hard for them to verify the connection between the discrimination adopted by the administration and the general interest. As was said, in a note to one case: 'In order to establish that the general interest does not benefit from such inequalities, it would be necessary to engage in appreciations of the situation which would never produce results conclusive enough to justify limiting the government's freedom of action. Thus, it is the uncertainty as to the effects of any economic policy which makes it impossible for the courts as well as for the legislature to place definite limits on the government's freedom of action'.[51] Secondly, since the different kinds of economic activity are closely connected with one another, the courts do not distinguish in this area, as they do in others, between the different aspects of the general interest. Lastly, in economic matters the courts do not examine the merits of the alleged grounds of the general interest, so that the administration disposes of a discretionary power of appreciation. Even so much so, that the administrative courts seem to admit that the actions of the administration benefit in a fashion from a presumption of conformity with the general interest.[52] Thus, although an applicant must always prove a charge of abuse of power, whatever the subject-matter of the case, in economic matters this requirement is apparently strengthened: 'The plaintiff company has not established that the measure was aimed not at developing the external trade of the colony, but exclusively at promoting certain privately-owned enterprises';[53] 'It has not been proved that this privilege was not justifiable in terms of considerations of the general interest'.[54]

In certain cases, however, the administrative courts consider that the administration is required, if not to show proof of the general interest, at least to explain that such grounds do exist: 'It was incumbent on the administration to state its considerations of general interest for the purposes of applying legislation in economic matters'.[55] The development of this line of authority is likely to continue, since the decision of the *Conseil d'Etat* in the case of the *Société Maison Genestal* in 1968, in which the court held that the administration, even if it cannot be formally required to give fully reasoned decisions, must at least make known to the judge in some detail the considerations of fact or law which led it to take the contested decision. It is also possible for the applicant to contest the presumption of compatibility with the general interest by producing proof of abuse of power by the administration, proof which may consist in the systematic nature of the discrimination.

Finally, it remains to be considered whether considerations of the general interest alone, without differences of situation, may justify infringements of the principle of equality. The question posed here is to decide whether the two conditions which may justify a breach of equality must operate cumulatively, or whether they may operate separately. This question is relevant to both general and economic litigation, but, in view of the importance of the reservation of general interest in economic matters, it is particularly incisive in this area. On a reading of certain conclusions of Government Commissioners,[56] it appears doubtful that these two conditions can operate otherwise than cumulatively: 'With the exception of imperative requirements of a technical order, we hardly consider it possible that the general interest could be invoked otherwise than to justify special treatment granted or refused to categories of citizens in different situations . . . The notion of the general interest does only come into play, in our view, to complete and define the obligation to extend identical treatment to persons in the same situations. It is with regard to the general interest that differences of situation in front of the public service must be appreciated, and it is the general interest which dictates the extent of the adjustments necessitated by these special situations'.[57]

In general terms, however, it appears that the general interest and the differences of situation operate as two alternative conditions; not that there is any contradiction whatsoever between the point of view which has just been stated, and the cases to which I am about to refer; but rather that that point of view is concerned with the application of the principle of equality before the public service, a principle which is particularly important in view of the fact that the rule of equality of access to the public service still remains one of the foundations of our administrative organisation. In other respects, however, the two conditions appear to operate in the alternative, but in slightly different ways.

In some decisions, no reference at all is made to the general interest. As soon as it was noted that differences of situation existed as between the citizens concerned, any indication as to the purpose of the administration seems to have been considered irrelevant. On the other hand, in other cases, the courts referred directly to the notion of the general interest, without having previously considered the differences of situation which might have justified a derogation from the principle of equality.[58] In a third series of decisions, the notion of the general interest intervened only in a subsidiary fashion: the differences of situation not apparently being of such a nature as to justify an infringement of the principle of equality, the court referred to the idea of the general interest.[59]

The differentiation in the application of a rule in response to the situations it is intended to govern, and the development of the reservation of the general interest, both factors being linked to the economic interventionism of the State, have posed difficult problems for the courts. But it could also be said that interventionism, which is what the cases we have considered were concerned with, had as its aim, at least in some of the cases, the restitution of a situation of equality which had broken down; and besides, that the means with which it accomplished this aim were of a legal character so that its implementation could be controlled by the courts, and was therefore, to a large extent, exempt from the mere discretion of the administration.

The discriminations operated by the administration in this area developed according to categories, so that, no matter how narrow the category to which the rule extended, it was at least possible for the courts to ensure that it was applied in an equal fashion to all those included in the category. However, it appears that things will be quite different with the appearance of a new form of interventionism, which is not restricted to establishing a transition from equality to 'justifiable privilege',[60] but which confronts the citizen with a prerogative of the administration of such a widely discretionary character as to result, in extreme cases, in depriving the principle of equality of all meaning.

B. From Privilege to Prerogative

A new kind of interventionism, connected with the planning and development of land, has come to graft itself onto the interventionism of the traditional type. It is no longer a question here of interventions by means of regulations, but rather of incentive measures which the administration may take on the basis of very wide discretionary powers, and which imply an appraisal of individual cases on their own merits, without reference to any general norm. Where the State's former interventions in the economy were made according to categories, the new discriminations are made case by case, and, in this new situation, with its new kind of interventionism, it may well be asked whether the principle of equality can still be effectively invoked, or even whether the principle can still be said to exist. 'The government', declared Mr. Combarnous in a contribution to the *'Journées Henri Capitant'* of 1961, 'often establishes special zones in France, called by different names according to the period they are established, and in which contractors enjoy special advantages, conversion zones, for example. It is difficult for me to predict what a court would reply, if, after the institution of one of these conversion zones on some rural or urban district, a neighbouring district were to come before it and say: We have fulfilled very similar conditions; there is unemployment in our area, too; we also have factories going out of business, and we don't see why we should not equally benefit from measures of this kind'.[61]

Here, too, the situation is not without precedents and equivalents in general administrative law.

a. It would be a mistake to believe that in general administrative law, the principle of equality is applied in an abstract or rigid manner. As far as public entrance examinations are concerned, for example, the principle can, to date at least, be reduced to the principle of equality of opportunity which must be ensured to all candidates, and to the principle of the impartiality of the selection boards, since the very nature of the selection procedure implies that only a certain proportion of the candidates will be proposed for nomination. The courts have also applied variegated solutions in cases involving the rule of the equality of members of the public with respect to the use of public property. It is clear that, where the property is used in accordance with its assignment to the public use, and not in an exclusive manner, the assignment creates a right in all members of the public to benefit equally from the use of the property. But as soon as the use, though not necessarily exclusive, begins to take on a somewhat abnormal character, the rule of the equality of users is already considerably diluted. For example: it was held that the abnormal use of the highway for trials of automobile chassis allows institution of a system of authorisations with a discriminatory character;[62] similarly, the abnormal use of the streets of a town by the public transport services was also held to permit submission of these services to a discriminatory system of authorisations.[63] Where exclusive use of public property is concerned, the fact that the use conforms to the purpose of the assignment of the property does not suffice to create a right to use it in this way. Once the use of property is exclusive, it cannot clearly, and as a matter of fact, remain open to everyone. The decision of the administration to grant a right of exclusive use of property, thus granting to one person what it refuses to another, cannot be made in an entirely discretionary manner; permission can only be refused on the grounds of the interests of the public service, of the public at large, or of public property; but the administration can still draw on such a wide category of reasons to support its decision, that the significance of the rule as to the equality of the users of public property may be reduced to virtually nothing. Finally, once there exist rights of use not in conformity with the assignment, other users can no longer assert a right to use the property for the purpose envisaged in the assignment, and in such a case the rule of the equality of users has no further importance whatever. Authorisations for use granted by the administration are acts of a purely discretionary character which do not create any rights to the benefit of other users.

Similar considerations to those relating to the nature of things in cases of public entrance examinations and of exclusive use of public property, and similar considerations to those relating to the discretionary power of the administration, in cases of public entrance competitions and of abnormal use of public property, crop up very frequently in the new law of economic interventionism.

b. The planning and the development of land imply choices between different possible courses of action, which are converted into as many discriminations. Whether it is a question of establishing a programme for public investment, of attracting private investment towards priority sectors, or of granting loans, the administrative authorities are always required to consider each case separately, without reference to a general norm; more precisely – reference to some kind of norm will be made, but it will consist either in considerations of general interest, which it is difficult for the judge to evaluate, or in a document whose legal value is questionable, such as the plan itself, or in legislative provisions which leave a very wide discretion to the competent authorities. Besides, the nature of things sometimes prevents the principle of equality from being effectively invoked: for instance, while the administration may wish to favour all enterprises in a given sector, the insufficiency of budgetary resources, together with a wish to avoid useless dispersal of these resources, will make it necessary to favour only certain enterprises; and while it is understandable that rival enterprises would feel that there had been a breach of the principle of equality, it is difficult to see how they could frame their claim against the administration in administrative litigation.

In order to avoid the risk of arbitrary treatment to which citizens may be exposed, it has been suggested that, where incentive measures of a financial and fiscal kind are concerned, the authority in question should have the power to fix general criteria for the selection of those who are to benefit from the measures. If this possibility were admitted, it would give back some scope to the principle of equality in the area under discussion; but it would meet with two obstacles. The first one consists in the administration's obligation, established in case-law, not to take a decision, in areas where it disposes of a power of discretion, until after a special examination of the circumstances of each case, an obligation which does not permit it to fetter its appreciation in advance with general rules and norms. The second obstacle consists in the fact that case-law does not allow to Ministers other powers of regulation than with respect to the organisation of their own departments, and therefore forbids them to lay down rules of substance. The sheer impossibility for Ministers to define general criteria to govern the exercise of their regulatory power should have been clearly illustrated by a decision of 1969, *Distilleries Brabant et Compagnie*; in spite of the submissions of the Government Commissioner, who had tried to urge the court to give a slight bend to its case-law, the *Conseil d'Etat* annulled for mistake of law a decision to refuse an exoneration from taxes, taken on the basis of criteria laid down in a ministerial circular: 'The Minister could not derive, either from legislative or regulatory provisions . . . or from the power he possessed to ensure the functioning of the department placed under his authority, any competence to exclude from the benefit of the exoneration all the operations undertaken by enterprises situated in the Paris area'.[64] The following year, however, in its decision *Crédit Foncier*, the *Conseil d'Etat* was to adopt a more flexible approach in recognising the legality of an administrative decision taken with reference to a body of rules defining general trends of policy; the applicants in the case did not rely on any distinguishing feature of their situation with respect to the rules in question, or on any consideration of the general interest of such a kind as to justify an exception; nor did they submit that the rules in question disregarded the aims of the legislator.[65]

It is apparent that this line of thought, in a manner characteristic of the administrative courts, recognises that the authority in question has a certain power, matching its power to apply a rule, to make reservations as to the principle of equality, reservations which correspond to the limits which the courts traditionally assign to this principle where the laying down of administrative rules is concerned. In spite of these reservations and in spite of the fact that this area of case-law, if it can ensure that a citizen excluded from the benefit of an incentive measure will not obtain it, cannot guarantee that another citizen belonging to the class eligible to this benefit, will in fact have it, this development should nevertheless make it possible for the courts to assure the enforcement of the principle of equality in a more effective way.

IV. *The Sanctions of the Principle of Equality*

It appears necessary, as far as the sanctions of the principle are concerned, to distinguish whether the measures which infringe the principle of equality are lawful or not.

A. Unlawful Infringement of the Principle of Equality

Where the infringement of the principle consists in an administrative decision which is irregular, the court can annul the decision as being *ultra vires* (*excès de pouvoir*). It should simply be noted that, since the principle can be infringed either by a unilateral act or by a contract, third parties may contest the legality of unilateral acts which for this purpose can be detached from the formation and execution of an agreement that they consider discriminatory. With regard, still, to proceedings for contesting the legality of an administrative act, it should also be noted that the ordinary civil courts may also be required to enforce respect for the principle; exceptionally, they may even be led to decide on the legality of a measure which purports to contravene this principle.[66]

Not only can an administrative decision which infringes the principle of equality in an irregular fashion be annulled by the administrative courts, it can also entail liability of the administration. Since any illegal act may constitute a fault, an illegal contravention of the principle of equality may, should the occasion arise, amount to a fault. This coinciding of illegality with liability was clearly brought out in a decision of the *Conseil d'Etat* of 1951, *Société des Concerts du Conservatoire*: 'The administration disregarded the principle of equality, which governs the functioning of the public service . . . This fault engages liability of the State'.[67]

With this in mind, we can recall how, in proceedings to contest the legality of administrative acts, the courts allow reservations to be made to the applications of the principle of equality, whether they are based on the existence of special circumstances or on considerations of the public interest. It is obvious, therefore, that applicants are inclined, in cases where the court is likely to decide that the contested measure is not illegal, and thus does not constitute a fault, to argue their claim on the basis of liability without fault.

B. Lawful Infringements of the Principle of Equality

A characteristic illustration of this situation is offered by a decision of the *Conseil d'Etat* of 1960.[68] The plaintiff company, the *Société d'exploitation des chantiers d'Ajaccio*, manufactured industrial products on the basis of certain kinds of wood, which could be found in abundance in Corsica and which could be bought very cheaply there. When it found itself in a difficult situation because of the rise in price of these raw materials, it was forced to cease operations. In an action alleging liability of the State, the plaintiff company argued that the rise in price which had caused its loss had been induced by the attitude of the services of foreign trade which had, in a systematic and irregular fashion, granted export licences to Corsican wood traders, with the effect of making it more difficult for the company to obtain the raw materials it needed in Corsica, as the terms offered on the world market were much more advantageous to the Corsican exporters. On the question of illegality and of fault, the claim had little chance of success. The *Conseil d'Etat* had, in fact, to decide that, in granting individual licences to the Corsican wood producers, no matter how great the number of such licences, the administration had not committed any fault, since the applicable legislation (ordinance of 22 June 1944 and decree of 30 November 1946) had the very aim of authorising the central licensing service to make individual exceptions for the export of certain products. Moreover, in response to the company's argument that the administration could not, without exceeding the bounds of its competence, systematically grant individual exceptions to all producers in the department of Corsica, the *Conseil d'Etat* went on to add that the decisions of the administration were, in the circumstances of the case, justified according to the general interest. So, leaving the question of liability for fault, the company argued that the infringement of the principle of equality to its disadvantage, and particularly of the equality of citizens with regard to public burdens, gave it a right of indemnification, even in the absence of a fault committed by the administration.

Once it is admitted that the administration was able, without exceeding the terms of its competence, to grant individual export licences in such a way as to amount to the grant of a generalised exception, could not the plaintiff company validly argue that there had been a breach of the principle of the equality of citizens in front of public burdens, and so demand reparation from the administration for their loss on the basis of liability without fault? Case-law has, in fact, admitted that the administration may, without committing an illegal act, take measures which have the effect of infringing this principle.

The principle of reparation was first stated, with respect to damage resulting from a statute, in a decision of the *Conseil d'Etat* of 1938, *Société des produits laitiers La Fleurette*.[69] In later cases, the *Conseil d'Etat* extended the principle of reparation to damage resulting from a regulation or legally-made individual decision. Thus, in a decision of 1963, *Commune de Gavarnie*, concerning a municipal regulation which harmed the interests of a tradesman, the *Conseil d'Etat* considered that the fact that the mayor's decision was properly taken did not prevent the injured tradesman from obtaining an indemnity 'because of the special nature of the damage, and provided that it constitutes a burden of a kind which he is not normally required to bear'.[70]

The admission of liability without fault for measures of a general and impersonal nature, because of the inequalities they may induce, was bound to lead to the application of the same solution in the case of individual decisions. In these, just a single person, a single situation, is involved; the prejudice resulting from the harmful act can be clearly distinguished from that inflicted on other citizens. Thus, in a decision of 1947, *Société Boulenger*, concerning the pressure exercised by the government on a company to induce it to cede its business to a workers' cooperative, the *Conseil d'Etat* held that the State was liable, even though no fault of the administration was involved, on the grounds that the interventions of the government representatives, though made in the general interest, had caused the company to suffer a particular prejudice, which, on account of its gravity, could not be considered as the kind of loss which would normally accrue to it.[71]

A similar conclusion was reached in another case, where the administration had refused a company the authorisation to dismiss its workers in order to avoid a serious economic upheaval, even though in this case the administration acted in conformity with the powers which it derived from an ordinance of 28 May 1945.[72] Finally, in a decision of 1962, *Société Manufacture des Machines du Haut Rhin*, the *Conseil d'Etat* considered that the liability of the State could be engaged, even in the absence of fault, on the basis of the principle of the equality of citizens in front of public burdens, 'in the case where a measure, though lawfully made, has the effect of causing to a person, whether an individual or a collectivity, a special loss of particular gravity'.[73] Whatever the clarity of this motive, it would be pointless to deny that it is only in a restricted range of cases that the liability of the administration is engaged for a lawfully-taken decision infringing the principle of equality. Thus, in the case of the *Société d'exploitation des chantiers d'Ajaccio* discussed earlier on,[74] in order to grant an indemnity to the company on the basis of the line of authority begun in the decision *Société des produits laitiers La Fleurette,*[75] it would have been necessary for two conditions to be fulfilled: that the indemnity should answer to the implied will of the legislator, and that the loss suffered should be exceptional and exceed the burdens normally accruing in everyday life.

In economic questions, these requirements are only satisfied in rare cases. Where the State directs the economy, economic policy has as its effect and as its objective the creation of discriminations and distortions; in pursuing a policy for the planning and development of land, the public authorities are unavoidably required to favour the installation of industries in certain regions, or, on the contrary, to discourage certain enterprises by economic measures. In the same way, the regulation of prices by public authorities necessarily creates inequalities between enterprises, and in this area the courts have been forced to limit the possibilities of having recourse to liability without fault. Thus, in the case of the *Société des chantiers d'Ajaccio*, the *Conseil d'Etat* held that, in view of the purpose for which the legislation on external trade was made, decisions lawfully made in application of this legislation could not engage liability of the State.

These case-law solutions are inspired by the idea that private enterprises should not be able to rely on their own special situation in order to contest the application of measures justified by the general interest, by calling into question the liability of the State with respect to the prejudice these measures may cause them.

This review of the sanctions of the principle of equality should not be concluded without mention of the possibilities opened, or half-opened, by the decision of the *Conseil Constitutionnel* of 16 July 1971, concerning contraventions of the principle of equality not attributable to acts of the administration, but rather to the legislator.[76] In this decision, which concerned the liberty of association, the *Conseil Constitutionnel* for the first time critized certain dispositions adopted by Parliament for violation of 'fundamental principles recognized by the laws of the Republic, and solemnly reaffirmed by the Preamble to the Constitution'. This way, the constitutional judge[77] explicitly and definitively affirmed the constitutional importance of the Preamble, and thus of the principle of equality, which is enshrined in the Declaration of 1789 as well as in the Preamble to the Constitution of 1946, to both of which the present Preamble refers. It has thus been established that the respect for the principle of equality is incumbent also on the legislator. But from this point onwards, things are less certain, as we run again into the overriding difficulty in this subject: what kind of equality are we talking about? The legal equality proclaimed by the Declaration of 1789, or actual equality, that is equalisation of situations which requires differentiation in the application of a rule, and which appears to be called for by certain provisions in the Preamble of 1946? According to this last conception of equality, would it be possible to authorise the legislator to operate discriminations in fiscal affairs, so as to ensure equality in the sacrifices demanded of citizens? Discriminations, at least within certain limits. In an important decision the *Conseil Constitutionnel* declared the dispositions of article 62 of the Finance Act for 1974, tending to introduce discrimination between citizens concerning their possibilities to supply counter-arguments to a decision taken by the tax-office, repugnant to the Constitution. The court took into consideration that these dispositions would infringe upon the principle of equality before the law as it is to be found in the Declaration of 1789 and solemnly reaffirmed by the Preamble to the Constitution.[78] So, if this actual equality permits the legislator to discriminate, to a certain degree, in fiscal affairs, would it then be necessary, in the name of the first conception – i.e. legal equality – to consider as unconstitutional legislative provisions which authorise the administration to grant fiscal advantages, not with a view to creating greater social justice, but in the context of a policy for the planning and development of land? Even though their content is not easy to define in a precise manner, 'the fundamental principles recognised by the laws of the Republic' do, perhaps, constitute a rather reliable foundation for the control of constitutionality, whether it is a question of equality in civil matters, or of the principle of equal access to public employment.

Whatever the extent of the efforts made to date to reduce inequalities, and in spite of the reactions aroused by the breaches of the principle which necessarily accompany a policy of experimentation on the part of the administration, and of interpenetration of the public and the private sector, the movement in favour of equality remains fundamental in France at the present time, and there would be no end to summing up its manifestations.

It is in the name of equality that, in the political sphere, the lowering of the voting age is demanded, and a revision of the electoral boundaries; and, in the sphere of taxation, greater justice generally. It is the same principle which inspires, in the field of labour relations, attempts to give an effective application to the principle of equal pay for men and women, or to the principle of equal eligibility of both sexes for employment in either the public or private sector.

On a more far-reaching and profound level, is not the whole problem of equal opportunities in life still very much a live issue? And is it not from the principle of equality that the various challenges to authority, which we witness today, take their source, no matter what the context in which they arise?

Is equality, therefore, a continuous creation? Certainly, it is; but where it is a question of translating it into legal terms, prudence and reflection are essential. Man is so fashioned that he is aware of the inequalities of which he is the victim, without his always noticing the privileges which may benefit him. And it is difficult to call for the rectification of the one, without at the same time renouncing to the benefit of the other.

Looking at the question in a more general way, would not the systematic challenging of authority in all its forms, if not accompanied by a detailed definition of a new scheme of relations, risk leading to the situation which Tocqueville described when he wrote: 'A kind of equality can be instituted in the political sphere even though political freedom as such does not exist there at all. Every man is the equal of his fellow men, except for one man who is, without distinction, the master of all, and who also chooses his subordinates from among the whole of the population'.[79]

NOTES

1. Of all the literature devoted in France to the study of the principle of equality, the following are particularly worthy of attention: the report presented by Jean Rivero to the 'Journées Henri Capitant' of 1961 on *'Les notions d'égalité*

et de discrimination en droit public français' (in: *Travaux de l'Association Henri Capitant* vol. XIV, Paris, 1965, p. 343), and the thesis of Pierre Delvolve on *'Le principe d'égalité devant les charges publiques'* (Paris, 1969); also the development relating to this principle discussed in the thesis of Benoit Jeanneau, *'Les principes généraux de droit dans la jurisprudence administrative'* (Paris, 1954), works drawn on by the author of this article.

2. G. Dupuis, *'Les privilèges de d'Administration'*, thesis, Paris, 1962 (typewritten).

3. René Savatier, *'L'enseignement du droit économique dans les pays non socialistes'*, Il Diritto Dell' Economia, Anno XIII, 1967, no. 1, p. 4-5.

4. Decree (*ordonnance*) of 4 February 1959, Article 18.

5. Rivero, op. cit. at p. 353.

6. Conseil d'Etat 3 August 1927, *Stade Olympique Chabanais,* Recueil p. 917; also *Société l'Eveil de Contres,* 23 December 1932, Recueil p. 1129.

7. Conseil d'Etat 7 July 1939, *Union corporative des travailleurs français et autres,* Recueil p. 460.

8. Conseil d'Etat 28 May 1954, *Barel,* Recueil p. 308.

9. Conseil d'Etat 25 June 1948, *Société du journal 'l'Aurore',* Recueil p. 289.

10. Conseil d'Etat 9 May 1913, *Roubeau,* Recueil p. 521.

11. Conseil d'Etat 26 June 1931, *Chambre syndicale des propriétaires loueurs d'autocars, Sieurs Ascagne et autres,* Recueil p. 707.

12. Conseil d'Etat 17 December 1948, *Société Ungemach,* Recueil p. 476.

13. Conseil d'Etat 28 September 1962, *Jourde et Malleville,* Recueil p. 508.

14. Conseil d'Etat 25 July 1939, *Demoiselle Beis,* Recueil p. 524; 3 May 1950, *Demoiselle Jamet,* Recueil p. 247.

15. Conseil d'Etat 3 July 1936, *Demoiselle Bobard et autres,* Recueil p. 721; 6 January 1956, *Syndicat national autonome du cadre de l'administration générale des colonies,* Recueil p. 4.

16. Conseil d'Etat 10 February 1928, *Chambre syndicale des propriétaires marseillais,* Recueil p. 222.

17. Conseil d'Etat 1 July 1936, *Veyre,* Recueil p. 713.

18. Conseil d'Etat 9 March 1951, *Société des Concerts du conservatoire,* Recueil p. 151.

19. Conseil d'Etat 19 February 1960, *Chambre syndicale des médecins de la Seine,* Recueil p. 133.

20. Conseil d'Etat 25 February 1928, *Société l'Eveil de Contres,* Recueil p. 272; also *Carlier,* 18 November 1949, Recueil p. 490.

21. Conseil d'Etat 2 June 1944, *Sieur Fays,* Recueil p. 159.

22. Conseil d'Etat 5 May 1922, *Fontan,* Recueil p. 386; 10 February 1928, *Chambre syndicale des propriétaires marseillais,* Recueil p. 222; 23 November 1936, *Abdouloussen,* Recueil p. 1015.

23. Conseil d'Etat 30 November 1923, *Couiteas,* Recueil p. 789; 3 June 1938, *Société de Cartonnerie et d'Imprimerie St. Charles,* Recueil p. 521.

24. Conseil d'Etat 21 November 1947, *Société Boulenger,* Recueil p. 436.

25. Conseil d'Etat 10 February 1950, *Dame Sornin de Leysat,* Recueil p. 102.

26. Conseil d'Etat 24 March 1922, *Chambre syndicale des fabricants d'eau gazeuse,* Receil p. 256; 23 May 1930, *Société Métropole Voitures,* Recueil p. 548.

27. Conseil d'Etat 26 June 1931, *Chambre syndicale des propriétaires d'autocars,* Recueil p. 707; 6 July 1934, *Société Van Outryve,* Recueil p. 786; 21 June 1935, *Le Gallo,* Recueil p. 698; 24 July 1936, *Société générale de défense des grands vins de la Côte d'Or,* Recueil p. 861.

28. Conseil d'Etat 1 April 1938, *Société l'Alcool dénaturé de Coubert,* Recueil p. 337.

29. Conseil d'Etat 7 October 1959, *Sieur Jacquier et autres,* Recueil p. 492.

30. Conseil d'Etat 6 January 1967, *Ville d'Elbeuf,* Recueil p. 1.

31. Conseil d'Etat 21 January 1944, *Darmon et autres,* Recueil p. 22.

32. Conseil d'Etat 22 March 1950, *Société des Ciments français,* Recueil p. 175.

33. Conseil d'Etat 29 April 1966, *Société Affichage Giraudy,* Recueil p. 293.

34. Conseil d'Etat 13 July 1963, *Aureille,* Recueil p. 829.

35. Conseil d'Etat 30 May 1962, *Parmentier,* Recueil p. 868.

36. Conseil d'Etat 7 October 1959, *Jacquier et autres,* Recueil p. 492.

37. Conseil d'Etat 28 October 1960, *Syndicat national des biologistes français,* Recueil p. 572.

38. Conseil d'Etat 13 July 1963, *Société de décorticage SODEC,* Recueil p. 433; 15 July 1959, *Chambre syndicale des bureaux d'études techniques,* Recueil p. 469.

39. Conseil d'Etat 6 January 1967, *Ville d'Elbeuf,* Jurisclasseur Périodique 1967 II 15019, with conclusions of Galmot.

40. Conseil d'Etat 24 October 1951, *Fédération nationale des travailleurs des PTT,* Recueil p. 495; 13 May 1960, *Molina et Guidoux,* Recueil p. 324; 30 June 1961, *Fallourd,* Recueil p. 458.

41. Conseil d'Etat 16 June 1972, *Dame le Marre,* Actualité Juridique 1973, p. 94.

42. See also intervention Combarnous at the 'Journées Henri Capitant' of 1961, Travaux cited in note 1 *supra,* p. 424.

43. See Rivero, Travaux cited in note 1 *supra,* p. 353.

44. Conseil d'Etat 12 February 1960, *Société Industrielle et commerciale d'approvisionnement,* Actualité Juridique 1960, p. 77, with conclusions of Kahn.

45. So Rivero, Travaux cited in note 1 *supra,* p. 353.

46. Conseil d'Etat 12 November 1958, *Syndicat de la raffinerie de soufre française,* Actualité Juridique 1959 p. 14, with conclusions of Fournier.

47. *Société Ungemach,* see note 12 *supra.*

48. Conseil d'Etat 13 June 1947, *Compagnie navale des pétroles,* Recueil p. 255.

49. Conseil d'Etat 29 June 1951, *Syndicat de la raffinerie de soufre française,* Recueil p. 377; 9 July 1958, *Gisquet et autres,* Recueil p. 480.

50. Conseil d'Etat 8 October 1958, *Société GENPA,* Recueil p. 472; 6 March 1959, *Totaliment,* Recueil p. 158.

51. Paul Reuter, in a note following Conseil d'Etat 21 November 1953, Jurisclasseur Périodique 1953 II 7468.

52. See, on all these questions, Delvolve, thesis cited in note 1 *supra,* p. 217 *et seq.*

53. Conseil d'Etat 15 March 1946, *Compagnie d'exportation de Madagascar,* Recueil p. 81.

54. *Syndicat de la raffinerie de soufre française* 1951, cited in note 49 *supra.*
55. *Totaliment,* cited in note 50 *supra.*
56. Government Commissioners give, as independent advisers, their 'conclusions' before the *Conseil d'Etat* formulates its decision; examples in notes 39, 44 and 46 *supra,* and in note 57 *infra.*
57. Conclusions of Combarnous in the case Conseil d'Etat 24 april 1964, *Société anonyme de livraisons industrielles et commerciales,* Actualité Juridique 1964 p. 308.
58. Conseil d'Etat 10 January 1964, *Ministre de l'Agriculture* v. *Simmonnet,* Recueil p. 19.
59. *Compagnie navale des pétroles,* cited in note 48 *supra.*
60. Expression used by the Conseil d'Etat in the 1951 decision *Syndicat de la raffinerie de soufre française,* cited in note 49 *supra.*
61. Intervention Combarnous, cited in note 42 *supra.*
62. Conseil d'Etat 27 July 1928, *Société des Usines Renault,* Dalloz Périodique 1929 III p. 15.
63. Conseil d'Etat 29 January 1932, *Société des autobus antibois,* Sirey 1932 III p. 65. See also conclusions of Mosset in the case Conseil d'Etat 2 November 1956, *Sieur Biberon,* Recueil p. 403, from which this analysis is taken.
64. Conseil d'Etat 29 May 1969, *Distilleries Brabant et Compagnie*, Actualité Juridique 1969, p. 640.
65. Conseil d'Etat 11 December 1970, *Crédit Foncier,* Conclusions Questiaux de France, Actualité Juridique 1971, p. 227.
66. Cour de cassation, chambre criminelle, 25 October 1961, *Jacques,* Bulletin No. 420 p. 800 (relating to the creation on public highways of parking zones reserved to a privileged class of drivers).
67. Conseil d'Etat 9 March 1951, *Société des Concerts du Conservatoire,* Recueil p. 151.
68. Conseil d'Etat 16 November 1960, *Secrétaire d'Etat aux Affaires Economiques* v. *Société d'exploitation des chantiers d'Ajaccio,* Recueil p. 621.
69. Conseil d'Etat 14 January 1938, *Société anonyme des produits laitiers 'La Fleurette',* Recueil p. 25. See also 21 January 1944, *Caucheteux et Desmond,* Recueil p. 22; 1 December 1961, *Lacombe,* Recueil p. 674.
70. Conseil d'Etat 22 February 1963, *Commune de Gavarnie,* Recueil p. 113.
71. Conseil d'Etat 21 November 1947, *Société Boulenger,* Recueil p. 436.
72. Conseil d'Etat 28 October 1949, *Société des Ateliers du Cap Janet,* Recueil p. 450.
73. Conseil d'Etat 29 June 1962, *Société Manufacture des Machines du Haut-Rhin,* Recueil p. 432.
74. See note 68, *supra.*
75. See note 69, *supra.*
76. Text of the decision in La vie judiciaire, 19-25, July 1971. See also note by Rivero in Actualité Juridique 1971 p. 537, and the article by the same author *Les principes fondamentaux reconnus par les lois de la République: une nouvelle catégorie constitutionelle?* Dalloz 1974, 41st cahier, Chronique.
77. French constitutional law recognizes only judicial review, in a particular form, since 1958; see articles 61-62 of the 1958 Constitution.

78. On this point see: L. Philip, *La portée du contrôle exercé par le Conseil Constitutionnel* (on the decision of 27.12.1973), Revue du Droit Public, March/April 1974.

79. Alexis de Tocqueville, Democracy in America, part II chapter I.

6

Chr. Osakwe

Equal Protection under Soviet Constitutional System

CONTENTS

Introduction

Equal protection under law, respect for individual freedom, vigorous and non-discriminatory law enforcement are among the professed cornerstones of Soviet justice and socialist democracy. Speaking of the central position occupied by these three principles in contemporary Soviet law the 24th Congress of the Communist Party of the Soviet Union (CPSU) noted:

> 'During the period under review the Central Committee and the Soviet Government have continued taking steps to strengthen legality and law and order,...
>
> It is not only the task of the state apparatus to strengthen legality. Party organizations, the trade unions and the Komsomol are in duty bound to do everything to ensure the strictest observance of laws and improve the working people's knowledge of the law. Respect for legality and for the law must become part and parcel of the make-up of every person. This is particularly true of persons in office. No attempt to deviate from or to circumvent the law is to be tolerated, no matter what the motive. Nor can we tolerate any violation of the rights of individuals and infringement of the dignity of citizens. For us communists, champions of the most humane ideals, this is a matter of principle.'[1]

This statement, coming from the Soviet Communist Party itself, sets in motion any discussion of the true nature of equal protection under the Soviet legal system.

If the essence of Soviet socialist law can be expressed in one phrase it would be: equal justice under law for all citizens irrespective of race, sex, nationality, religious belief, social, property or educational status, or party membership. All citizens are equal before the law. All citizens have the same standing before Soviet courts and the same legal duties are imposed on all persons that come within the territorial jurisdiction of the USSR irrespective of citizenship status.[2]

However, Soviet justice is 'class justice': the 24th Congress of the CPSU condemned any attempt to speak of universal justice (which may be equally true for all social systems) or of a universal concept of individual freedom (that is devoid of a class approach). Rather the Party Congress feels that '[t]here is no freedom in general, just as there is no democracy in general. There is a class concept (to both freedom and democracy)'.[3] It follows that the equal protection clauses of the law may not necessarily and do not in fact apply to 'class enemies' within the Soviet society. The possible rationale for this exclusion of class enemies from under the protective umbrella of Soviet equal protection privileges is that Soviet law itself looks upon class enemies as legal non-persons and in fact as the objects which the law is out to destroy in the first place. The raison d'être of early Soviet law was condensed in the phrase 'death to the class enemy'. The concept and number of persons who qualified as class enemies, however, varied from one historical era to another. With the ultimate physical annihilation of these class enemies it became possible to restore full equality under law to all surviving citizens within the Soviet society.

> Soviet legal theoreticians maintain that the Soviet Union today is a 'state of all the people' in which there are no longer any antagonistic classes. Rather there are two friendly classes - the proletariat and the peasantry whose economic interests do not conflict and whose separate existence the state is working to eliminate in the long run. The convergence of these two classes into one will eventually take place under the classless society known as communism.

This class approach to Soviet justice also means that the individual is only a part of the society and therefore the exercise of his freedoms must not and cannot be incompatible with the general social purpose of the state – which is the universal march toward general happiness under communism. The closer the state approaches this state of affairs known as communism, the wider the scope of individual rights and freedom the law would grant to its citizens. This means that Soviet law views individual rights in their historical perspective: depending on a combination of objective and subjective factors at any particular time citizens would tend to enjoy more or less individual freedom.

> For example, it would be correct to say that Soviet citizens perhaps had more rights during the NEP than they probably had during the period of War Communism. Similarly Soviet citizens certainly enjoy more freedom now than they ever did either during Stalin's collectivization of agriculture or during the period of industrialization of Soviet national economy or in fact at any time during Stalin's regime. To attribute all the suppressions of individual liberty during Stalin's regime to just Stalin's Caucasian personality would be incorrect.

Since it will be futile to evaluate equal protection under Soviet law by using the same standards that are applicable to other legal systems this study proposes to put forward some of those basic principles of Soviet law which should be constantly borne in mind in looking at the equality of citizens under that law. First and foremost it should be borne in mind that when Soviet law confers rights on its citizens it imposes certain reasonable obligations to go with those rights. Rights and duties in this context cannot be divorced one from the other. The fundamental rights and duties of Soviet citizens represent juridical form for the expression of the freedom and responsibility of the individual under socialism. 'In these rights and duties are manifest the dialectic unity of society and individual, of the state and the citizen, of the group and its members'.[4]

In discussing the rights and duties of citizens under Soviet law the following principles should govern:

1. The dialectical relationship between rights and duties presupposes that there can be no right without an attendant duty. Rights are conferred in reasonable expectation that its recipient will reciprocate by performing certain duties toward the society that so conferred the right. Failure to perform these duties may lead and, in fact, in many instances has led to either a denial of such rights (where the rights have not been exercised) or to a demand from society for compensatory payment to atone for the rights where the latter have been taken advantage of in bad faith.

2. In the hierarchy of rights under the Soviet system the rights of the society at large are superior to those of the individual. This means that an individual right may be exercised only to the extent to which it does not conflict with the rights of the society. Any conflicts between the rights of the individual and those of the society should invariably be resolved in favor of the latter. No citizen shall place himself above the society of which he is only a part. By the same token a law designed to grant equal protection to all Soviet national or ethnic cultures can be interpreted only in the light of public policy.

3. A legally created right of one citizen necessarily presupposes the active or passive duty of another citizen not to interfere with that right. Thus, in order for one citizen to subjectively realize his objective rights he would need the cooperation of other citizens not to deny him such a possibility. For example, a statute which confers on all Soviet citizens the objective right to hold a particular job irrespective of race, sex, religious belief, or natural origin creates a duty in those officials charged with hiring persons for such jobs not to discriminate along the lines mentioned above. In other words '[a] legally created right always expresses not just a unilateral, but at least a bilateral link between subjects of that law. The right of one citizen consequently corresponds to the active or passive duty of another . . . In the very concept of right is contained a dialectic unity of rights and duties, their organic relationship. Rights may be defined only through duties. When there are no duties for some, there cannot be rights for others'.[5]

4. Since rights and duties are social categories which cannot exist in isolation, the responsibility for coercing the performance of these duties falls upon the state – the ultimate guarantor of the rights of citizens. In the words of Professor N. Aleksandrov '... each subjective right represents the unity of three possibilities: the appearance (and measure) of possible behavior of the possessor of such subjective right; the possibility of demanding a corresponding behavior (to carry out a particular act or, on the reverse, to desist from such act) from other (obligated) persons; finally, the possibility of resorting, in the light of necessity, to the aid not only of society, but also to state apparatus."[6]

In other words, 'the constitutional rights of Soviet citizens, like no other rights, represent a real possibility guaranteed by the state to enable (the holders of such rights) to enjoy the available social gifts. By social gifts within this context one understands not just the various types of material wealth, but also all the different demands of man the enjoyment of which the law considers permissible.'[7]

This also means that the timing and the scope of these objective rights will depend upon the periodic determination to be made by the state as the ultimate guarantor. The right of the state to grant, deny, suspend, cut back or expand these rights is an absolute legislative privilege which is subject only to those due process requirements which the lawmaker has set down to guide it in its legislative activities. The legislative powers of the Soviet lawmaker are absolute and the relative ease with which the USSR Constitution can be amended is intended to accomodate the freedom with which such power may be exercised. It should be borne in mind that even though the Soviet Constitution is the fundamental law of the land, it was never intended to be a dogma. It is no more than a legal platform for social, economic and political action and if any of its provisions outlives its social usefulness it is immediately amended under the procedure outlined in art. 146 of the USSR Constitution of 1936.

5. The conferment of individual right by Soviet law on its citizens is not an end in itself but rather only a means to an end. The aim is to give the Soviet citizen all the freedom he needs so that he could maximize his personal input into the national construction of a communist future for the entire society. Failure to use this right for its designated purpose, or worse still, any attempt to use this right to the detriment of those goals established by society, will leave the state with no choice but to take away such right. A kind of master-servant relationship exists here between the Soviet state, the Soviet Government and individual Soviet citizens: the state is the master, the government is the servant and individual citizens are subservants. This means that whatever incidental individual freedom these subservants have is subject to the actual or possible control of the master as well as of the servant. The declared business of the master is the construc-

tion of communism and to this end the subservants owe to the master the duty of obedience, absolute loyalty, subservience, full disclosure and total accountability for all knowledge or information acquired in the course of such 'employment' – i.e., as long as he or she remains a Soviet citizen. In the words of a Soviet commentator '[legal] duties are established both for the purpose of furthering the interests of the entire society, the state as well as the interests of each individual Soviet citizen. Duties, just like legal rights, cannot be divorced from their aims which are only an expression of these interests.'[8]

Rights and duties of citizens under Soviet law being what they are – historical categories – this study purposes to analyze equal protection under Soviet constitutional system as it evolved in the post-1936 era and especially in the post-1958 period of Soviet legal history. Whereas the Soviet constitution represents the most fundamental embodiment of equal protection laws in the land, most of the constitutional provisions have been re-articulated and elaborated upon in the various other branches of Soviet law. We propose to look at the question in four interrelated parts. Part I deals with the substantive equal protection provisions of the USSR Constitution of 1936; part II with the re-articulations and elaborations of these provisions in Soviet electoral law, Soviet labor law, Soviet education law, Soviet family law as well as Soviet civil law. These two parts contain the body of the argument; they stress the fundamental importance of equality in Soviet legislation, as applied to various branches of law. Part III deals with substantive legal guarantees of equal protection through the legal sanctions imposed under Soviet criminal law, Soviet civil law and Soviet administrative law. Part IV deals with the due process provisions (procedural guarantees) in the Codes of Civil and Criminal Procedure. It also looks at the special roles of the courts, the procuracy and the militia (the Soviet police) in guaranteeing the rights to all citizens on a basis of equality for all.

The term 'equal protection of the law' means that equal protection and security shall be given to all persons (irrespective of race, sex, color, religious belief or natural origins) under like circumstances. Since all men are equal before the law this principle requires that equal rights be granted them and that equal obligations be imposed upon them. However, since the circumstances of all men in life are not alike, this principle does not bar a compensatorily discriminatory application of the law in favor of a particular disadvantaged group nor does it bar the dispensation of individualized justice under law.

The principle of equal protection under law can be found in the various aspects of contemporary Soviet law. Naturally the USSR Constitution provides the fountainhead in this regard and the general principles of the constitution are eventually concretized in the other independent branches of the law. The Soviet definition of the concept of equal protection under law is offered by a leading Soviet commentator on the subject as follows:

> 'Equality of citizens before the law means that the laws of the Soviet state are equally binding upon all citizens irrespective of their social, property or official status, national or racial identity, religious belief. Each person who violates the law, notwithstanding the official position he holds within the state, notwithstanding any decoration that may have been conferred on him in the past, is subject to liability for such violation on equal terms with all other citizens. All citizens have the same rights to defend their legal rights before a court of law. Neither official position nor property status, neither party membership nor social origins shall confer any privileges on any citizen before a court of law. For all Soviet courts the law establishes a uniform procedure.'[9]

Since the Soviet Constitution is the supreme law of the land any legal analysis of equal protection under contemporary Soviet law should start with the 1936 Constitution.

I. *Equal Protection Under the 1936 Soviet Constitution*

Professor Voevodin, a leading Soviet constitutional lawyer defines a constitutional right as 'that possibility which is fixed in the constitution and guaranteed by the Soviet state and which makes it possible for each Soviet citizen to freely and independently elect the type and measure of his behavior, to create and utilize those social benefits granted to him both in his own personal interest and in the interest of the society.'[10] By the same standards he defines a constitutional duty as 'that necessity which is established by the Soviet state in the interest of all members of the society and fixed in its constitution and thus imposes upon each citizen a specific type and measure of behavior and liability for its negligent performance.'[11] These rights and duties are so fundamental that they may not be derogated from by any other organic statutes. These rights however are not inherent in the nature of man but rather they owe their origins clearly to the constitution which only can confer them. A right that is not specifically granted under the constitution cannot be assumed to be inherent in the Soviet citizen. The enumeration of rights under the Soviet Constitution is intended to be exhaustive of those legal rights which Soviet citizens have. Any so-called 'inherent right of man', for one thing, may not be asserted as a defense against any constitutionally created duty. Whereas the enjoyment of these constitutional rights is not necessarily confined to Soviet citizens only, it is to be understood that the law may specifically deny the enjoyment of a particular right to aliens or stateless persons residing in the Soviet Union, to certain categories of Soviet citizens who lack the legal capacity for such enjoyment or to those Soviet citizens who have been stripped of their Soviet citizenship by a competent organ of the Soviet state.

Generally speaking, contemporary Soviet constitutional legal theory[12] categorizes all constitutional rights and duties of Soviet citizens into three major groups: rights and duties of Soviet citizens in their capacity as workers (these refer to their rights and duties in the sphere of socio-economic and cultural life); rights and duties of Soviet citizens in their capacity as social and political activists (these refer to the rights and duties of Soviet citizens with regard to their participation in the socio-political aspects of Soviet life); rights and duties of Soviet citizens in their capacity as individuals (these include all those rights and duties which relate to the individual life of each citizen).[13] Such a division is intended to underscore the tripartite role of the Soviet citizen who at any given time is a socialist worker, a social and political activist and an individual in his own right. One category of these rights and duties should not conflict with the others. The true nature of the rights and duties of a Soviet citizen can only be seen in a dialectic unity of these three categories.

A. Constitutional Rights and Duties of Soviet citizens in the Sphere of Socio-Economic and Cultural Life of State: the Right and Duties of a Soviet Citizen as a Socialist Worker

Central to these rights and duties are the right of the Soviet citizen to work, the duty to work, and the obligation to observe labor discipline. The work of a socialist worker can be satisfactory and effective only if he is adequately prepared to meet the demands of such work. To this end the right to education becomes fundamental and not just incidental to his rights and duty to work. Also important to his status as a socialist worker is his right to rest and leisure, to free medical treatment, to social security as well as his duty to protect the fruits of his labor. This means in effect that the category of rights and duties of a Soviet citizen as a socialist worker includes the following: the right to work, the right to free education, the duty to work, the duty to observe labor discipline, the duty to preserve and enhance socialist property, the right to own and inherit personal property, the right to rest and leisure, the right to free medical treatment as well as the right to social security.

Art. 18 of the USSR Constitution establishes the right of all Soviet citizens to work. This right to work means 'the right to guaranteed employment and payment for [one's] work in accordance with its quantity and quality.' According to para. 2 of art. 118 of the USSR Constitution '[t]he right to work is ensured by the socialist organization of the national economy, the steady growth of the productive forces of Soviet society, the elimination of the possibility of economic crises, and the abolition of unemployment.' This right to work is so fundamental that it may not be denied to any Soviet citizen on the basis of race, sex, religious belief or national origin. The right of citizens to obtain work creates in the state an obligation to provide the jobs to each citizen according to his qualifications and individual ability and to be paid for such job accordingly.

The right to work in the Soviet Union is guaranteed from violations not only by the state (through an extensive network of criminal and civil sanctions for their violations) but also by the Soviet trade union organizations and other social groups. Under the Marxian theory of evolution it was work that helped man evolve from the level of the ape to that of a 'homo sapiens'. If man ceases to work he shall degenerate into the level of the ape and in order to prevent this historical regression art. 12 of the USSR Constitution makes it a legally enforceable duty for all able-bodied Soviet citizens to work. It states: 'Work in the USSR is a duty and a matter of honor for every able-bodied citizen, in accordance with the principle: 'He who does not work, neither shall he eat.' The principle applied in the USSR is that of socialism: 'From each according to his ability, to each according to his work.' ' No man shall be a parasite on his fellow men. No able-bodied citizen shall live off the labor of society. To prevent this from happening the Soviet Constitution forever condemns all acts of vagrancy and voluntary unemployment as anti-social and incompatible with the Soviet way of life.

Art. 130 of the USSR Constitution makes it a duty of all Soviet citizens to maintain labor discipline. Generally these rules of Soviet labor discipline can be found in numerous organic statutes, rules, regulations and model instructions – the aim of which is to guarantee maximum compliance with safety standards by all Soviet workers.[14]

If the result of the collective labor of Soviet citizens is to be used to the benefit of all citizens, the law makes it the duty of all citizens to protect these results. Accordingly, art. 131 of the USSR Constitution provides: 'It is the duty of every citizen of the USSR to safeguard and fortify public, socialist property as the sacred and inviolable foundation of the Soviet system, as the source of wealth and might of the country, as the source of the prosperity and culture of all the working people. Persons committing crimes in respect of public, socialist property are enemies of the people.'

By the same token every citizen is entitled to enjoy the fruits of his own labor. To guarantee him this right art. 10 of the USSR Constitution states: 'The right of citizens to own, as their personal property, income and savings derived from work, to own a dwelling-house and a supplementary husbandry, articles of household and articles of personal use and convenience, is protected by law, as is also the right of citizens to inherit personal property.'

Art. 10 as quoted above establishes four things: it recognizes individual property as one of the permissible forms of socialist property ownership in the Soviet Union; it defines the objects of such ownership rights; it limits the use of such personal property to the satisfaction of the personal needs of citizens and no more; it recognizes the right to own personal property as a fundamental right of all Soviet citizens.[15] Any attempt to use this personal property for an illegal purpose (e.g., to derive an un-earned income, to subvert a legitimate public policy or to aid a foreign enemy of the Soviet state) will result not only in a retaliatory curtailment of this right by the state but possibly in some criminal action against the particular individual. These limitations on the use of personally acquired individual property applies equally to inherited property. Personal property, whether acquired through self-effort or through inheritance is only designed to aid the owner in attaining individual self-fulfilment and no more.

The right of Soviet citizens to rest and leisure is enshrined in art. 119 of the Soviet Constitution which provides, in part: 'Citizens of the USSR have the right to rest and leisure. The right to rest and leisure is ensured by the establishment of a seven-hour day for industrial, office, and professional workers . . .; by the institution of annual vacations with full pay for industrial, office, and professional workers and by placing a wide network of sanatoriums, holiday homes and clubs at the disposal of the working people.'

Finally, art. 120 of the USSR Constitution grants to all citizens the right to social security in the following provisions: 'Citizens of the USSR have the right to maintenance in old age and also in case of sickness or disability. This right is ensured by the extensive development of social insurance of industrial, office, and professional workers at state expense, free medical service for the working people, and the provision of a wide network of health resorts for the use of the working people.' The fundamental rights contained in art. 120 above have been extended through social legislation to include: the granting of state aid to un-wed mothers as well as to mothers with many surviving children, the establishment of a wide network of state orphanages and children's institutions for children whose parents cannot afford to bring them up properly, a humanistic and generous old age pension scheme and a special job placement scheme for invalids.

The right to receive free medical treatment is so fundamental that the Program of the Communist Party of the Soviet Union insists on its being treated separately from the right to social security.

Art. 121 of the 1936 USSR Constitution confers the right to free education[16] in the following provision: 'Citizens of the USSR have a right to education. This right is ensured by universal compulsory eight-year education; by extensive development of secondary polytechnical education, vocational-technical education, and secondary specialized and higher education . . ., by free education in all schools; by a system of state scholarship grants . . .' The right to free education in the USSR extends to all stages in the educational process – from kindergarten to the university.[17]

Under art. 14, para. (5) the jurisdiction of the federal government covers the definition of the basic principles in the spheres of education whereas the immediate task of the practical enforcement of the Soviet education statute is vested in the local councils and their executive organs. The duty to send ones children to school is not only a moral but also a legal duty of all Soviet citizens. Women in the USSR are granted equal right to education under art. 122 of the USSR constitution which states: 'Women in the USSR are accorded all rights on an equal footing with men in all spheres of economic, government, cultural, political and other social activity.' All Soviet citizens, irrespective of their national origins have the same right in the sphere of education. In order for this equality to be fully realized by all, however, the state grants special compensatory privileges to members of ethnic minority groups in the Soviet Union in the form of established quota system in the admission of students to Soviet colleges and universities.[18]

B. Constitutional Rights and Duties of Citizens in the Sphere of Socio-Political Life of the Society: Rights and Duties of Soviet Citizens in their Capacity as Political Activists

The Soviet Constitution seeks to guarantee the right of all citizens, irrespective of race, color, sex, creed, national origin or party membership, to equally participate in the social and political life of the country. Such right may not be denied or abridged on the basis of economic or property status. The full rights of a Soviet citizen in his capacity as a political activist are enumerated in arts. 134-142 of the USSR Constitution. Under art. 134 all elections in the USSR are conducted on the basis of universal, equal and direct suffrage and by secret ballot. Art. 135 explains the element of universality of Soviet elections to mean that 'all citizens of the USSR who have reached the age of 18, irrespective of race or nationality, sex, religion, education, domicile, social origin, property status or past activities, have the right to vote in the election of deputies, with the exception of persons who have been legally certified insane.' It also means that 'every citizen of the USSR who has reached the age of 23 is eligible for election to the Supreme Soviet of the USSR, irrespective of race or nationality, sex, religion, education, domicile, social origin, property status or past activities.' According to art. 136 elections in the USSR are equal in the sense that 'each citizen has one vote; all citizens participate in elections on equal footing.'

Cognizant of the relative sparsity of the rural population as compared with the urban population, realizing the apparent inequality in the contribution of population among the 15 union-republics which make up the Soviet Union, art. 34 of the USSR Constitution provides that: 'The Soviet of the Union [which is one of the two chambers of the Soviet federal parliament – the Supreme Soviet] shall be elected by the citizens of the USSR voting by election districts on the basis of one deputy for every 30,000 of the population,' whereas art. 135 establishes the following quota for the other chamber of the federal parliament: 'The Soviet of Nationalities is elected by the citizens of the USSR voting by Union Republics, Autonomous Republics, Autonomous Regions and National Areas on the basis of 32 deputies from each Union Republic, 11 deputies from each Autonomous Republic, 5 deputies from each Autonomous Region, and one deputy from each National Area.' Apportionment under these guidelines totally disregards the race, sex or nationality of the voters. If all are to participate equally in the election of deputies to the USSR Supreme Soviet the vote of one segment of the country should not weigh more than that of the other subdivisions of the USSR. To apportion electoral districts along racial, ethnic or nationality lines would be a violation of the principle of one man-one vote contemplated under art. 136 of the USSR Constitution. Art. 137 makes special effort to state that 'women have the right to elect and be elected on equal terms with men.' Even 'citizens serving in the armed forces of the USSR have the right to elect and be elected on equal terms with all other citizens.' Under art. 130 elections for public offices in the USSR are direct, i.e., the deputies are elected by a direct vote of the citizens rather than through any indirect voting system. The right to nominate candidates for these public offices 'is secured to mass organizations and societies of the working people: communist party organizations, trade unions, cooperatives, youth organizations and cultural societies.'

Other fundamental political freedoms of Soviet citizens are contained in arts. 124 (freedom of religious worship and freedom of anti-religious propaganda); 125 (freedom of speech, of the press, of assembly and of movement); 126 (freedom of association).

> The freedoms granted under art. 125 of the USSR Constitution are often misunderstood in the West and therefore need some clarification: freedom of speech under art. 125 of the USSR Constitution does not mean freedom to slander the Soviet state or its social system nor does it mean the freedom to aid and abet the foreign enemy through any form of communicative art. The freedoms granted under this provision contemplate only those freedoms which are necessary for individual fulfilment and for the spiritual development of one's self. The exercise of this freedom need not and should not conflict with a superior state interest. 'A genuine freedom of speech does not include an unimpeded circulation of all sorts of ideas, concepts, etc., but rather protects only a free propagation of avant-garde, revolutionary opinions, ideas, and concepts which will serve the interests of the popular masses - the standard bearers of social progress, the locomotive of history. Only in this context can one speak of genuine freedom of thought and particularly of the freedom of speech, press, assembly, etc.'[19]
>
> To slander the Soviet state is not a constitutionally protected freedom. Since the right of free speech is designed to further the propagation of

revolutionary and progressive ideas and since the right to determine what ideas are revolutionary or reactionary is vested in the state itself acting as a mouthpiece of the Soviet Communist Party, the right to disagree with promulgated state policies and to openly polemicize with Party doctrine is not a constitutionally protected right of free speech. The Party certainly welcomes any intra-Party communications on any points concerning Party ideology. The Party organization is amenable to criticisms from below. The state also welcomes any constructive criticisms of its policies so long as such criticisms are made known to it through established channels. But to take one's case directly to the people over the head of the Party or of the State Government becomes an impermissible arrogation of unprotected free speech.[20]

The right of association under art. 126 of the USSR Constitution, like all the other rights granted under the Constitution, is not an absolute right. It is subject to certain limitations the purpose of which is to make sure that this right is not abused to the detriment of the state: only those associations which further cultural, spiritual, political and educational needs of its members are protected by law. Whereas all legally constituted associations enjoy organizational autonomy from state interference, the law nevertheless requires that all existing organizations (with few exceptions) be registered with the designated state agency before they can operate. The law also requires that a newly created association should not attempt to duplicate or unnecessarily compete with an already existing organization which satisfies the same needs and most important, that admission to membership of any of these organizations should not be predicated upon considerations of sex, race, religious belief, national origin, economic or property status. This in practical terms means that Soviet citizens may not set up a rival political party since one already exists in the Soviet Union.[21]

The duties imposed under arts. 132 (universal military service)[22] and 133 (the duty of all Soviet citizens to defend the motherland) are among the many duties of the Soviet citizen as a political activist but art. 130 imposes one of the most fundamental constitutional duties on all Soviet citizens when it provides that 'it is the duty of every citizen of the USSR to abide by the Constitution of the USSR, to observe the laws, to maintain labor discipline, and to respect the rules of socialist society.' As to what art. 130 actually contemplates, Professor Voevodin explains that '[t]o abide by the Constitution means to conform one's behavior to the prescriptions of this law. He who violates the Constitution, does not observe its provisions, voluntarily or involuntarily subverts the stability of the Soviet system which has found recognition in its basic law.'[23] Since organic statutes are only an elaborate concretization of the prescriptions of this Constitution the duty imposed by art. 130 of the Constitution includes the obligation to unquestionably and unconditionally obey all constitutionally valid Soviet laws.

However, since the determination of the constitutionality of a Soviet federal statute is a prerogative of the Presidium of the USSR Supreme Soviet (art. 49, para. (c) and (f) of the USSR Constitution) it follows that all Soviet statutes are prima facie constitutionally valid until otherwise declared invalid by the Presidium of the USSR Supreme Soviet. To predicate any ostensible violation of Soviet law upon its unconstitutionality (prior to such a law being declared unconstitutional by the Presidium of the USSR Supreme Soviet) smacks of arrogation and therefore constitutes not only a violation of the duty under art. 130 of the USSR Constitution but also a crime under art. 200 of the RSFSR Criminal Code.[24]

Among the many duties imposed by art. 130 of the USSR Constitution is the duty to respect the rules of Soviet socialist society. This represents a positive attempt on the part of the state to legally enforce the observance by its citizens of the rules of public morality. Among these moral duties of the Soviet citizen are: the duty to serve the society in good faith, the duty to subject one's personal interests to those of the state, the duty to voluntarily carry out all impositions and assignments by the state, by the society at large or by the various social organizations of which the individual citizen is a member. What is interesting about this duty is its attempt to obliterate the differences between law and morality. Rules of morality (to the extent to which they have not been enacted into positive law) have traditionally been enforced through extra-legal coercion but art. 130 of the USSR Constitution imposes a legal sanction for a violation of a non-legislative norm of socialist morality.

One possible danger in enforcing such a duty is the possible harassment to which Soviet citizens can be subjected by an overzealous law enforcement officer. Since the only comprehensive codification of the rules of Soviet socialist morality which can be found in the so-called *Moral Code of Builders of Communism* is replete with vague and overtly broad propositions, the determination of some of these moral duties becomes a highly subjective thing. As to what constitutes these un-legislative rules of socialist morality Professor Voevodin writes: 'The rules of socialist morality include all those social norms, operative within the Soviet society, which were either created directly by society itself, or by those individual associations existing within the society and designed to regulate the conduct of their members in the light of the tasks before such associations.'[25] This means that all Soviet citizens are under an obligation to respect the rules established even by social organizations to which they happen to belong and to 'honestly' perform their obligations before the Soviet society at large.[26] One Soviet commentator defines 'honesty' under art. 130 of the USSR Constitution to mean the moral duty 'to behave in accordance with one's conscience, with one's convictions, and with the demands of justice.'[27] Whatever the substantive contents of these rules are what is important is that they are equally binding on all Soviet citizens irrespective of sex, race, nationality, religious belief, social or property status, official position or Party membership.

The question here is: when a state law requires all Soviet citizens irrespective of Party membership to obey an internal rule of the Communist Party organization, is this not a subtle form of discrimination against those non-members of the Communist Party who may not have internalized the particular rule to begin with? The answer to this question is a negative one. Art. 120 of the USSR Constitution describes the CPSU not just as one of the many social organizations that exist in the USSR, but as 'the vanguard of the working people in their struggle to build communist society and as the leading core of all organizations of the working people, both government and non-government.' From this it follows that norms of the Party are voluntarily binding upon party members by virtue of their membership in the Party and universally binding on all Soviet citizens irrespective of their membership of the CPSU, just by virtue of the Constitution and all other laws of the state which seek to make them binding on all alike.

C. Constitutional Rights and Duties of Citizens in the Sphere of Personal Life and Individual Freedom

The sphere of individual life and personal freedom of citizens is a sphere preeminently governed by rules of communist morality. Nevertheless, Soviet law establishes very close links between the Soviet state and its citizens through an intricate network of laws designed to protect the personal freedoms of the citizen. Prominent among these rights of individual freedoms are the rights of privacy protected under art. 127 which states: 'Citizens of the USSR are guaranteed inviolability of the person. No person shall be placed under arrest except by decisions of a court of law or with the sanction of a procurator.' Art. 118 provides that 'the inviolability of the homes of citizens and privacy of correspondence are protected by law.'

The rights granted under this section are strictly personal – they are granted to the individual himself and not to the group to which he belongs. For example, art. 127 essentially confers on all citizens taken individually the right to be protected by the state from illegal transgressions on his life, health, freedom, honor and dignity. These freedoms are guaranteed through a network of criminal sanctions. However, art. 127 grants protection only against illegal transgressions and not necessarily against those transgressions which are sanctioned by law or carried out in conformity with the law. The right of privacy may not be asserted against any authorized actions by the competent state agencies. Among the state organs that may temporarily override these individual freedoms are the courts, the procuracy, organs of the State Comittee on Security (KGB), Commanders of Military Formations. In fact art. 127 of the Soviet Constitution grants special privilege in this regard to the courts and the procuracy.[28]

Similarly the right guaranteed under art. 128 of the Constitution is statutorily waived in favor of those state agencies charged with state inspection of residential homes as well as organs of state fire departments. Since the law provides for regular sanitation, insurance, tax and fire inspections of residential homes, the right of the residents to the privacy of their homes may not obstruct this legitimate state purpose. The right to inspect residential homes is also granted to directors and managers of state housing administration as well as to designated agents of communal services. A newly enacted Police Code[29] also grants to the Soviet police the right to enter any residential homes, right of privacy notwithstanding, in the course of the investigation of an individual who is suspected of having committed a crime or in an attempt to uncover a crime or other violations against public order or against the personal security of citizens. The Code also grants the police the right to enter private homes (during daylight hours) in order to verify any suspected violations of the Soviet passport rules.

The privacy of one's correspondence is guaranteed not only under art. 128 of the USSR Constitution, but also under the 1971 Postal Ordinance[30] which imposed upon postal workers the duty to respect the secrecy of private correspondence of Soviet citizens. The privacy of one''s correspondence thus may be violated only in accordance with the law.

Art. 124, among other things, grants Soviet citizens the much cherished freedom of conscience in the following provision: 'In order to ensure to citizens freedom of conscience, the church in the USSR is separated from the state, and the school from the church. Freedom of religious worship and freedom of anti-religious propaganda is recognized for all citizens.' Freedom of conscience permits one to embrace and practice any religious faith in the USSR. It protects such believers against any illegal harassments. However, whereas it permits the conduct by any citizen of anti-religious propaganda, it strictly prohibits any form of religious propaganda. He who believes in any religion should keep his faith to himself and it is against public policy to attempt to contaminate other innocent citizens with such 'opiate.'[31] In the Soviet Union freedom of religion does not mean freedom to propagate religion. It does, however, mean the right to propagate anti-religion for those who embrace the state ideology of atheism. Any citizen who is already a convert however is free to join any religious organizations of his choice, to switch from one faith to another at his option. The right to participate in any religious group however does not include the right to solicit new members for such a group. The law permits citizens to unite either in religious societies (the law defines a religious society as a religious organization with membership of more than 20 persons) or in religious groups (i.e., religious organizations with less than 20 members) but all such religious associations must register with the competent state agency before they can commence their activities. The removal of such associations from a state list of approved religious organizations means that the group must stop all its activities. The name of such organizations may be removed from this state list under any of the following circumstances: voluntary dissolution of the group by its members, decline of its membership below the established minimum by state law, violation of state law by the group.

> Some typical examples of violations of state law by religious groups in the Soviet Union would include the following: if the religious group takes a strong stand against compulsory military service by its members for reasons of incompatibility of military service with their religious belief; if the group engages in any collective form of religious indoctrination of the children of its members; if the group sets up a parochial school and discourages the children of its members from attending state schools (Soviet citizens may obtain religious knowledge but only through private arrangement since state law permits the establishment of religious schools only in the form of seminaries solely for the education of priests and ministers of a particular religion and no more); if the group uses its place of worship for purposes other than religious services; if the group takes any common stand on any national issues that have no bearing on religion, etc. Any of the above actions would constitute a violation of state law and therefore a ground for closing down the group itself.

By definition all social organizations in the USSR enjoy organizational autonomy from any state interference in their internal affairs. This privilege applies also to those religious groups which operate legally in the Soviet Union. However, since the general orientation of these religious groups is contrary to the ideology of the state (state ideology looks upon religion as the opiate of the people and therefore as incompatible with the atheistic posture of the communist-oriented society) they do not enjoy the other rights accorded to other social organizations under art. 126 of the USSR Constitution. For one thing these religious associations may not take part in the economic, socio-political or cultural life of the state; they may not own any buildings in the USSR.[32] That the Soviet Government merely tolerates but does not encourage the existence of religious associations cannot be gainsaid. This attitude results in a series of regulatory schemes designed to emphasize the unequal status of religious groups in the Soviet Union.

Art. 110 of the Constitution grants equality to the languages of all the Union Republics, Autonomous Regions, and Autonomous Republics in court proceedings. It also guarantees to anyone who does not speak the language of the particular republic the right to an interpreter in a court of law. Art. 123 epitomizes the equality of all Soviet citizens before the law in its provision: 'Equality of rights of citizens of the USSR, irrespective of their nationality or race, in all spheres of economic, government, cultural, political and other social activity, is an indefeasible law. Any direct or indirect restriction of the rights of, or conversely, the establishment of any direct or indirect privileges for, citizens on account of their race or nationality, as well as any advocacy of racial or national exclusiveness or hatred and contempt, are punishable by law.'

In order to demonstrate the equality of industrial and agricultural workers in the Soviet Union (workers and peasants) the arms of the USSR (under art. 143 of the Constitution) and the state flag of the USSR depict the hammer and the sickle – the working symbols of these two friendly classes.

The Constitution merely grants the so-called fundamental and basic rights and duties of Soviet citizens. In most cases the details of these rights and duties are left to the various other branches of Soviet law and it is to those branches of the law that one should turn in order to fill in the gaps that may have been left by the constitutional provisions just discussed in the above paragraphs. Before this is done however a few things should be said about the notion of Soviet citizenship as a legal category as well as the legal status of aliens under contemporary Soviet constitutional system.

1. Concept of Soviet citizenship

Citizenship is the status of being a citizen and a citizen is a person who, under the constitution and laws of a particular state, is a member of the political community, owing allegiance and being entitled to the enjoyment of full civil rights. The status of a citizen imposes certain duties as well as it confers certain rights. Soviet citizenship therefore guarantees to its possessor the enjoyment in its fullest sense and on equal terms with all other citizens of all the constitutional rights and freedoms as well as the fulfilment of all the legal duties imposed upon all such citizens.[33] In the USSR today there is a uniform federal citizenship according to which all citizens of the various union republics are considered citizens of the USSR ipso facto. The citizen of one Union Republic is treated equally in another Union Republic. Under the citizenship law of August 19, 1938 all persons who as of Nov. 7, 1917 were subjects of Imperial Russia, and had not lost Soviet citizenship or those persons who have acquired Soviet citizenship by other means as of that time were to be considered as Soviet citizens.

The 1938 Act which is still in force today put an end to the anarchy and confusion which had surrounded the whole question of Soviet citizenship prior to that date. For example, under the pre-1938 Soviet decree any person who was resident in the USSR and could not show any proof that he was a citizen of another country was automatically considered to be a Soviet citizen even against his will. Not only was this an imposition of Soviet citizenship on those aliens who perhaps did not want to be so 'honored', but it left unclear the issue as to who exactly was a Soviet citizen and who was a non-citizen alien or a stateless person.

Art. 3 of the 1938 citizenship law granted to all aliens resident in the USSR, irrespective of race, color, creed or national origins the right to be admitted to citizenship upon application to the Presidium of the USSR Supreme Soviet and to the Presidium of the Supreme Soviet of the Union Republic where they were resident. The Presidium in all such cases shall decide to grant or deny the request.

In connection with Soviet citizenship law certain equal protection questions generally asked are: does a Soviet citizen have an inherent right to his citizenship status? If so is a state decree depriving him of this citizenship right valid under Soviet law? Can the Soviet Government deny a petition by a Soviet citizen seeking to be relieved of his citizenship?

The answers to these three questions lie in the nature of the power of the state to grant or deny citizenship status. One Soviet commentator has suggested that 'citizenship, if seen as the defined legal relationship between a person and the state, is for that person an objective fact. The official decision to alter, for example, the citizenship status of a particular individual who possesses Soviet citizenship is a prerogative only of the Soviet state. This is its inherent sovereign right. Presumably, a Soviet citizen may enter into relation with his state through an application to the Presidium of the USSR Supreme Soviet requesting to be relieved of Soviet citizenship. However, in such a legal relationship the citizen only has the right to apply to be relieved from citizenship.'[34] The decision to so grant his request is a sovereign decision which only the Soviet Government may take. What this means is that: no Soviet citizen has an inherent right to Soviet citizenship; if citizenship right is only an objective rather than a subjective right it follows that the Soviet state, acting through its competent organ, may grant or deny citizenship privileges at will;[35] a decision to that effect is a sovereign act of the Soviet state and is not subject to appeal to any superior body; by the same token the Presidium of the Supreme Court of the USSR at its will may reinstate to Soviet citizenship a person who was previously deprived of such citizenship.

In the Soviet Union there are no second class citizens. One is either a citizen, an alien or a stateless person in the Soviet Union. The legal status of the alien is in many instances similar but not necessarily identical with that of a Soviet citizen.

2. Legal status of aliens in the USSR

Soviet law defines an alien as any such person resident in the USSR who is not a citizen of the USSR and owes allegiance to a foreign government. The legal status of such aliens is regulated by federal law and by such international conventions to which the Soviet Union is a party. The alien in the USSR enjoys either the national regime (in which case they are treated on the same terms as Soviet citizens) or the most-favored-nation regime (in which case all aliens are treated alike except that the Soviet Government establishes retaliatory restrictions on those aliens whose home governments also discriminate against Soviet citizens). Either regime is granted on the basis of reciprocity. Whereas most aliens in the USSR enjoy the national regime the law finds it necessary to impose certain limitations on the rights of such aliens. Among such specific regulatory limitations on the rights of aliens in the USSR are the following: all aliens are required to obtain a residence permit in order to live in the USSR; all aliens are required to first obtain exit and entry visas before travelling across Soviet state lines; an alien needs to obtain a police permit before he can travel inside the Soviet Union; an alien may not participate in the Soviet electoral process (he may neither vote nor be voted for nor participate in electoral campaigns of any sorts); an alien in the USSR is not subject to compulsory military service and may not hold any job involving the security of the state. Absent any of these specific limitations an alien in the USSR enjoys just about the same rights and is held to the same obligations as his Soviet counterparts. Among the many rights which an alien enjoys are: the right to work, the right to free education, the right to receive state social security; the right of free speech, freedom of assembly, freedom of street demonstrations; freedom of illegal search and seizure; full legal personality under Soviet private law. Among the many obligations of an alien are the following: the duty to abide by all Soviet law; the duty to respect local morals; the duty not to insult the national feelings of Soviet people or their human dignity through his behavior – in short, the duty to comport himself in a manner that is expected of a guest. Failure to live by this rule of thumb might result in the alien being thrown out of the USSR.

In sum, the alien resident in the USSR is presumed to be covered under the equal protection clauses of the Soviet Constitution unless the law specifically provides otherwise.

II. *Substantive Equal Protection under Soviet Law*

A. Equal Protection Under Soviet Electoral Law

The provisions of Chapter XI of the USSR Constitution – the electoral system – have found specific articulation in the Federal Elections Statute of 1950.[36] This statute re-states the general principles governing Soviet elections at all levels. This section of our study merely analyzes those provisions of the 1950 statute which specifically deal with the equality of Soviet citizens in the exercise of their rights to vote and be voted for.

Art. 1 establishes the principle of universal, equal, direct elections by secret ballot whereas art. 2 grants to all Soviet citizens who have attained the age of 18, irrespective of race, national origin, sex, religious belief, residential requirements, educational or economic status or past activities the right to vote at elections for the USSR Supreme Soviet. The only category of persons who have been denied this fundamental right are those who have been declared incompetent by a court of law or persons actually serving a prison term at the time of such elections.

Art. 3 of the 1950 Federal Elections Statute provides that any Soviet citizen who has attained the age of 23[37] irrespective of race, national origin, sex, creed, educational status, residential requirements, social background, property status or past activities may stand for election to the USSR Supreme Soviet.

At the last election to the USSR Supreme Soviet (which was held on June 16, 1974) the following data were given: 1517 deputies were elected out of which 767 were elected to the Council of the Union and 750 to the Council of Nationalities. Of the registered 161,724,222 voters in the USSR 161,689,612 participated in the elections and thus accounted for 99.98% of all the voters. Distribution of seats in the Council of the Union among the 15 Union Republics was as follows: RSFSR-423, Ukraine-150, Belorussia-28, Uzbekistan-35, Kazakhstan-39, Georgia-15, Azerbaidzhan-15, Lithuania-10, Moldavia-11, Latvia-7, Kirgizia-9, Tadzhikistan-8, Armenia-7, Turkmenia-6, Estonia-4 (Total 767). In terms of party membership: 1,096 (72.2%) were members of the CPSU (this figure includes candidate-members of the CPSU), 421 (27.8%) were non-party members; this figure for non-party members includes members of the Young Communist League who accounted for 174 (11.5%) of these. Thus in actual fact non-party members in the strict sense accounted for only 247 (16.3%) of all members of the USSR Supreme Soviet. In a country where only 9% of the adult population are members of the Communist Party (the figures released by the 24th Congress of CPSU in 1971 show that there were 14,455,321 Communists in the Soviet Union out of which 645,232 were candidate members of the CPSU: supra note 1 at. p. 111) the number of communists elected into the USSR Supreme Soviet is highly disproportionate to the number of non-communists. In terms of sex 1042 (68.7%) of the deputies elected were men and 475 (31.3%) were women.[38]

Art. 5 makes a special effort to emphasize the fact that women exactly enjoy the same rights (to vote and be voted for) with men. The law makes special efforts to guarantee the right to vote and be voted for to persons who by virtue of their official duties may be absent from the USSR on election days: a decree of Feb. 22, 1950 grants such right to crew members of Soviet merchant vessels that may be situated at sea on election day;[39] a decree of March 19, 1966 extends this right to members of Soviet armed forces stationed outside the USSR on election day.[40]

Art. 9 denies the right to vote or be voted for at Soviet elections to all aliens resident in the USSR. In order to give all Soviet citizens an equal economic opportunity to run for elections art. 11 provides that all campaign expenses shall be borne by the state.

Under art. 57 of the statute only the following social organizations may nominate candidates for elections: the CPSU, trade union organizations, youth and cooperative organizations, cultural and educational groups. In each case both the central and the local units of these organizations may nominate candidates independently. The right to nominate candidates for elections generally are also granted to the general meetings of workers, to various units of Soviet military formations, to the general meetings of collective farms as well as to the general meetings of state farm workers. One category of organizations that is obviously excluded from nominating candidates for elections or in any way influencing the course of elections in the USSR is the religious association.

Under art. 59 a candidate may stand for election only in one electoral district. A new law now permits more than one candidate to compete for election from one district. This element of multiple choice marks a departure from the past practices by which an electoral district had only one candidate on the ballot and the voters were given the choice of either voting for or against such candidate. In this sense multiple choice at Soviet elections is an improvement in Soviet electoral law. However, since these competing candidates generally do not have competing platforms (they all invariably declare support for the party platform even if they are not party members and thus focus their campaign efforts on the question of their personal suitability to better help carry out that party platform) it is hard to see how the establishment of multiple choice at Soviet elections really marks a radical departure from the past practices.

Art. 70 grants to all those organizations that have put up candidates for election the right to vigorously campaign for their candidates at campaign meetings, in the press or by any other methods compatible with art. 125 of the USSR Constitution.

Glaringly obvious from a reading of the Soviet Electoral Statute is the equal treatment of civilians and members of the Soviet armed forces, men and women, literate and illiterate citizens, members of the various nationalities and ethnic groups, town and country dwellers, rich and poor, ex-convicts and persons without previous criminal records, sick (but not declared mentally incompetent) and the healthy citizens. The unequal treatment in this regard of minors, legally declared incompetents and incarcerated citizens is justified under Soviet public policy.

B. Equal Protection Under Soviet Labor Law

Under the Soviet socialist economic system the right of citizens to work as well as their right to be free from capitalist exploitation of their labor are among their most sacred rights. Like any other rights guaranteed under Soviet constitutions the right to work and to be paid for a job well done has found articulation in separate legislations aimed at granting currency and fulfilment to those skeletal provisions of the Constitution. In addition to the Soviet constitutions, other major sources of Soviet labor law include: the Fundamental Principles of Labor Legislation of the USSR and the Union Republics (adopted on July 15, 1970),[41] the labor codes, of the various union republics,[42] other statutes and *polozheniia* (regulations) as well as internal rules and regulations adopted either by the trade union organizations or by the respective enterprises (e.g., safety regulations, fire regulations, etc.). No doubt the most important of these sources of Soviet labor law, second perhaps only to the Constitution of the USSR is the Fundamental Principles of Labor Legislation of the USSR and the Union Republics. This section of the study will be devoted almost entirely to an analysis of the relevant provisions of these Fundamental Principles.

> Under art. 14, para. (t) of the USSR Constitution the jurisdiction of the Soviet federal government extends to the definition of the fundamental principles of labor legislation. These fundamental principles serve as a mandatory guideline which the respective union republics are required to internalize into their own union republican laws. Matters not covered by such union republican laws are directly regulated by the Fundamental Principles and in case of conflict between the Fundamental Principles and the union republican codes the Fundamental Principles takes precedence under the supremacy clauses of the USSR Constitution – arts. 14, para. (d); art. 20; art. 69.

These Fundamental Principles establish in the preambular provisions the principles of Soviet labor law. In a concluding paragraph the preamble to these Fundamental Principles states: '[I]n accordance with the USSR Constitution citizens are guaranteed equality in the sphere of work, irrespective of nationality and race. Women in the USSR are granted equal rights with men with regard to work, wages, rest and social security. The working rights of citizens are guaranteed by law. The protection of these rights is carried out both by state organs as well as by trade unions and other social organizations'.

Art. 2 enumerates the following avenues in which the right to work in the USSR are concretely realized: the right to guaranteed wages commensurate with the quality and quantity of one's work, the right to rest and leisure in accordance with the law which establishes working hours and regulates workers' annual vacations, the right to work under healthy and safe conditions, the right to receive free professional and vocational training, the right to freely choose one's profession, the right to unite in trade unions, the right to participate in the management of the enterprise, the right to social security payments as well as old age pension. These rights are complemented by the following reciprocal obligations: the duty to observe labor discipline, the duty to conscientiously handle or use state property, the duty to work according to those labor norms established by the state.

These rights and obligations constitute two sides of the same coin and there is no doubting the fact that these rights are conferred upon the citizens in reasonable expectation that each recipient of such right agree to carry out the attendant duties. Under the Soviet system of justice there are no rights without obligations and in most instances certain rights are only a compensation for an obligation well performed. Since the Soviet Constitution provides that 'he who does not work neither shall he eat' (art. 12) the analogy extends also to the following balancing of rights and obligations: he who does not work, neither shall he rest; he who does not work, neither shall he receive free professional, technical and vocational education. The right to receive free education implies the duty to use that education to the benefit of society that made such free education possible. Anything short of this would be tantamount to unjust enrichment on the part of the citizen who receives free education but refuses to work for the state. Such a behavior is offensive to the socialist sense of social justice.

Art. 5 of the Fundamental Principles provides that any work agreement (entered into by the worker and his employer under chapters 2 and 3 of these Fundamental Principles) which imposes work conditions on workers other than those provided in these principles, is illegal and invalid. Under art. 9 any unjustified refusal to hire any worker is a violation of the law because under the USSR Constitution '. . . any direct or indirect limitations on these rights or the imposition of any direct or indirect preferential hiring practices based on sex, race, nationality or religious belief is prohibited.'

Whereas art. 21 establishes a 41-hour week as the normal working time for all workers, art. 22 establishes a different regime for minors and other special categories of workers: for those workers between the age of 16-18, no more than 36-hour week; for persons between 15-16, no more than 24-hour week; for those persons engaged in work under unhealthy conditions, no more than 36-hour week. In addition to these exceptions, Soviet statutes also establish separate working hours for certain other categories of workers – school teachers, medical doctors, etc. Every worker is entitled to rest on those public holidays established by state law which art. 31 enumerates. In addition to these public holidays each worker is entitled (under art. 32) to an annual paid vacation which may not be denied him or substituted by any form of payment.[43]

On the question of workers' wages art. 36 stipulates that 'work in the USSR is compensated according to its quantity and quality, but absolutely without consideration for sex, age, race or national origin.' This means that no one may receive less compensation than that which is established by law.[44] Chapters 8 and 9 of the Fundamental Principles are devoted to a detailed regulation of the labor of women and minors – the two categories of Soviet workers that are generally given special treatment under Soviet labor law. Most of the provisions of Chapter 8 not only reassert the equality of women with their male counterparts, but also create special favor for women. These preferential favors conferred on women are justified on the grounds of women's physical weakness and maternal functions.[45] Art. 68 illegalizes the employment of women's labor in heavy-duty jobs as well as in jobs which pose health hazards, or in any undergrounds jobs (except if the latter does not involve actual physical work). Art. 69 prohibits the employment of women during night shifts (which the law defines as any time between 10 p.m. and 6 a.m.) 'except in those areas of national economy where such employment [of women's labor] is an extreme necessity and is therefore permitted as a temporary measure.' Upon certification by a medical doctor (as to the fact of their pregnancy) pregnant women shall be transferred to a lighter job with retention of their medium wage for their original job (art. 70).

Art. 71 grants to expectant mothers ante-natal leave of 56 calendar days and a post-natal leave of 56 calendar days and the retention of her right to return to her job after the childbirth. During these 112 calendar days she shall be paid from state social security funds.[46]

If she decides to return to work upon the completion or her regular maternity leave art. 72 provides that she be granted extra time off from work (during her working hours) to enable her to feed her child. Such extra break shall be given her no less than every 3 hours and shall not be less than 30 minutes each time. This privilege shall continue until her child attains the age of one. In a most categorical language art. 73 provides that any refusal to hire or rehire or any attempts to demote, fire or reduce the pay of any worker on the grounds of her pregnancy or out of consideration of time she spends on feeding her less-than-one-year-old child would be illegal. Firing will be permissible, as in all other cases, in those instances when the the enterprise is closing down completely. But even then the administration of the enterprise that is winding up is under an obligation to provide another job for all such displaced workers. All these benevolent provisions of the Fundamental Principles tend to make the Soviet woman more equal than her male counterpart. These preferential treatments of the Soviet women however do not violate the equality doctrine under Soviet labor law. The principle of equality under Soviet labor law, just like in the other areas of Soviet law, means that no one shall enjoy less rights or be bound by less duties on the grounds of sex, race, religious belief or national origin. The law may confer more than the minimum rights on certain individuals on the basis of sex and age. By the same token the law may demand less than normal duties from these persons.[47] Thanks to these shield laws the Soviet woman today rubs shoulders with her male counterparts almost in all spheres of the national economy. In some areas, in fact, women outnumber men: of all persons engaged in health services in the Soviet Union about 90% are women and about 70% of those engaged in education are women whereas only 38% of scientific workers in the USSR are women.[48]

Chapter 9 of the Fundamental Principles extends certain privileges and protection to infant workers in the USSR: under art. 74 no persons under the age of 16 may be employed, but 'in exceptional situations, in agreement with the factory committee of the trade union organization, persons who have attained the age of 15 may be employed.' Even then, persons who are less than 18 years of age will not be employed in heavy-duty jobs, or in jobs with health of safety hazards or in underground jobs. No person below the age of 18 shall be employed except upon a preliminary medical examination and all such persons shall be required to file similar annual medical report with the employer until they attain the age of 18 (art. 76). By this provision Soviet law shows concern for the health of its youth.

Under art. 77 even though persons below the age of 18 are required to work less hours per day (as compared to their adult counterparts) they shall receive the same full wages that are paid to adult workers performing the same job. In other words, a minor who works just 36 hours per week (if he is between 16-18) or merely 24 hours per week (if he is between 15-16) receives the same wage as an adult working 41 hours a week on the same job. Art. 78 bars the employment of minors in night shifts, in overtime work or during public holidays; persons below the age of 18 shall take their annual vacation during the summer months or, if they so request, at any other time of the year; art. 82, in addition to the regular guarantees against arbitrary firing of workers by employers, grants extra protection to those workers who have not attained the age of 18 – they may not be fired except with the express approval of the state regional commission on youth affairs.

Generally, arts. 83-85 grant to all Soviet workers the privilege of being able to combine work with study – among the many privileges the Soviet worker has in this regard is the ability to apply for an unpaid leave from work in order to prepare for college entrance exams or for semester exams while studying in a college or university.

Since the Soviet trade union organization plays a very significant role in the enforcement of Soviet labor legislation the right of Soviet workers to join trade union organizations becomes a very fundamental one.[49] He may not be forced into membership of the trade union. He may not be denied employment for failure to be a trade union member. This right is granted under art. 95 of the Fundamental Principles of Labor Legislation of the USSR and the Union Republics. In an effort to re-affirm the independence of the trade union organizations from state interference art. 95 stipulates that 'these trade unions operate on the basis of their own statutes and are not subject to registration with any state agency.' However, any impression created by art. 95 as to the actual independence of Soviet trade unions from government or communist party supervision is a fallacious one.[50]

An analysis of the rights of Soviet trade unions under art. 96 shows that the trade union organization is a de facto enforcement agency of the Soviet government. Among the rights of the trade unions enumerated in art. 96 are: the right to participate in the adoption and implementation of state economic development plans, the authority to act as a mechanism for involving workers in the management process. The Soviet trade union organization participates in the establishment of conditions of labor and wages, helps in the overall enforcement of labor legislation, caters for the housing needs of workers and their families, operates the state social security program as well as runs the state sanatoria, rest homes, cultural, educational, tourist and sporting camps throughout the USSR.

Speaking through the All-Union Central Council of Trade Unions – the central organ of the Soviet trade union – the Soviet trade union organizations have the right to propose legislation in the Supreme Soviet of the USSR. In paying tribute to the role of the trade union organization in the Soviet socio-economic system the 24th Congress of the CPSU had this to say:

> 'The trade unions are one of the key links in the general system of socialist democracy, in drawing the working people into the administration of the affairs of the state and society. They participate in solving many problems of economic development - from the drawing up of state plans to the management of each enterprise. They play an important role in the production and social work of the personnel of factories, building projects and offices. They help to inculcate a communist attitude to labor and social property, and work to satisfy the cultural and everyday requirements of the people and protect their health.'[51]

Under art. 97 of the Fundamental Principles of Labor Legislation every Soviet worker has a right to participate in the discussion and decision of questions connected with the improvement of productivity and to make suggestions for the solution of other industry-related problems.

Chapter 13 of the Fundamental Principles deals with state social insurance program and under art. 100 all workers are subject to compulsory state social insurance to be paid by the state. For this insurance no deductions whatsoever are made from the wage of the insured worker and its coverage includes: payments for temporary incapacity, maternity leave payments to women workers, old age pension as well as pension for permanent incapacity, loss of breadwinner or pension for long service (in the case of certain categories of workers). State social insurance also covers treatment in sanatoria and health resorts, services in profilactoria and rest homes as well as payments toward the upkeep of young pioneer camps and various other programs. In conclusion, art. 106 states that federal law, as well as union republican law (where the latter is not inconsistent with the former) may create special exceptions for those workers who work in extreme northern regions of the USSR or in those other regions where the working conditions are comparable to the harshness of the extreme north. Thus, this provision establishes climatic conditions as a third permissible ground upon which preferential treatment may be granted under contemporary Soviet labor law – the other two are sex and age. Preferential treatments on any other grounds are constitutionally suspect.

We include some observations about the right to strike, as misunderstandings of the Soviet legal position in this respect are pervasive. To the mind of the Soviet lawyer, the question of the right to strike is closely linked to the principle of equal treatment of workers. No distinctions are being made between a private and a public sector, or between vital and non-vital branches of the economy, or between those professions where national security considerations can be invoked for denying certain rights to workers and those where such considerations do not come into play. All workers are in an equal position, and this applies to their right to organize in trade unions, implied by the freedom of association under art. 126 of the USSR Constitution, as well as to their exercise of the right to work. As no specific regulations exist, one could say that in the Soviet Union the question of the right to strike is uniformly unregulated. We shall therefore briefly look into some of the questions one might raise in this regard.

> The questions generally asked are: can Soviet workers operating through the trade union organization go on strike; if his right to strike is guaranteed under law what legal limitations are placed on that right; if there is no such right are they any specific legislations banning strikes in the USSR. To the first question the answer is that no law specifically guarantees to the Soviet worker the right to strike against his employer. Soviet commentators have maintained that in order to truly speak of the need and subsequently of the right to strike one ought to look at the background economic situation: in an economic system where the worker himself is a co-partner in the ownership of the means of production and distribution, to strike would be self-defeating. He would be striking against himself. In order for any strikes to be justifiable there ought to be a situation of class antagonism between the striking workers and the employers. In the Soviet Union the Soviet Government, which is the single largest employer in the Soviet Union, is a government of all the people and has no conflicting class interest opposed to those of the workers. The unity of purpose between the Soviet Government, the Communist Party, and the trade union organizations and the Soviet workers precludes any social or economic needs for labor strikes.
>
> To provide a legal right to strike under these circumstances will be an empty gesture because '[t]hat for which workers in the capitalist countries are required to fight [and strikes are only one form of workers' fight with

the employer] has long become a reality for the Soviet worker as well as for the workers in other socialist countries.'[52] The need to strike necessarily precedes the right to strike and in the Soviet Union there is no such need.

Furthermore, Chapter 12 of the Fundamental Principles of Labor Legislation of the USSR and the Union Republics enumerates the rights of the Soviet trade union organizations. The enumeration does not include the right to organize a disruption of the production process at a Soviet enterprise. Art. 3, para. (g) of the Charter of USSR Trade Unions makes it a duty of all trade union members 'to strictly observe state and labor discipline, to put to full and rational use all working hours for the purpose of raising the quality and quantity of productivity and to fight with any violations of labor discipline' by other workers.[53] This provision creates in every Soviet worker the duty to help police the industrial and production process. This duty certainly precludes any resort to strike actions since such strikes would not be 'a full and rational use' of one's working time nor would it be an action aimed at improving the quality and quantity of productivity.

The resort to strike actions, therefore, would technically be tantamount to a violation of a duty to obey labor discipline both under the Constitution of the USSR, the Fundamental Principles of Labor Legislation of the USSR and the Union Republics as well as under the Statute of Trade Union Organizations. Strike actions in the USSR would constitute a crime under art. 190-3 of the Criminal Code of RSFSR - in short, not only is the right to go on strike not constitutionally protected, there is a legal as well as a moral duty not to strike.

C. Education Law in the USSR: Equal Access of all Citizens to Free Education

Art. 121 of the USSR Constitution grants to all Soviet citizens the right to receive free education at all levels of the education ladder. In a country where almost all able-bodied citizens are receiving one form of education or the other the right to free education occupies a central place in the social, economic and political life of the society. To be denied the right to free education in the Soviet Union is to be made a second class citizen. To stop this from happening the Soviet Union recently adopted a comprehensive statute – The Fundamental Principles of the USSR and the Union Republics on Popular Education[54] – to regulate all the intricate aspects of this fundamental right. Without attempting to discuss all the provisions of this important statute this portion of our study merely seeks to draw attention to those provisions dealing with the equal treatment of all citizens in the sphere of popular education.

Art. 3 proclaims the right of all citizens to receive free education at all levels of the Soviet educational system as well as the duty of all citizens to go through, at least, the compulsory primary education. Among the fundamental principles governing Soviet popular education are, under art. 4: 'the equality of all citizens of the USSR to receive education irrespective of racial or national origins, sex, religious belief, property or social status', the right to receive education in one's native language or in the language of any other Soviet nationality, the unity of educational and communist upbringing, the foundation of Soviet education on humanistic and high moral standards, co-education of both sexes and the exclusion of all religious elements from popular education. Art. 20 states that 'pupils in high schools are given the opportunity to receive their education in their own native tongue or in the language of another Soviet nationality.' Parents or legal guardians have a right to choose for their children a school where the language of their choice is used. In addition to the language in which lessons are taught in that school pupils may elect to study another language of one of the Soviet nationalities. This provision is no doubt intended to guarantee the equality of all the national languages in the USSR. This writer's experience in the Soviet Union is that the rule promulgated in art. 20 is not always given effect in practice: a Russian child resident in any other Union Republic than RSFSR can easily find a school where the language used is Russian. This is so thanks to the progressive 'russification' of the entire USSR. But a Georgian kid or a young Kazakh who happens to reside in Moscow or Leningrad or, in fact, in any central portions of the Russian Federation (RSFSR) can hardly count on finding a school of his choice where his native language is used. To this extent the granting of Soviet pupils the right to freely choose the language in which they may be educated is a farce.

Art. 42 grants to all Soviet citizens who have completed high school, irrespective of race, sex, nationality, religious belief, social or property status or party membership 'the right to be admitted to a college or university, in accordance with the rules established by the Ministry of Higher and Specialized Education in the USSR.'

> As a rule admission to Soviet colleges and universities is based on an entrance examination in which applicants with better high school background and who are invariably from urban areas (as opposed to those from rural areas) often perform better. This means that the high school graduate from a rural area may never get to some of the best Soviet colleges unless under a special quota system. The Moscow University, the best university in the Soviet Union today, has a preparatory school from which its freshman class is almost invariably recruited. The standards of admission are very high and for any student from the rural area to get into this university he/she must rely on some form of preferential admissions policy.

Art. 46 in a most detailed fashion enumerates the rights of Soviet students to include the following: the right to free use of laboratories, reading rooms, library services, gymnasiums and other education and recreational facilities of the college or university, the right to receive monthly stipends, free residence in dormitories and other halls of residence operated specially for students, free medical treatment, free or substantially subsidized use of all means of public transportation (not including taxis) throughout the USSR, the right to combine work and study without having to give up one's job, the right to a guaranteed job upon completion of one's education (such a job to conform to one's qualification and training), the right to participate (through membership in the various social organizations) in the decision-making process connected with the social, ideological and disciplinary aspects of the internal life of the college or university.

Soviet students do not have the right, per se, to participate in curriculum planning or in the hiring or firing of faculty members. These are matters left exclusively in the hands of the college administration working in close collaboration with the Communist Party organization. The decision to hire or fire a faculty member should not be made 'from below', the Soviets would argue.

To compensate for these rights art. 47 imposes the following duties on the Soviet college or university student: he has a duty to systematically and conscientiously immerse himself in the acquisition of knowledge and practical know-how; he has a duty to attend all classes and to complete all his class assignments as contemplated by the school curriculum. To increase the level of his ideological and cultural education, to participate in a socially-useful work, to respect all internal rules of educational discipline, to obey orders before complaining about them. 'All students must be disciplined and organized, must respect the rules of socialist society, must protect and strengthen socialist property, must show an uncompromising attitude toward any anti-communist manifestation [by anyone in his presence] and must participate in the social life of the group.'

As in many other instances where Soviet law confers rights on its citizens the rights granted under this statute are not intended to be used to the detriment of the interests of the Soviet society. The right to free education carries with it the implied duty to use the knowledge so required to help the state. This obligation includes the duty to stay in the USSR and work for the state or cooperative organizations. The right of the individual Soviet citizen to emigrate to another country after receiving free education in the USSR is subordinate to the interest which the state and the society at large have in her personal services. Current Soviet legislation requires that in order for any citizen to secure a release from this superior duty to serve the state, he has to pay back the state the approximate amount expended on him by the state.[55] The actual amount of this compensatory payment varies not only with the level of education received by the individual who so wishes 'to abandon his duty', but also with the quality of such education.[56] The quality of this education depends upon the location of the school (in the Soviet Union this means that the nearer the school is located to Moscow or to the various state capitals the better the quality of education received by the students), as well as upon intangible factors which go to make up a 'good school'.

D. Equal Protection under Soviet Family Law: Rights and Duties of the Members of a Soviet Family

The Soviet family is a sacred institution. Since the family is the most intimate union of any two given citizens the law is designed to grant maximum protection to this union to the extent to which this is compatible with state interest. Under art. 14, para. (w) of the USSR Constitution the jurisdiction of the federal government covers the 'definition of the fundamentals of legislation on marriage and the family.' Under such powers the USSR Supreme Soviet on June 27, 1968 adopted a set of Fundamental Principles of the USSR and the Union Republics on Marriage and the Family.[57] Without attempting to analyze all the provisions of these Fundamental Principles this portion of our study will only discuss those sections of the Act which relate to the rights and duties of members of the Soviet family.

Art. 3 states that in family relations man and woman have equal personal and property rights. This 'equality of rights in the family is founded upon those provisions of the USSR Constitution which grant equal rights to men and women in all spheres of state, socio-political, economic and cultural life of the country.' No direct or indirect limitation on the rights of any citizen to establish a family shall be predicated upon race, nationality or religious belief (art. 4).[58]

Art. 9 stipulates that the rights and duties of spouses arise only out of marriage that is properly registered with the state organ charged with the registration of civil acts. Since marriage is a consensual act art. 10 provides that the mutual consent of both spouses is a prerequisite to their marriage. No spouse shall be given into marriage (either by the parents or by the guardians) without his/her consent. Among the many individual rights which the spouses equally share under art. 11 are: the right to freely choose a second name upon marriage; each spouse is free to decide upon a job, profession, or place of residence. This in effect means that a husband may not stop his wife from working in any job of her choice or from practising any profession for which she was trained nor can he require her to reside in the same plase as he does. The mere act of marriage does not deny the wife of her basic right under the Constitution – the right to freely choose her place of residence.

Cohabitation is an essential element of any family relationship and this free choice of a place of residence granted to the spouses is only designed to emphasize the equality of the spouses. They have to agree to a common home or face the danger of a broken marriage.[59]

It is not clear from the present law whether they have equal rights when it comes to deciding whether or not the wife should undergo an abortion. The liberalized Soviet abortion statute grants to the woman the freedom to decide the issues of motherhood herself.[60] Thus, the present law permits abortion to be performed, on demand by the woman upon consultation with her physician,[61] by a medical doctor in a hospital.

In the same vein the principle of equality of the spouses means that the consent of the wife is a prerequisite to any sexual act between husband and wife. A Soviet wife does not abandon her rights to give or deny consent to sexual relationship by the mere fact of her entry into marriage. If she refuses to give such consent the husband may not legally compel it. Consistent denial of such consent by a married woman over a long period of time may constitute a ground for divorce, however (under art. 14 of the Fundamental Principles).

Art. 12 of the Fundamental Principles speaks of the property rights of the spouses: any property belonging to a spouse before marriage as well as any property received by him or her during marriage (either through gift or inheritance) remains his or her personal property; any property acquired by the spouses jointly or separately during marriage remains the common property of the family, i.e., community property. With regard to this community property each spouse has equal right to its ownership, use or disposition. Should the need arise to devide such property each spouse shall receive equal share even in those circumstances where one of the spouses was the sole breadwinner and the other spouse merely attended to domestic work and just took care of the children.

Under art. 13 both spouses are under an obligation to support each other. Failure to grant such material support to the spouse in need (the spouse in need might be either the woman or the man) might give the other spouse the right to compel such support in a court action. It is important to note here that art. 13 does not grant the right to be supported only to the wife. The provision does not relate the notion of breadwinner to masculinity.

The divorce clause (art. 14) provides that, inter alia, any spouse or both spouses may file for divorce in the course of the marriage.[62] Upon such petition for divorce the court shall first attempt to reconcile the parties[63] but once convinced that the marriage has irretrievably broken down it shall proceed to grant a divorce. In granting the divorce the court shall decree such measures that are aimed at protecting the interests of the children as well as take care of the interests of the spouse that is in need of material support. If however the spouses do not have any infant children their mutual agreement to petition for divorce will be enough to grant them one in an administrative proceeding before the organ of civil registration. Such administrative divorce shall take effect three months after it was granted by the

Divorce Registry. Art. 14, therefore, in its pertinent provisions, grants full equality to the spouses even in divorce proceedings.

Art. 18 establishes the equal rights and duties of parents toward their children: parents shall bring up their children in a spirit of communist morality; both parents shall show concern for the physical wellbeing of the child and shall see to it that the child receives the proper training and education that would prepare him for a socially useful employment. Both parents have an equal duty to maintain their infant children and to render material help to those adult children who, due to physical incapacity, are unable to provide for themselves. It is the joint duty of the parents to protect the interests of their children, and in fact, parents may not exercise their parental authority against the interests of these children. Parents have a delegated authority from the state – the pater familias – to take good care of the interests of these state children and not to harm them. As if to reaffirm the equality of the spouses in this regard art. 18, para. 7 states: 'Parents enjoy equal rights and bear equal responsibility in regard to their children, even after they have been divorced.' Since parental rights may not be exercised either against the interests of the child or against the interests of the society at large, any abuse of these rights may result in their being taken away.

A petition to deny parental rights to both or one of the parents may be instituted by any state or social organization, by one of the spouses or by the custodian, or by the procurator.[64] What this process reaffirms is the concept according to which there are no rights without attendant duties and that the failure to perform these duties will invariably lead to a denial of the rights forthwith.

Still in an effort to support the legal equality of the spouses in a marriage, the Fundamental Principles reject the discriminatory notion according to which citizenship of the husband determines the subsequent citizenship of the wife. If both spouses are equal both should be able to retain their citizenship status even after marriage unless one of the spouses takes special steps to conform his/her citizenship with that of the other spouse. To require that the wife automatically loses her citizenship and picks up the citizenship of her husband is an invidious discrimination based on the sex of the spouses. Accordingly, art. 31 of the Fundamental Principles stipulates that marriage between Soviet and foreign citizens in the USSR is regulated on equal basis – viz., 'The entry into marriage by a Soviet citizen with a citizen of another country does not entail the change in the citizenship status.'

If a child is born to parents of different citizenships but one of whom is a Soviet citizen the child is considered a Soviet citizen if at the time of the birth of the child at least one of the parents (this could be either the father or the mother) was resident in the USSR. If however both parents resided outside the territory of the USSR the citizenship of the child shall be decided by mutual agreement of the parents.

The conclusion to be drawn from these provisions is that: the Soviet husband or the Soviet wife is still the same full-fledged citizen that he or she was before the marriage; marriage per se does not operate the erosion of the fundamental rights granted to all Soviet citizens and these include the right to a free choice of profession or place of residence, the right to join any social or cultural organizations. Once the husband and wife decide to form a family union they shall be equal partners to that association: this applies to their property rights, rights to bring up their children jointly, the right and duty to support each other, the duty to support their infant children, and if necessary, their adult children. Any agreement by spouses to deny any spouse any of the above rights is against public policy and therefore void ab initio. Similarly, none of these rights shall be adbridged, denied or suspended on the basis of race, nationality or creed. Legal guarantees of the rights granted under Soviet family law can be found in other branches of the law particularly in criminal and civil law.[65]

E. Equal Protection under Soviet Civil Law: Rights and Duties of Soviet Citizens under Soviet Private Law

In the Soviet legal system the traditional division of laws into public and private is often disregarded. No law, it is contended, can afford to be exclusively private in the sense that the state has no legitimate interest to intervene in the transactions between private individuals. Even private contracts in the Soviet Union have sufficient public policy implications as to justify state intervention if and when appropriate. In short, in the USSR 'all law is public law.'[66] If however by private law one means that branch or department of law which, in contradistinction to public law, is concerned with the definition, regulation and enforcement of rights in cases where both the person in whom the right inheres and the person upon the obligation is incident are private individuals, then the Soviet legal system has an approximate equivalent of private law even though it is not so designated. Most norms of Soviet private law are grouped into a department of Soviet law referred to as Civil Law (*grazhdanskoe pravo*). Soviet civil law is presently codified into a series of Union Republican Civil Codes but basic to all of these codes is the Fundamental Principles of Civil Legislation of the USSR and the Union Republics which was adopted by the USSR Supreme Soviet on December 8, 1961.[67]

This section of our study deals with those pertinent provisions of the 1961 Fundamental Principles dealing with the rights of Soviet citizens in the realm of private law. As one of its basic provisions the Preamble to the 1961 Act recognized the right of citizens to own personal property. 'Personal property is a derivative of socialist property and it serves the purpose of satisfying the needs of citizens. As the state advances toward communism [however] the personal demands of citizens will to a considerable extent be satisfied out of public funds' and thus the needs for individual property will tend to diminish. Under full communism there will be no need at all for individual property but until such time, it is the task of Soviet civil law to protect individual property rights (art. 1).

Art. 5 states that the 'private law rights [of citizens] are protected by law with the exception of those instances when such rights are exercised contrary to their designated purpose in a socialist society that is engaged in the construction of communism. In exercising their rights as well as in carrying out their duties citizens and organizations must observe the laws, respect the rules of a socialist society and the moral principles of a society that is building communism.' Art. 5 in effect means that under no circumstances may a right granted under these Fundamental Principles be used to frustrate a legitimate state purpose – the construction of communism. Any conflict between individual rights and the interest of the society will invariably be resolved in favor of the latter.

Art. 6 establishes those legal remedies which are available to individuals whose private law rights may have been violated: they may resort to a court of law or to a permanent court of arbitration or to an ad hoc arbitral tribunal to seek a declaratory judgment, restitution, injunctive relief, specific performance, damages or other types of remedies granted by law. Remedies, in specific cases, may also be sought either in a comrades' court, through the trade union organizations or other social organizations.

Art. 8 recognizes all citizens on equal basis as legal persons and provides 'that legal personality commences from the time of birth and terminates at death.' However, legal capacity is acquired only upon attainment of age of majority – 18 years. The law may concede partial legal capacity to persons who have not attained the age of majority. 'No person may be denied this legal personality or legal capacity except by law. Any act aimed at limiting such legal personality or capacity is invalid.' In short, all persons have equal rights under Soviet private law. This equality may not be abridged by any bilateral agreements between private citizens. The law and only the law may establish limitations on these rights.

The actual contents of this legal personality under art. 9 include the following: the right to own personal property, the right to use living quarters and other property, the right to inherit and will property, the right to freely choose one's profession and place of residence, the right to authorship of one's scientific, literary and artistic works, the right to one's invention as well as other property and individual rights compatible with law. Each of these rights is subsequently elaborated upon in the following sections of the Act: Section 2, for example, deals with the right to own personal property and provides, among other things, that the right of ownership of personal property includes the right to own, use and dispose of one's property as established by law (art. 19), that each individual may own as items of personal property the following objects which are only designed to satisfy his material or cultural needs – his income and savings, a dwelling house (or part thereof), items of domestic and personal convenience and comfort. Any item of personal property however may not be used to derive un-earned income. This provision further states that a citizen may own only one dwelling house. Should public interest so require the state may take over (requisition) any individually owned dwelling house at any time. On the other hand, if the individually owned house is not properly taken care of (the state establishes minimum standards which all dwelling houses must meet) the state may confiscate the house. The requisition or confiscation of individually owned property, however, is regulated by law.[68]

The owner of an individual dwelling house may enter into a contract with someone else to rent out a portion of the house under art. 56 of the Fundamental Principles. Rental payment, however, for such private lease may not exceed the tariff established by law (art. 52). It is not clear from the present statute whether an individual house owner is under an obligation to rent out any excess space in his dwelling house. One would surmise that there is such an unwritten obligation. For one thing, in the USSR, the law establishes the maximum amount of living space that an individual family may occupy (with few exceptions for certain categories of citizens – honored citizens, scientists, literary personalities, military personnel, etc. – whom the law considers as deserving more living space). This established norm would apply both to those living in state, cooperative or individual homes. If a family has more space than it can legally occupy in an individually owner house public policy would require such family to make that excess space available to the less fortunate citizens who do not own their own homes. Even if there is no law specifically requiring this, one would imagine that the rules of communist morality would so require. A good citizen should live and let live.

Chapter 4 of the Fundamental Principles deals with the right of authorship: any citizen is entitled to the right of authorship of his scientific, literary and artistic works. This right of authorship extends not only to published works but also to all such works which, even though not published, exist in any objective form that is capable of reproduction (this includes manuscripts, drawings, illustrations, public speeches, public performance, records, tape or other recordings, etc.). An acknowledged author of any work has a right, under art. 98, to publish, reproduce or circulate his work by all legally permissible methods under his own name, under a pseudonym or even anonymously. He also has a right to the inviolability of his works as well as a right to be compensated for any use of his work by other persons except in those instances where the law permits free use of such works. The amount of payment for use of an author's work is regulated by state law.[69]

Finally, art. 106 grants to the state the absolute right to buy the right of authorship from any individual authors. Here, as in many other instances, the interests of the state are superior to those of any individuals and public policy demands that any author should transfer to the state the right to any work in which the state might have a legitimate interest. The right of ownership of one's invention is discussed in arts. 107-116 and the provisions are analogous to those regarding the right of authorship as discussed above.

The right of citizens to inherit property is analyzed under Chapter 7. The right of citizens to inherit property either by operation of law or by a will is recognized under art. 118. He who inherits property is obligated to satisfy the obligations of the decedent to the extent of the actual value of the property so received (art. 120). As to the capacity of foreigners to inherit or will property, the applicable conflict of law principles are articulated under art. 127, except that under art. 128 any foreign law which violates Soviet public policy may not be applied in the USSR. In case of any conflicts between the rules articulated in these Fundamental Principles and other rules contained in an international agreement to which the USSR is a party, the latter shall prevail.

It should be re-emphasized that all the rights discussed above are to be accorded to all Soviet citizens, irrespective of sex, race, national origin or creed. The right of all Soviet citizens to own personal property is a fundamental one which may be subject only to those limitations imposed by law and justified under public policy. Not even the right of a citizen to authorship of his own work or invention is free from this legitimate state intervention.

So far we have examined the substantive equal protection provisions taken from these selected areas of Soviet law. These rights will be destroyed if not granted adequate protection under law. Legal sanctions for their violation would depend upon the nature of the particular right one is dealing with. For violations of any of these rights the sanctions might range from nullity, in the case of illegal contracts, to incarceration in the extreme case of criminal transgression. The legal guarantees of due process can be considered also as protections of the substantive equal protection provisions. For an overview of these legal guarantees we turn to the parts III and IV of this study.

III. *Substantive Legal Guarantees of Equal Protection under Soviet Law*

The creation by law of the rights and duties discussed in the foregoing paragraphs presupposes an underlying undertaking by the state to guarantee their performance by all persons concerned. Rights without adequate guarantees are an empty promise. In order to carry out this inherently sovereign duty the state establishes a set of legal sanctions which may attach to any specific violations of these rights or to non-performance of specific obligations established by law. Depending on the seriousness of the violations the sanctions might be criminal, civil or administrative. Besides, one violation may involve more than one sanction. For example, a pregnant woman who is illegally dismissed from her job may be reinstated by a court order, may be paid her due wages for the involuntary leave of absence and on top of that the official responsible for violating her right to work may indemnify the state for the payments to the woman and possible criminal charges for the same act. Similarly, a person who suffers civil damage resulting from a criminal action may be entitled to civil remedies on the one hand while on the other hand the person who caused the damage may face criminal charges. Since the most serious of these legal sanctions is the criminal sanction, we shall begin this analysis with an examination of those substantive legal guarantees under Soviet criminal law.

A. Legal Guarantees under Substantive Soviet Criminal Law

The general purpose of Soviet criminal law is, according to Art. 1 of the 1958 Fundamental Principles of Criminal Legislation of the USSR and the Union Republics,[70] 'to protect the Soviet social and state structure, socialist property, the person and the rights of citizens as well as the entire socialist legal order from criminal transgressions. In order to accomplish this task the criminal law of the USSR and of the Union Republics defines which socially dangerous acts constitute a crime and establishes penalty which is to be applied to persons who commit crimes.' The Fundamental Principles leave to the various criminal codes of the Union Republics the task of establishing the different categories of crime. A typical union-republican criminal code is that of RSFSR which was adopted in 1960[70] and it is to that code that we shall now refer in order to articulate those provisions which specifically deal with guarantees against criminal transgressions of the civil and political rights of Soviet citizens.

Chapter 4 of the Code deals with crimes against the political and labor rights of citizens. Under art. 132 the obstruction, through force, deception, threat, or bribery of the exercise by a USSR citizen of the right to vote shall be punished by deprivation of freedom for a term not exceeding one year.

Art. 134 also stipulates that the obstruction of a woman from participating in state, social or cultural activity, thereby substantially violating the women's equal rights, if combined with force or threat of force is a crime. Art. 135 criminalizes the violation of the secrecy of citizen's correspondences. Similarly, art. 136 imposes a possible sentence of up to one year imprisonment for any illegal search, illegal eviction or other illegal actions violating the inviolability of citizen's dwelling space. Under art. 138 the illegal dismissal of a working person from work for personal motives or the failure to execute the decision of a court concerning his reinstatement to work or any other intentional substantial violation of labor legislation if committed by an official of a state or social enterprise or institution is a crime. The refusal to employ or the dismissal from work of a woman because of her pregnancy as well as the refusal to employ or the dismissal from work of a mother who is nursing a child is a crime under art. 139. Any violation of the right of authorship or right of invention of any citizen is punishable under art. 141. The right of citizens to freely practise their religion is protected under art. 143 which makes it a crime to obstruct the performance of religious rite by law-abiding citizens.

Chapter 5 of the Criminal Code deals with crimes against personal ownership of citizens. Since the right to own individual property is guaranteed under the USSR Constitution, any infringement upon that right is criminalized under art. 144 (theft), 145 (open stealing of personal property), 146 (assault with intent to rob), 147 (swindling), 148 (extortion), 149 (intentional destruction or damaging of personal property of citizens), and 150 (negligent destruction or damaging of personal property of citizens).

Finally, chapter 11 deals with crimes constituting survival of local customs. Since the right of citizens to marry and raise a family is implicitly recognized under the Fundamental Principles of the USSR and the Union Republics on Marriage and Family as a fundamental one and since marriage is a consensual affair into which no man or woman should be coerced, to compel a woman or a man to enter into marriage or, on the reverse, to obstruct his or her entry into such marriage is a crime under art. 233 of the RSFSR Criminal Code. All in all Soviet criminal law, through an extensive network of criminal sanctions, establishes a legal guarantee for most of the fundamental rights and privileges of Soviet citizens discussed in Part I of this study.

B. Legal Guarantees under Soviet Civil Law

For those violations of individual rights for which the law deems criminal sanctions inappropriate or insufficient other guarantees have been established – these include, inter alia, civil sanctions. Depending on the nature of the specific violation the 1961 Fundamental Principles of Civil

Legislation of the USSR and the Union Republics in art. 6 establishes the following legal remedies: declaratory judgment (recognizing the right so denied or violated); restoration (of the status quo before the transgression occurred); specific performance; injunction (against a contemplated violation of such right); imposition of payment for damages; other types of compensatory payments or any other remedies granted by law. For defamation art. 7 establishes retraction as a possible remedy. A special form of civil sanction under art. 14 is nullity which is designed to negate ab initio any illegal private contracts. Like in the case of criminal sanctions, civil sanctions are intended to guarantee the rights of Soviet citizens. For every civil wrong there is a civil remedy.

C. Legal Guarantees under Soviet Administrative Law

Soviet administrative law is one of the many branches of Soviet public law which still lacks any clear-cut definition. It is also one of the least systematized. The guarantees provided by Soviet administrative law against violations of individual rights are not only nebulous but often-times not vigorously enforced. They therefore tend to be less reliable as legal guarantees. The probable reason for this is that the offender, in most cases, is not an individual citizen as in the case of criminal and civil violations, but state or social agencies.[71] One recurrent form of violation of individual freedom by an administrative agency is the so-called administrative arrest. The incessant abuse of this power by Soviet agencies has been a cause for concern to many Soviet commentators.[72]

IV. *Due Process Guarantees of Equal Rights under Soviet Law*

Soviet criminal, civil, and administrative procedure laws guarantee to all parties due process in these respective actions. Thus, any person whose rights have been criminally violated is entitled to due process under this code. Art. 3 makes it the obligation of a court, the procurator, the investigator or the state agency of inquiry, within the limits of their competence, to institute a criminal case in every instance in which indicia of a crime are disclosed and to take all measures provided by law for ascertaining the occurrence of the crime and the persons guilty of committing it, and for punishing them. Other due process guarantees under the RSFSR Code of Criminal Procedure are: art. 11 (which states that no one may be subjected to arrest except by decree of a court or with the sanction of a procurator); art. 12 (which guarantees the inviolability of a citizen's dwelling space and the secrecy of his correspondences); art. 13 (which states that 'justice in criminal cases shall be administered only by courts' and that 'no one may be deemed guilty of committing a crime or subjected to criminal punishment except by judgment of a court'); art. 15 (establishing the right of a criminal defendant to be tried only by a court made up of judges and people's assessors duly elected in accordance with the law); art. 17 (the right to be provided with adequate translation in cases where the judicial proceedings are conducted in a language of which the defendant does not have command); arts. 19 and 47 (the rights of a criminal defendant to a defense counsel). Other rights of the criminal defendant and of other parties in the proceedings are enumerated in arts. 46-51.

Similar due process rights are granted to the civil defendants and other parties to a civil proceeding in the following provisions of the 1964 RSFSR Code of Civil Procedure: art. 3 (the right to apply to a court for protection); art. 5 (which states that 'Justice in civil cases is administered solely by a court based on the principle of equality before the court and before the law of all citizens irrespective of their social, economic and official status, their race or nationality or religious denomination'); art. 6 (the right to go before a court in which judges and people's assessors are sitting); art. 8 (the right to be provided with adequate translation at the proceeding); art. 9 (the right to a public trial); etc.[73]

Two important institutions charged with the guarantee of these due process rights are the court and the procuracy.[74] The Statute on Procuracy Supervision in the USSR[75] establishes the Procuracy of the USSR as the organ charged with supervising the enforcement of all laws in the USSR. Art. 2 of that Statute states that 'The Procurator General of the USSR and procurators subordinate to him shall be obliged to watch over proper and uniform application of the laws of the USSR and of the Union and Autonomous Republics, notwithstanding any local differences and despite any local influences.'

The Procuracy shall protect from any infringements 'the political, labor, housing, and other personnel and property rights and legally protected interests of citizens of the USSR guaranteed by the Constitution of the USSR and by the Constitutions of Union and Autonomous Republics' (art. 2, para. 2). Art. 23, para. 5 grants the procurator the authority to 'lodge protests, in the procedure established by law, against illegal or unjustified judgments, decisions, rulings, or decrees of judicial agencies,' the authority 'to exercise supervision over execution of judgments of a court' (art. 2, para. 7) and a very wide power of subpoena under art. 24. In short, if the procuracy notices any violations of the law by any agency of the government or by any social or cooperative organization it shall immediately take actions to restore the rights so violated and to take actions, where appropriate, to bring to justice those persons who violated the law. Endowed with these enormous powers the procuracy today is the most effective guarantor of the rights of all citizens in the USSR.

The Statute of the Supreme Court of the USSR[76] establishes the USSR Supreme Court and charges it with 'supervision over the judicial activity of judicial agencies of the USSR, as well as of judicial agencies of Union Republics within the limits established by the present statute. The Supreme Court of the USSR shall verify the application of all-union legislation by union-republican judicial agencies, as well as the execution [by them] of degrees of the Plenum of the Supreme Court of the USSR.'

In addition to the guarantees provided by the Procuracy and the courts, Soviet citizens may resort to other methods for the protection of their rights. Among such methods is the possibility given to the citizen to lodge his complaint directly with the state or social organizations and demand immediate resolution of his grievances. Under art. 1 of a 1968 federal statute[77] the state, social or cooperative organization with which such citizen's complaints are lodged are under an obligation to receive them and resolve the issues as expeditiously as possible, assuming the substance of the complaint is within the jurisdiction of the agency in question. Under art. 11 of this statute citizens may also lodge their complaints with any of the Soviet newspapers or periodicals who in turn will turn over the complaints to the appropriate state, social or cooperative organization for immediate investigation of their substance and take action on their merits. The aggrieved citizen may take his complaint to any of the local offices of the organs of Peoples Control in the USSR,[78] or to the Comrade's Court. In all instances he is guaranteed a thorough investigation of his complaint and a speedy remedy if he is entitled to. Moreover the Soviet militia is certainly at his service to help him protect his rights. Art. 1 of the 1973 Police Code[79] specifically calls upon the Soviet militia to stand in the defense of the rights and legal interests of all citizens.

Among the many other Soviet statutes which guarantee the equality of all Soviet citizens before the law are: the Fundamental Principles of Court Procedure in the USSR, the Union and Autonomous Republics,[80] art. 5 of which proclaims the equality of all citizens before the law and in a court of law irrespective of their social, property or official status, nationality, race or religious belief; the Fundamental Principles of Civil Procedure in the USSR and the Union Republics,[81] which reiterates the equality of all parties in a civil litigation irrespective of social, property or official position, national or racial considerations or religious belief (art. 7); the Fundamental Principles of Criminal Procedure in the USSR and the Union Republics[82] which in art. 3 proscribes any form of unequal treatment of parties in a criminal litigation.

A combination of all these procedural and substantive guarantees would tend to maximize the possibility that a Soviet citizen would realize the rights granted him both under the Constitution of the USSR and under those laws adopted in pursuance of the Constitution. In this sense equal protection and due process constitute two sides of the same coin – individual liberty under Soviet constitutional system.

Conclusions

Equality of all citizens before the law has always been a cornerstone of Soviet socialist law. This equality, however, is denied to enemies of the state against whom the law is directed in the first place. If law is only a concentrated form of politics, then socialist law is aimed against those class enemies who seek to destroy socialism and its fundamentals. Those who seek to destroy the Soviet state shall neither seek nor expect to receive equal protection under the law. With the completion of the physical liquidation of these enemies of the state and with the establishment af 'a state of all the people' in the Soviet Union Soviet law now guarantees to all citizens, irrespective of race, color, sex, social or property status, national origins, religious belief or party membership equal treatment under the law.

Equality of all before the law also means that all citizens shall equally obey the commands of the law. V. I. Lenin once demanded that 'all [citizens] shall sacredly obey the laws and commands of the State authority, and see to it that all other citizens do the same.'[83] Socialist legality should be enforced equally throughout the land. No one should be above the law. Speaking on the question of uniform enforcement of the law throughout Russia V. I. Lenin in a 1922 letter to the Politburo of the Central Committee of the Bolshevik Party stated: 'Legality cannot and must not be different for [the different regions of Russia] but rather must be uniform throughout the Russian Federation.'[84]

One Soviet commentator added: 'In the Soviet state, there must not be any privileged treatment [of certain individuals] before the law in the sense that the law is mandatory for some persons but not for others. No official, no matter the position occupied by him, has a right to violate the law. Any manifestations of disrespect for the law, its violation or circumvention will be vigorously prosecuted . . .'[85]

This does not mean, however, that the Soviet law maker, acting in his sovereign capacity may not create special privileges for certain underprivileged categories of its citizens, the provision of the Constitution notwithstanding. In order to properly speak of equality before the law all persons must operate from an equal platform. Equal status deserves equal treatment. But where certain persons, to start with, are unequally placed in the society (either because of a previous or current de facto inequality) they operate at a disadvantage vis-a-vis other citizens. To remedy this obvious disparity the law creates certain compensatory privileges for members of underprivileged groups. By reserving special places for members of the minority ethnic national groups in Soviet institutions of higher education the Soviet Government seeks to achieve this balancing of educational opportunity among its citizens. The provision under art. 123 of the USSR Constitution that '. . . the establishment of any direct or indirect privileges for citizens on account of their race or nationality' does not apply to a legislatively created privilege in favor of disadvantaged ethnic minority groups, particularly so if such privileges are created by the central government.[86]

By the same reasoning, the law creates certain added privileges for women and minors in the areas of labor law. By granting the Soviet woman such things as paid maternity leave and time off from work in order to feed her child, the law merely seeks to give her a real chance to be equal with her male counterpart in the sphere of labor relations.

It should also be noted that when the law confers rights on the individual these rights in themselves do not constitute a license for him to subvert the interests of the state. Individual liberty in the Soviet Union is only a privilege which, if abused, may be taken away. In the words of a leading Soviet commentator: 'Marxism-Leninism sees real [individual] freedom not in man's isolation from society by his subjective rights, but his direct, active, day-to-day participation in the administration of the affairs of the state and society in deciding the destiny of the country and his people hence his own destiny with the aid of these rights.'[87] To be free is to be responsible and responsibility calls for self-restraint on the part of all free men. There is no such thing as absolute freedom, for freedom is only a cognitive necessity.

In conclusion, it should be said therefore that classifications are a necessary part of lawmaking and the equal protection doctrine does not of necessity require an end to all classifications based on the recognition of human differences. Equal protection under Soviet law forbids the use of race, sex, national origin, religious belief, social or property status, or party membership as the basis for legal classification but it permits and perhaps will continue to permit (until all men are placed equally in society) the Soviet lawmaker to classify on the basis of real differences in the life situations and characteristics of its citizens. As long as there exists a rational relationship between the classification and the objects of the statute in question Soviet public policy would not only permit, but even would compel such classification. A classification based on national origin, religious belief or sex, as long as it is designed to further a compelling state interest, would not be a violation of equal protection under contemporary Soviet law.

NOTES

1. Documents of the 24th Congress of CPSU (March 30-April 9, 1971). Published by Novosti Publishing House (Moscow, 1971) at p. 97.

2. Permissible exceptions to these rules may be made in the case of diplomatic personnel or those other foreigners who under a treaty arrangement enjoy extraterritorial privileges in the Soviet Union.

3. Documents of the 24th Congress of CPSU, supra note 1 at p. 99.

4. L. Voevodin, Konstitutsionnye Prava i Obiazannosti Sovetskikh Grazhdan (The Constitutional Rights and Duties of Soviet Citizens) II (Moscow, 1972). On the interlocking relationship between individual rights and the rights of society under Soviet law see generally: V. Chkhikvadze (ed.), Problemy Sovetskogo Sotsialisticheskogo Gosudarstva i Prava v Sovremmenyi Period (Problems of Soviet Socialist State and Law in the Contemporary Period) (1969); V. Chkhikvadze, Gosudarstvo, demokratiia i Zakonnost'-Leninskie idei i sovremennost' (The State, democracy and the rule of law - Lenin's ideas and contemporary times) (1967); V. Chkhikvadze, Lichnost' i gosudarstvo: vzaimnai otvetstvennost' (The individual and the State: Mutual Responsibility), I Soviet State and Law 22 (1972) [Soviet State and Law is hereafter cited as S.S.L.].

5. L. Voevodin, supra note 4 at 16, 17.

6. N. Aleksandrov, Pravo i Zakonnost' v period razvernutogo stroitel'stva komnunizma (Law and the Rule of Law in the period of comprehensive construction of communism) 225 (1961). See also, S. Kechekian, Pravootnosheniia v sotsialisticheskom obshchestve (Legal Relations in a socialist society) 57 (1958).

7. L. Voevodin, supra note 4 at 23.

8. L. Voevodin, supra note 4 at 34.

9. Iuridicheskii Spravochnik dlia naceleniia (Pocket Size Legal Encyclopedia for Members of the public) [Iuridicheskaia Literatura, (Law Publishers) Moscow 1968] at pp. 375-376.

10. L. Voevodin, supra note 4 at p. 35.

11. I. Voevodin, id. at p. 35.

12. See: L. Voevodin, id.; L. Voevodin, Razvitie svobodi lichnosti i osnoynykh prav sovetskikh grazhdan v period razvernutgo stroitel'stva kommunizma (Evolution of individual freedom and fundamental rights of Soviet citizens in the period of comprehensive construction of communism), I Vestnik M.G.U. - Seriia X. Pravo (1962) (I Moscow State University Review - Law Series No. 10, 1962); L. Voevodin, Teoreticheskie voprosy pravovogo polozheniia lichnosti v sovetskom gosudarstve (The theoretical questions over the legal status of the individual in a Soviet state), 2 S.S.L. (1963); L. Voevodin, Svoboda lichnosti i pravovoe polozhenie grazhdan v sovetskom obshchenarodnom gosudarstve (Individual Freedom and the Legal Status of citizens in the Soviet state of all the people) (Moscow, 1963).

13. A few Soviet constitutional lawyers disagree with the tripartite division of the rights and duties of Soviet citizens. The substance of their disagreement is discussed by professor Voevodin who openly takes issue with them. See L. Voevodin supra note 4 at pp. 251-257.

14. On labor discipline in the USSR see generally P. Vas'kov, Gosudarstvenaia ditsiplina v SSSR (State discipline in the USSR) (1960).

15. The component elements of this fundamental right to own personal property are defined in greater details in art. 25 of the Fundamental Principles of Civil Legislation of the USSR and the Union Republics and the legal guarantees of this right can be found in the respective provisions of Soviet criminal law. See respectively the sections below en Soviet Civil and Criminal Law.

16. The origins of the right to free education in the USSR are analyzed in: E. Pichugina, Prava na Obrazovanie v SSSR (The Right to Education in the USSR) (1957).

17. For details see the section below dealing with Soviet education law.

18. For details as to the constitutionality of such quota system see the section below on education law.

19. L. Voevodin, supra note 4 at p. 288.

20. See generally: A. Khomenok, Politicheskia Svobodi grazhdan SSSR (The political freedoms of Soviet citizens) (1963).

21. See generally: A. Brianskii, Poniatie obshchestvennoi organizatsii i soderzhanie prav grazhdan na obedinenie, (The concept of social organization and the content of the right of citizens to associate), 9 S.S.L. (1963).

22. Art. 3 of the 1967 Fundamental Law on Compulsory Military Service makes it a duty of all able-bodied, Soviet, adult, male citizens to serve in the armed forces of the USSR without regard to race, national origin, religious belief, educational status, place of residence, social or property status. See art. 3 of Zakon o vseobshchei voinskoi obiazannosti, (Act on compulsory military service) 42 VVS-SSSR (1967). This law makes no room for conscientious objectors nor does it grant special privileges to members of the Soviet intelligensia. The law also grants to appropriate Soviet military organs the right to enlist women with medical, veterinary or special technical training.

23. L. Voevodin, supra note 4 at 279.

24. Art. 200 of RSFSR Criminal Code defines arrogation as 'the unwarranted exercise in violation of the legally established order, of one's actual or supposed right, causing substantial harm to citizens or to state or social organizations ...' The message is clear - no man shall take the law into his own hands.

25. L. Voevodin, supra note 4 at p. 298.

26. See generally: Iu. Andreev and V. Strunnikov, Pravila sotsialisticheskogo obshchezhitiia (Rules of socialist communal life) (1961).

27. L. Voevodin, supra note 4 at p. 283.

28. For procedural safeguards against illegal search and seizure or illegal arrests see sections on Criminal and Administrative law below.

29. Fundamental Duties and Rights of the Soviet Militia in the Protection of Public Order and Fight Against Crime, adopted on June 8, 1973. 23 Vedemosti Verkhovnogo Soveta SSSR (1973) [News Bulletin of the Supreme Soviet of the USSR - hereafter cited as VVS-SSSR].

30. See Ustav Sviazi SSSR (USSR Postal Regulations), 10 Sbornik Postanovlenii SSSR (1971) [hereafter cited as SP-SSSR].

31. Generally on the question of freedom of conscience in the USSR, see F. Rudinskii, Svoboda sovesti v SSSR (Freedom of Conscience in the USSR)

(1961); Iu. Girman, V chem sushchnost' svobodi sovesti? (What does freedom of conscience consist of?) (1966).

32. Under a decree of January 23, 1918 [Ob otdelenii tserkvi ot qosudarstva i shkoli ot tserkvi (On the separation of church and state as well as school and church), 18 Sbornik Uzakonenii, RSFSR 263 (1918) [18 Collected Statutes of RSFSR 263 (1918)] the buildings and other property placed at the disposal of these religious groups belong to the state and are under the direct administration of the local councils from whom the groups may receive them under an agreement but free of all charges. These groups are responsible for the upkeep of such buildings in accordance with state law.

33. See V. Chkhikvadze (ed.) Entsiklopedicheskii Slovar' Pravovykh Znanii (Encyclopedia of Soviet Law) 90-91 (Moscow, 1965); F. Feldbrugge (ed.), 1 Encyclopedia of Soviet Law 108-111 (1974).

34. V. Shertsev, Sovetskoe Grazhdanstvo (Soviet Citizenship) 42 (Moscow, 1965).

35. Under art. 7, para. (a) of the 1938 citizenship law Soviet citizenship could be taken away by a decree of a court as a form of legal sanction. The adoption in 1958 of the Fundamental Principles of Criminal Legislation of the USSR and the Union Republics has put an end to judicial deprivation of citizenship status and now concentrates all such powers only and exclusively in the hands of the Presidium of the USSR Supreme Soviet.

36. Polozhenie o vyborakh v verkhovnogo soveta SSSR (Statute on elections to the Supreme Soviet of the USSR) adopted on January 9, 1950 (as amended), 2 VVS-SSSR (1950). The major provisions of this federal statute have been reaffirmed in the various other subordinate electoral statutes: Statutes on Elections to the Supreme Soviet of the Union and Autonomous Republics Statute on Elections to the local Soviets. These Statutes as well as the Constitution of the USSR and the various constitutions of the Union Republics and the Autonomous Republics constitute the primary sources of Soviet Electoral Law.

37. In the case of local councils the minimum age in order to qualify to be elected thereto is 18 years and for the Supreme Soviets of the Union Republics and Autonomous Republics the minimum age limit is 21 years.

38. The above statistics are given in: 25 Vedomosti Verkhornogo Soveta SSSR 467-471 (June 19, 1974).

39. Postanovlenie ob uchastii v vyborakh v verkhovnyi sovet SSSR lichnogo sostava sudov, nakhodiashchikhsia v den' vyborov v plavanii [Regulation on the participation in elections to the USSR Supreme Soviet by Members of the Crew of Soviet Vessels, Located in the High Seas on Election Day], Feb. 22, 1950. 1 Sbornik Zakanov SSSR [Collected Statutes of USSR] 1938-1967, 235 (1968).

40. Ukaz (Law) of March 19, 1966. 12 VVS-SSSR (1966).

41. 29 VVS-SSSR (1970).

42. The RSFSR Labor Code, for example, was adopted on Dec. 9, 1971 and went into force on April 1, 1972. See: Kodeks Zakonov o trude RSFSR (Labor Code of the RSFSR), Official Text issued by the Ministry of Justice of the RSFSR (Moscow, 1972).

43. Art. 33 established a minimum 2-week annual vacation for all categories of workers and a minimum of 1 month for workers who have not attained the

age of 18. Art. 34 establishes 'complementary vacation period' for certain categories of workers. During such annual vacation the Soviet worker receives half of his regular pay. He may however go on extra leave if he so desires but this shall be without pay (art. 35).

44. During the last 5-year economic plan the minimum wage for a Soviet worker was raised to 60 rubles per month. The 24th Congress of the Soviet Communist Party called for the increase of this minimum wage in the 9th 5-year plan period to 70 rubles per month. At the same time the medium wage for a Soviet worker during the current 5-year plan period rose to 146-149 rubles per month while the medium wage for a collective farm worker rose to about 98 rubles per month. Statistics are provided in L. Voevodin, supra note 4 at p. 268.

45. See: V. Tolkunova, Prava Zhenshchin na trud i ego garantii (The rights of women to work and their guarantees) (Moscow, 1968); A. Abramova, Okhrana truda zhenhchin (The protection of women labor) (Moscow, 1967); T. Chumakova, Okhrana prav materi i rebenka (The protection of the rights of the mother and child) (Minsk, 1967).

46. Under a 1973 decree of the Presidium of the USSR Supreme Soviet [adopted on August 10, 1973 and went into force on Dec. 1, 1973, 3 VVS-SSSR (1973)] the woman shall be paid her full salary during the entire period of her regular maternity leave, i.e., during the 112 days in case of a normal childbirth or 126 days in case of an abnormal or complicated childbirth.

47. An example of a law which imposes less duties on women on the basis of sex is the compulsory military service statute which exempts women from military service. It has never been contended that this exemption violates equal protection of all persons under the law.

48. See *Statistics on Woman and Children in the USSR* published by the State Statistical Publishers (Moscow, 1969) at pp. 62, 71.

49. As of 1971 available statistics put the membership of the Soviet trade union organization at 93 million. 'This is practically the entire working class, the whole of the working intelligentsia and numerous sections of rural workers.' See Documents of the 24th Congress of CPSU, supra note 1 at p. 95. To be excluded from the trade union organization is a serious blow for any Soviet worker.

50. For a brief discussion of the interdependence of the trade unions, the government and the Soviet communist party see C. Osakwe, The Participation of the Soviet Union in Universal International Organizations 52-63 (1972).

51. Documents of the 24th Congress of CPSU, supra note 1 at p. 95.

52. I. Smirnov, Profsoiuzi SSSR: 100 voprosov - 100 otvetov [Trade Unions in the USSR: 100 questions - 100 answers], 1972, p. 35.

53. See Ustav Profsoiuzi SSSR [Model Charter of USSR Trade Unions] (Profisdat, 1972).

54. Adopted on July 19, 1973 by a law of the Presidium of the USSR Supreme Soviet and went into effect on January 1, 1974. 30 VVS-SSSR (1973).

55. See Ukaz (law) of the Presidium of the USSR Supreme Soviet: O vozmeshchenii grazhdanami SSSR vyezzhaiushchimi na postoiannoe zhitel'stvo za granitsu, gosudarstvennykh zatrat na obuchenie, [On the Repayment by USSR Citizens, who wish to take up Permanent Residence Abroad, of Money expended on

their Education by the State] 52 VVS-SSSSR (1972).

56. The following table compares the differences in payments for education received at the Moscow State University Law School and at other Soviet Law schools: LL.B.-7,300 rubles at MSU and 3,600 rubles at all other law schools; LL.M.-12,200 rubles at MSU and 6,000 rubles at other law schools; PH.D.-17,700 rubles at MSU and 11,400 at all other law schools. This is the first time the Soviet Government indirectly conceded that there is a clear hierarchy among its universities and that Moscov State University is at the apex of this educational pyramid.

57. See 27 VVS-SSSR (1968). These Principles went into effect on October 1, 1968. The RSFSR adopted its family code (officially entitled Code of Marriage and Family of the RSFSR) immediately after the Federal Principles were promulgated and it went into effect on November 1, 1969.

58. Art. 4 certainly is not a one hundred percent proof against de facto discrimination in this regard. Marriage is a consensual affair and if a Russian father does not want his daughter or son marry a Soviet Asian, for example, all he needs to do is to influence the son or daughter not to consent to such marriage. True enough if the state authority finds out about this and can prove it the action itself will be a violation of the law. But racial or, in fact, any other discrimination, is a state of the mind which is not totally amenable to state regulation.

59. An extended de facto separation, however, might constitute a ground for divorce under art. 14 of the Fundamental Principles.

60. See art. 38 of the Fundamental Principles of Legislation of the USSR and the Union Republics on Health, Dec. 19, 1969, 52 VVS-SSSR (1969).

61. As a practical matter this writer has personal knowledge of instances in which married Soviet women underwent legal abortions without the husband's knowledge not to talk of his consent.

62. The husband, however, without the consent of his wife may not be allowed to petition for a divorce either during the pregnancy of the wife or within one year after her childbirth.

63. The court may not designate more than 6 months as a period during which the spouses should attempt a reconciliation.

64. A decision by a court to deprive any parent(s) of their (his/her) parental rights may be reversed and those rights reinstated if the court later finds it in the best interest of the children to do so.

65. For a detailed discussion of the legal guarantees of these rights through the norms of other branches of Soviet law see: N. Malein, Zashchita Semeinykh prav (The protection of family rights), 3 S.S.L. 35-42 (1972); E. Vorozheikin, Vina kak sub'ektivnoe osnovanie otvetstvennosti v semeinom prave (Guilt as the subjective basis of responsibility in family law), 20 Sovetskaia Institsii 13 (1970).

66. The classical phrase 'all law is public law' was first used by Lenin in a reference to the Soviet legal system and has since provided inspiration for subsequent Soviet doctrinal position that the distinction between public and private law is a myth founded in bourgeois ideology. See Lenin, 29 Collected Works 419 (2nd Ed.).

67. 50 VVS-SSSR (1961). It went into force on May 1, 1962. Art. 14, para.

(u) of the USSR Constitution extends the jurisdiction of the federal government to the definition of the fundamental principles of civil legislation of the USSR and the Union Republics. On the basis of these Fundamental Principles the respective union republics adopt their own civil codes and in case of any conflicts between a provision of the Fundamental Principles and of any of the union republican codes the former shall prevail.

68. For details about requisition and confiscation under Soviet law see F. Feldbrugge (ed.), 2 Encyclopedia of Soviet Law 585-586 (1974); also Vol. 1 of same at pp. 288-290.

69. For details as to the legal enforcement of the right of an author under Soviet law see: V. Chertkov, Sudebnaia Zashchita prav i interesov avtorov (Juridicial protection of the rights and interests of authors) (Moscow, 1972); V. Kamyshev, Izdatel' skyi dogovor na literaturnye proizvedeniia (Author's contract on literary works) (Moscow, 1969).

70. See the Criminal Code of RSFSR, adopted on Oct. 27, 1960 (as amended).

71. For details about Soviet administrative due process see: F. Feldbrugge (ed.), 1 Encyclopedia of Soviet Law 18-30 (1974); A. Korenev, Kodifikatsiia Sovetskogo Administrativnogo Prava [Codification of Soviet Administrative Law] (1970); N. Sulishcheva, Grazhdanin i Administrativnaia Iuridiktsiia v SSSR [Citizen and Administratieve Jurisdiction in the USSR] (1970).

72. See V. Ivanov, Guarantii prav lichnosti v sfere administrativnogo prinuzhdeniia [Guarantees of Individual Rights in the sphere of administrative Enforcement], 8 SSL 55-62 (1972).

73. For a current discussion of the procedural rights of civil and criminal defendants under contemporary Soviet law see: A. Mel'nikov, Sub'ektivnye protsessual'nye prava storon v grazhdanskom protsesse [Subjective Procedural Rights of Parties in a Civil Action], 3 S.S.L. 18-26 (1972); M. Shakarian, Sub'ekti sovetskogo grazhdanskogo protsessual'nogo prava [Subjects of Soviet Civil Procedural Law] (Moscow 1970); R. Gukasian, Problema interessa v sovetskom grazhdanskom protsessual'nom prave [Problems of interest in Soviet Civil Procedure] (Saratov 1070); E. Kutsova, Garanti prav lichnosti v sovetskom ugolovnom protsesse [Guarantees of Individual Rights in Soviet Criminal Process] (Moscow Univ. Press, 1972).

74. For the Procuracy see Boim, Morgan and Rudzinski, Legal controls in the Soviet Union, especially part II, in: Law in Eastern Europe, XIII (ed. Z. Szirmai), Leyden 1966.

75. Adopted on May 24, 1955 by the USSR Supreme Soviet, 9 VVS-SSSR (1955).

76. Adopted on Feb. 12, 1957 by the USSR Supreme Soviet, 4 VVS-SSR (1957).

77. Ukaz [Law] of April 12, 1968; Oporiadke rasmotreniia prodlozheniia zaiavlenii i zhalob grazhdan [On the procedure for handling of citizens' suggestions and protests], 17 VVS-SSSR (1968).

78. Organs of People's Control in the USSR were set up by a law of Dec. 9, 1965, which constituted the earlier organs of Party-State control of the USSR into Organs of People's Control in the USSR, 49 VVS-SSSR (1965).

79. Ukaz [Law] of the Presidium of the USSR Supreme Soviet: Ob osnovnykh

obiazannostiakh i pravakh sovetskoi militsii po okhrane obshchestvennogo poriadka i bor'be s prestupnost'iu [On the fundamental duties and rights of Soviet Militia in discharging their function of protecting Social Order and Fight against Crime], 24 VVS-SSSR (1973).

80. Osnovy zakonodatel'stva o sudoproizvodstve SSSR, Soiuznykh i Autonomynkh Respublik [The Fundamental Principles of Judicial Process of the USSR and the Union and Autonomous Republics], adopted on Dec. 25, 1958. 1 VVS-SSSR (1959).

81. Osnovy grazhdanskogo sudoproizvodstva SSSR i Soiuznykh Respublik [The Fundamental Principles of Civil Procedure of the USSR and the Union Republics], adopted on Dec. 8, 1961. 50 VVS-SSR (1961).

82. Osnovy ugolovnogo sudoproizvodstva SSSR i Soiuznykh Respublik [The Fundamental Principles of Criminal Procedure of the USSR and the Union Republics], adopted on Dec. 25, 1958. 1 VVS-SSSR (1959).

83. V. I. Lenin, 39 Collected Work 156 (4th Russian Edition).

84. V. I. Lenin, 45 Collected Works 198 (4th Russian Edition).

85. V. Boldyrev, Sovetskii Sud. [The Soviet Court], (Moscow 1966) at p. 7.

86. This particular type of compensatory discrimination in favor of these Soviet minority groups has been construed as constitutionally permissible by some Soviet commentators. See L. Voevodin, supra note 4 at p. 263.

87. V. Chkhikvadze, The State, Democracy and Legality in the USSR - Lenin's Ideas Today 294 (Moscow, 1972).

7

T. Koopmans

Comparative Analysis and Evaluation

CONTENTS

1. *Equality as a Problem*

a. A self-radicalizing concept

The five foregoing chapters dealt with quite different problems, even with different kinds of problems. Nevertheless, the legal systems under consideration seem to share one common experience: the efforts for realizing equality principles have come down from the spheres of abstract ideas to those of concrete issues. Conceived as an ethical and theological guideline, the notion of equality first made its way to the family of legal concepts, in order to become then, in the gradual process of penetrating into the day-to-day life of the law, a legal instrument for deciding controversial social problems.

It was Leibholz who summarized this development very clearly, when he wrote, already in 1925:[1]

> 'Modern democracy is characterized by the generalization of the idea of equality. This process seems to represent some sort of historical necessity; but it also shows the inherent tendency of the equality notion to radicalize itself. And the basis of this evolution consists of the abstract and general orientation of the concept itself.
>
> Man in this natural condition, or the notion of man as a personality, or the *'éminente dignité de la personne humaine'* forms the unifying feature, the general link between human beings, and thus symbolizes the element of equality; individual differences may be empirically established, but they fade away when confronted with the idea of equality, although the latter is bound to presuppose the differences. The doctrine derives its impetus from its simplicity and clarity, the more so as it is capable of being boldly stated and implemented.
>
> Although the origin of the concept goes back to Stoic ideals of humanity and to hellenistic mysticism, it was only completely understood by early Christianity, which gave it its full weight. It emerges again in the Digest, had a new appeal to Hobbes, was further developed by Christian Wolff and found its classical and most enchanting form in French 18th century literature (Voltaire, Helvetius, Rousseau)'.[2]

One could only add that the birth and growth of socialist ideas gave new dimensions to the equality concept.

b. The influence of legal thinking

Reviewing historical evidence, we have to admit that egalitarian tendencies make themselves felt with particular force in the 20th century. The causes of this development are of course – like those of any great historical movement – manifold and complex; for a lawyer, it would be hazardous to venture explanations. Nevertheless, some factors might be singled out which have to do with the evolution of law and jurisprudence itself.

First of all, belief in legislation as a main instrument for settling legal questions diminished to a marked degree. The early 19th century legal doctrine professed such a belief, explicitly or implicitly. This belief manifested itself in such different currents of legal thought as constitutionalism, political liberalism, the *'Rechtsstaat'* theory, the movement for codification, the legalistic approach in the fields of private and criminal law – in short, in the idea of 'being governed by law' under representative government. The great commentators of the *Code civil,* like Demolombe and Laurent, translate this general feeling as well as the political writings of Jeremy Bentham. To put it in more historical terms: the inclination to rely on legislation, which was so characteristic of French revolutionary thinking,[3] prolonged itself well into the 19th century; and so did the implicit belief in the effectiveness of legislative solutions to social problems. This set of ideas was first shaken when lawyers came again to realize that law is not merely legislation: in so far, the legal realists in America and Scandinavia and the school of Gény in France worked to the same end. But it received its final blow when the development of social science on the one hand, the experiments with economic policy on the other, brought us the modern conception that law is only one of a series of instruments for governing a society – and that in some cases it may even be a poor instrument. No wonder that in this new climate of thought the solemn declaration of equality principles in constitutions and statutes looked different: as the beginning, and not as the end of the efforts to establish some kind of equality among the citizens.

A second factor reinforced the working of this first one. The conception of 'citizen' of recent literature is not the same as that of early 19th century doctrine. That doctrine considered citizens in the abstract: it was founded on the idea of the autonomous individual, free from all interference except when he consented to it. The *'homo oeconomicus'* of classical liberalism had its counterpart in a *'homo juridicus'*. This conception was silently abandoned during the last hundred years. We seem to start from a different assumption now, which Burdeau eloquently qualified as that of *'l'homme situé'*: man in his situation.[4] Actually, when we think of citizens, we don't refer to men who are defined by their belonging to a certain uniform and abstract type or model, but to men whom we meet in our daily lives – men belonging to families, groups and organizations, and characterized by their professions, their habits, by their tastes and inhibitions, their wants and needs and their ways of looking at life; in short: men conditioned by their environment. It is obvious how the mere statement that all citizens shall be equal before the law conveys a different meaning in the new context. It could easily be applied to the abstract and reasonable citizens who formed the population of much of legal and political literature in the 19th century – citizens of a type that reminds one slightly of some curious mixture of Jefferson and Emerson. Difficulties are bound to arise when we think of equality between Montana housewives and unemployed Negroes in Alabama, between lorrydrivers and stockbrokers, between Indians in a reserve and civil servants in the capital. If basically, few citizens are quite comparable to others, we are to redefine our notion of equality – in whatever sense we use the word.[5]

c. Impact of social developments

Under these conditions, equality problems seem more embarrassing than ever. Indeed, the changes in legal and political ideas and beliefs cannot be isolated from developments in the world of facts; and these had again their own impact on our problem.

A first indication in this direction has already been given in the chapter on France.[6] Modern government rules by management. Attacking problems of unemployment, industrialization, rural and urban development, monetary and credit policy, public health etc. cannot be done by fixing general rules, but by organizing and implementing programs of action – legal and factual – which aim at specific situations.[7] In this climate, the idea that the general character of the law constitutes a guarantee for equal treatment of citizens vanishes – it more or less 'evaporates'. But if the law is only one of the tools for managing a society, and if this management concerns industry, agriculture, commerce and transport as well as education, culture, recreation and the conservation of nature, what is then the distinction between equality before the law, and equality in general? And perhaps we could go one step further: if interventionism by public authorities addresses itself to specific situations, doesn't it then impair the very idea of equality before the law? And isn't this even the case where government measures aim at achieving more social equality among citizens?

American experience seems to confirm this shifting of the scene. It would be naive to propose that the racial issue in the United States concerns only the concept of equality before the law. There is more veracity in the statement that a struggle is going on for equality in political, social and economic matters and – perhaps first and foremost – at the level of human relations; and that equality before the law is one of the weapons in this struggle, that it is a means to attaining a broader end: equal treatment in general.[8] The law is then, whatever its intrinsic quality and significance, instrumental in providing a basis for a comprehensive process of social change.

This thought, however, leaves us with one other query. Why did this happen in some instances, and not in others? It can, for example, easily be perceived with regard to the Negro problem in the United States, but not with regard to Anglo-French relations in Canada.[9] True, the equality principle was embodied in the Constitution of the United States more than a hundred years ago, and it made only its appearance in the Canadian Bill of Rights in 1960, but it is doubtful whether the moment of enactment of broad legal principles can possibly have so far reaching effects upon social developments. Of course, the adoption of the Canadian Bill of Rights can not be isolated from the general course of Canadian constitutional history. It seems extremely probable, nevertheless, that the different ways in which the United States and Canada deal with their minority problems, have deep roots into American and Canadian tradition and culture. It may well be, then, that some profound differences in social structure have animated the particular characteristics of American as compared to Canadian legal developments. If such is the case, a new and most arduous problem must be introduced into the comparative discussion of the protection of equality: that is, that some problems seem, at a certain point of time, ripe for being discussed in terms of equality whilst others are not. And this 'ripeness' may well depend on a great number of diverging elements, legal as well as non-legal.

d. Main themes

So far, we have alluded to some problems which are familiar to students of legal theory: the relation between 'law in the books' and 'law in action', of abstract concepts to concrete issues, of ethical and philosophical views to legal developments, of politics to law, of legal to social problems.[10] They can be discovered throughout the foregoing chapters on national developments, and they form the background to the comparative conclusions which are to follow.

We shall first take up the main themes announced in chapter I: the legal basis of the constitutional protection of equality (par. 2); its legal structure, and in particular the methods of realizing the citizen's claims to equal treatment under the law (par. 3); its social impact in the countries whose constitutional systems have been considered (par. 4); and finally, we shall return to the analysis of the notion of equality, always bearing in mind the general problems which seem so intimately connected with its way through legal history (par. 5).

2. *Legal Basis*

a. Declarations and bills of right

In a first category of countries, the equality principle finds its basis, not in the constitution, but in a declaration or bill of rights. This is not the case in the United States: the 'equal protection of the laws' is established in the XIVth amendment to the American Constitution, which belongs – just as the first ten amendments, together called American 'Bill of Rights' – to the Constitution itself. In this respect, the American situation is entirely comparable to that of the Federal Republic of Germany.

In France and Canada, however, the situation is different. Both countries have a written and 'rigid' constitution, the *Constitution du 4 octobre 1958* and the British North America Act, 1867, respectively; but neither of these documents can be said to contain any broad principle on equal protection. Such principles are stated in the French Declaration of the Rights of Man and of the Citizen of 1789, and in the Canadian Bill of Rights of 1960. And thus some questions arise as to the constitutional significance of these declarations.

In France, the position of the 1789 Declaration has always been somewhat peculiar. Politically, it remained more or less part and parcel of the French tradition, but legally, it had to endure many vicissitudes. First, it figured as a heading to the Constitution of 1791. The subsequent constitution, that of 1793 (or the year I), contained its own, more elaborate declaration of rights, and the constitution of 1795 (or the year III) had again another declaration as its preamble. Further constitutional documents stop this tradition. They do sometimes repeat some of the principles laid down in the different declarations, and particularly the equality principle; both the *Charte constitutionnelle* of 1814 and of 1830 provide in their first article that 'all French are equal before the law, whatever their titles and their ranks.' But they are not introduced by a solemn declaration of rights. The 1848 Constitution, however, again has a preamble reminiscent of its older predecessors. It is the 1852 Constitution which chooses a new model: its first article simply states that 'the Constitution recognizes, confirms and guarantees the great principles proclaimed in 1789, which form the basis of French public law'. The wording is not without importance, because it seems to imply that the 1789 principles belong, by tradition or otherwise, to the body of French constitutional law, and that the new constitutional document had to do nothing but recognizing and confirming these principles.

This model was taken up in the 1946 and 1958 constitutions. The 1946 document is preceded by a long preamble, which forms part of it and which states that the French people 'solemnly reaffirms the rights and liberties of the man and citizen laid down in the Declaration of Rights of 1789 and the fundamental principles recognized by the laws of the Republic'. After that, it sets out to define also some new rights of a social and economic character ('social rights', like the right to trade union freedom, to strike, to equal pay of men and women). And the 1958 preamble provides a link with this code of fundamental rights and principles by its very opening words: 'The French people proclaims solemnly its attachment to the Rights of Man and to the principles of national sovereignty as they have been defined by the Declaration of 1789, confirmed and completed by the preamble to the 1946 Constitution'.

This summing up of the errant course of the Declaration through French constitutions amounts to more than a piece of legal folklore. The French courts have been inventive enough to make use of the references to the 1789 Declaration; availing themselves of constitutional history, they were able to consider the 'rights of man' in their 1789 formulation indeed as constitutional and fundamental principles. Under the 1958 Constitution, the *Conseil d'Etat* set the tone in a famous judgment of 1959.[11] The reference to the Declaration, made in the preamble, has the effect, according to the court, of making the equality principle as stated in the Declaration one of the 'general principles of law' (*principes généraux du droit*); and administrative decisions which violate such principles are illegal and can therefore be annulled by virtue of the general competence of the administrative courts.

The *Conseil d'Etat* only controls administrative action; it cannot annul Acts of Parliament (*lois*), which form on the contrary the basis for its controlling activities. Nevertheless, under the limited powers of judicial review which the 1958 Constitution confers on a special court, the *Conseil constitutionnel*, the same conception of the effect of the 1789 Declaration could make its way. Bills introduced in Parliament run the risk of being annulled by the *Conseil* if they infringe upon the principle of equality as stated in the 1789 Declaration: so much is clear from a decision of 1971, which was already quoted in the chapter on France.[12] Thus, the development of case-law resulted in strengthening the meaning of the equality notion, in changing it from a mere principle to a constitutional guarantee.

Developments in Canada appear less involved, but nevertheless the situation is less clear from a legal point of view. Strictly speaking, the 1960 Bill of Rights is only a federal statute, an Act of Parliament which can legally be repealed or amended by any ulterior Act of Parliament. For the moment, the Canadian constitution is and remains the British North America Act, only to be amended by the British Parliament at Westminster. Still, the Bill of Rights is a pretentious piece of legislation, not only because it embodies very broad principles, but also because its wording seems to imply that it has another status than an ordinary statute. Part I of the Bill of Rights provides indeed that every law shall be so construed and applied as not to violate the fundamental rights and freedoms 'unless it is expressly declared by an Act of the Parliament of Canada that it shall operate notwithstanding the Canadian Bill of Rights' (section 2). This so called *non obstante* clause seems to suggest that Parliament cannot implicitly repeal or amend the Bill of Rights: it can only expressly make an enactment to the contrary. The question raised by this construction is then whether a statute without such an express reservation, which nevertheless constitutes an infringement upon the Bill of Rights, may be rendered inoperative by a judgment of the courts.[13] The Supreme Court of Canada seems to have given an affirmative answer to this question, in its decision *Regina* v. *Drybones*,[14] by rendering inoperative a section of the Indian Act which it deemed inconsistent with the Bill of Rights. This is, however, by no means sure, as the Indian Act was anterior to the Bill of Rights and might therefore be considered as overruled by virtue of the *lex posterior* rule. Unfortunately, the reasoning of the Court majority is not perfectly clear on this point. But as it makes reference to the *non obstante* clause, the decision may have the meaning of accepting the general thesis that the federal Parliament is not only limited by the federal division of powers under the British North America Act, but also by the Canadian Bill of Rights – unless, in the latter case, Parliament itself has expressly declared otherwise. Under these conditions, the *Drybones* case may be a first step towards a system of full judicial review, in which the courts do not only control the boundaries between federal and provincial powers, but also the protection of human rights, and therefore, of the equality principle.

The Canadian Bill of Rights is not drafted in such a way as to include a general rule on equal protection. It only states that certain enumerated rights and freedoms shall continue to exist 'without discrimination by reason of race, national origin, colour, religion or sex' (Part I section 1). But in general, this non-discrimination principle is interpreted as entailing the right to equality before the law.[15] The courts follow the same line, although their appreciations of the meaning of this right to equality may differ from case to case.[16] On the whole, then, Canadian constitutional practice seems to have come somewhat closer to the American model these last years.

b. Constitutions

The constitution itself embodies equality principles in the United States, the Federal Republic of Germany and the Soviet Union, but these principles are differently framed in each of the three documents.

The American Constitution confines itself to enunciating 'equal protection of the laws' in its XIVth amendment. This equal protection clause was, together with the 'due process' clause of the same amendment, intended to prevent discriminations by State governments; taken literally, it does not apply to actions by the federal government. However, due process also figures in the Vth amendment, applicable to the powers of federal institutions, and the American courts are of the opinion that due process more or less implies equal protection.[17] Nevertheless, the XIVth amendment is the only provision which expressly establishes equal protection, and it does so in very general terms.

The Soviet 1936 Constitution, on the other hand, does not proclaim any general principle of equal protection or equal treatment; it only mentions specific instances, like equal access to education, equality in labour law etc.[18] Soviet ideology and Soviet legislation are perhaps more relevant to the equality problem than constitutional provisions, and the chapter on the U.S.S.R. did indeed concentrate on these aspects. As there is no judicial review, and no general judicial control of administrative action, the practice of legislation and administration are necessarily prominent in Soviet law.

The German Constitution is interesting in its effort to combine both systems: a general clause on equal protection and specific provisions on equal treatment in certain situations. Its article 3 states that all persons are equal before the law; but it goes on by saying that men and women have equal rights and that nobody shall be favoured or disfavoured because of his sex, origin, race, language, home country, religion or religious or political convictions; and other articles add some more provisions on equality in specific situations, like article 6 paragraph 5, instructing the legislator to create equal conditions for physical and psychical development of illegitimate and legitimate children.[19] At first sight, therefore, the German Constitution contains practically everything: a general rule on equal protection, a general interdiction of discrimination, and some particular equality rules for specific situations. And this strong legal position of the equality principle is strengthened by other elements of the German constitutional system; the catalogue of human rights embodied by the Constitution is immediately applicable at the State (*Land*) as well as at the federal level; it starts by proclaiming the inviolability of the dignity of man as a basic rule intended to govern all provisions of the Constitution; and judicial protection is assured by judicial review of legislation and by a system of judicial control of administrative action. No wonder, therefore, that German case law offers so many materials illustrative of the legal issues involved in the implementation of equality principles.

However, the question what the courts can do to put equality principles into effect may not so much depend on the wording of these principles in constitutional documents, but rather on judicial attitudes in general. It is obvious that in systems with judicial review of legislation the judge plays a much more active role in giving shape to constitutional concepts than in systems which deny that power of review to the courts. The total lack of case law in our chapter on the U.S.S.R. is characteristic in this regard. We could state the matter more explicitly: if there is no judicial review of legislation, the courts show also a reserved position in cases where they do have the power of interpreting constitutional notions. In the Netherlands, for example, where statutes can not be challenged before the courts for being contrary to the Constitution, the constitutional provision that 'everybody on Dutch territory will enjoy equal protection of his person and property',[20] did not give rise to any significant body of case law: that is, even if municipal bye-laws are challenged because of violation of the equality provision, the courts, although quite competent for annulling the bye-law, show their usual reserve.[21] To put the same argument in another way: differences between American and German case law seem slight if compared to differences between both of them together and case law in countries without judicial review of legislation – whatever the wording of the constitutional provisions in question. This does not mean, of course, that the wording would have no implication at all: we saw, for instance, in the chapter on Germany, how the Federal Constitutional Court may admit certain differentiations under the general equality clause, which would be forbidden if that same differentiation was the object of a specific constitutional provision on equal treatment. More generally, specific equality rules give rise to stricter application.[22] Nevertheless, the United States Supreme Court, in developing its rules on 'suspect classifications',[23] might well come to the same practical results as its German sister-institution. And if it does not do so, this might be due to the kind of social problems that present themselves before the court in litigation, or to prevailing American ideologies, rather than to the general wording of the equality clause in the XIVth amendment.

c. Legislation

In ordinary legislation, it is much more difficult to discover the equality component than in the more general and solemn formulas of declarations and constitutions. Normally, legislators do not consistently make attempts at realizing constitutional or other principles one after another; they come in action, usually, when political pressure, economic difficulties, new social developments, a change of the moral climate or some such factors urge them to solve particular problems. And from this point of view, legislative process in democracies is more chaotic than that under more monolithic government: democratic policy making is more quickly liable to being influenced by popular emotions or public nervousness. This state of affairs may explain partially the very complete and nearly exhaustive way in which Soviet legislation seems to cover different aspects of equal treatment in education, in employment, in economic life etc.

In other countries, there are also occurrences in which the very aim of a statute is to realize equal treatment in a certain field. The American Civil

Rights Acts provide the most notable examples:[24] their professed purpose is to bring about equal treatment of black and white as far as voting rights, or employment, or other subjects are concerned. German law gives further examples: the federal statutes on parental power and on illegitimate children were intended to perform the duties that, according to the Federal Constitutional Court, were imposed on the legislator by the constitutional equality principles.[25]

But mostly, things are not as clear-cut as in these instances. French laws on the legal status of married women, or on matrimonial regimes, may be invoked as examples of legislative efforts to realize equality;[26] but it is by no means sure that French legislators felt any constitutional obligation to do so at that moment. They may have responded to ideas of justice, or simply to political pressure: the result, anyway, is a further realization of equal treatment of all citizens. Most probably, different elements come together in bringing about such legislative steps; and the strength of the equality notion in constitutional tradition is one of them.

In many cases, however, the connection between certain statutes and equality before the law is still more dim. Supreme courts may discover constitutional dimensions in problems like malapportionment of electoral districts,[27] or admission of students to universities;[28] but the odds are that legislative bodies dealing with such problems are inspired by quite a number of considerations, articulated or not, which rank from financial concerns, or considerations of political expediency, to high ideals about justice. Even if constitutional notions or traditions come into play during this process, and do so in an articulated form, it will be extremely difficult to establish their influence, let alone any relationship from cause to effect. Or, to put it into more abstract terms, legislators do not so carefully rationalize their preferences among conflicting values as judges do. This observation is not meant as a reproach – the actual result may be admirable – but simply as a statement of fact that helps to explain why the search for equality legislation is harder than the one for equality cases.

Nevertheless, one could venture the assumption that modern law reform more than once shows the influence of equality notions – from whatever source thay may come. We could refer to enactments in Western Europe about the legal and social position of women and of illegitimate children, about homosexual intercourse between adults, about student participation in university management, about parental power and nationality etc. More specifically, one could suppose that, if certain reforms in Germany were necessitated by art. 3 *Grundgesetz,* the same reforms in other countries might also have to do something with the realization of equality. This is particularly clear in the case of legislation on the status of married women and illegitimate children.

Twilight remains in many areas. Take the case of graduated taxes, with progression of rates on higher incomes. Some would certainly claim that this system is contrary to equality, as it manifestly subjects one citizen to a fiscal treatment which is different from the one applied to another citizen, although the object of the tax may be entirely identical. Others will be as sure in defending the opposite view: equality will be favoured by leveling incomes by fiscal means; or – other argument – high incomes present a situation of fact which is so different from that of low incomes that unequal treatment is justified. In countries with judicial review of legislation the constitutional judge will have the final and authoritative word in this conflict of opinions. In countries which do without judicial review, prevailing ideology or the professed conviction of the legislator may settle the matter. If neither of them does – an assumption which will be true for most Western countries – we can all have our convictions or beliefs but, as lawyers, we can never be sure.

d. Case law

After declarations, constitutions and statutory law, case law is the next formal source of equal protection. Partially, of course, it is not a source in its own right: this is particularly true of judicial review of legislation which tends, at least formally, only to give effect to principles and rules laid down in constitutions. However, we should also examine whether the courts give effect to equality concepts not because such concepts have been fixed by statute or by the constitution, but because the courts consider them as general principles of law.

We saw already that the French administrative courts have a tendency of doing so: equality is, according to their practice, a general principle of law, and its violation is thus a ground for annulling an administrative ruling or decision; but equality holds this position also because it is embodied in the 1789 Declaration of the Rights of Man.[29] Under French law, therefore, our problem does not arise in its pure form.

It does so, however, in English law and in the law of the Commonwealth countries, as far as judicial control of delegated legislation is concerned. By virtue of the doctrine of parliamentary sovereignty, the English courts cannot control any statute, but they do have power to control delegated legislation: if orders or regulations are not authorized by statute, the courts consider them as *ultra vires* and therefore void. But the courts go one step further by assuming that the legislator, or Parliament, never intends that powers of delegated legislation will be exercised in an unreasonable way. Unreasonable regulations can thus be challenged as being *ultra vires*. It is obvious that, under English law, Parliament has full power of authorizing unreasonable regulations, but it is deemed not to have done so unless its intention to the contrary is explicitly and unequivocally laid down in the text of the empowering statute.[30] In order to determine whether a regulation is unreasonable, the courts are having recourse to general principles of law. And it is interesting to note that equality belongs to the first principles to be invoked. According to much quoted words of Lord Russell, unreasonableness exists, 'if, for instance, bye-laws were found to be partial and unequal in their operation as between different classes, if they were manifestly unjust, if they disclosed bad faith . . .'.[31] Commonwealth judges are used to apply the same unreasonableness test to delegated legislation – perhaps under the influence of the Judicial Committee of the Privy Council, which for a long time acted as supreme appellate court for Commonwealth countries; Canadian courts also rely on the British approach in this field.[32]

The British case is interesting for a good understanding of judicial attitudes. In establishing a link between equality and reasonableness, and between reasonableness and legality, British courts seem to admit that equal treatment is essential to the administration of justice. This is hardly surprising. On the one hand, there is a close connection between equal treatment and the idea of justice itself: as H.L.A. Hart puts it, 'treat like cases alike and different cases differently' is 'a central element in the idea of justice'.[33] On the other hand, the notion that similar cases should be treated equally is more or less the general assumption underlying the lawyer's work; it is his first axiom, without which he would scarcely be able to do his duty. In a way, the principle of *stare decisis* in the common law and the idea of codification in civil law countries both reflect this general assumption. Both the application of precedents and of abstract codified rules to new cases must have a certain degree of predictability, for otherwise the resulting uncertainty would be greater than any organized society would be able to bear. Viewed in this light, the principle of equality before the law is self-evident, and the courts will apply it, consciously or unconsciously, without any constitutional or legal underpinning.

If this is true, however, the question remains how this general assumption of equal treatment could be adhered to in times when nobility and clergy had a privileged position in Europe and when Negro slavery existed in the Americas. The answer is of course simply that unequal treatment was legally possible because the cases were thought unequal at that time. The idea of equal treatment – to quote Hart again – 'must remain an empty form . . . until it is established what resemblance and differences are relevant.'[34] If we treat red-haired murderers in the same way as others, but differently the sane and the insane, we start not only from our general assumption of equal treatment of similar cases, but also from an assessment of what is similar and dissimilar.

Although judges will therefore, in their capacity of trained lawyers, tend to apply the principle of equality before the law, their assessment of similarities in the factual situations confronting them depends on legal tradition and on values prevailing in their society, in short on the cultural world they belong to. And in this respect, constitutional or legal underpinning of equal treatment may have the effect of making explicit certain choices between values, and of embodying them into the law. More precisely, one could say that such great historical events as the American Independence, the French Revolution, and the American Civil War and its aftermath resulted in such new choices; the importance of the Declaration of Independence, the Declaration of the Rights of Man and of the Citizen and the post-Civil War amendments to the American Constitution was not so much their bold proclamation of equality principles, but their explicit or implicit manifestation of the irrelevancy of certain dissimilarities. The courts drew only the full consequences of these choices after a considerable amount of time: the XIVth amendment was enacted in 1868, but the series of desegregation cases of the United States Supreme Court started in 1954;[35] the 1789 Declaration found its elaboration in 20th century French case law. The reasons for this time lag are not identical: in France, it took a long time before the *Conseil d'Etat* felt able to interpret its competence in such a way as to include violation of the law, as a general ground, in the notion of '*excès de pouvoir*'; in the United States, the courts were hesitant to tackle the subject of race in a way American society seemed not yet prepared to accept.

We conclude, therefore, that case law shows no reluctance in accepting equality before the law as a general principle, but that its role in determining relevant factual resemblance and differences varies according to diversities in legal tradition and social climate. The mere historical fact that for centuries Great Britain kept aloof from revolutions, and from constitution making, may have had a profound influence on judicial attitudes in this regard. British judges show mostly a very reserved position when it comes to making policy choices. The courts of Commonwealth countries inherited these British attitudes; if they have to make any value choices, they usually couch them in the phraseology of legal positivism and they avoid policy-type arguments.[36] And this makes the embarrassment of Canadian courts with regard to the Diefenbaker Bill of Rights all the more understandable.

e. Relation to private law

There is one subject that still deserves some separate attention: in what way, if at all, the equality principle makes itself felt in the field of private law, in the relations between private persons? This is the problem that German doctrine discerns, and calls the 'third party effect' or *'Drittwirkung'*. The underlying idea is then that equality is one of the fundamental rights (*Grundrechte*) of the citizen and that these fundamental rights are traditionally intended as a defense of citizens against interference of public authorities. In classic thinking about fundamental rights and liberties, their purpose is to protect the citizen against the State, not against his fellow citizen.

The *Drittwirkung* problem then results from two propositions which are both perfectly correct but nevertheless contradictory. On the one hand, modern conditions show that often private persons and institutions possess a considerable amount of power which may as much constitute a menace to the citizen's liberties as do the State's powers. On the other hand, relations between private persons are governed by private law which is in principle founded on the liberty of contract and, more generally, on the autonomy of the parties.[37] Keeping private persons and institutions within the limits of constitutional rights and liberties would obviously amount to a firm encroachment on party autonomy, particularly when one thinks of such rights as the freedom of expression.

The German Federal Constitutional Court tried to strike the balance between these two competing sets of fundamental principles by stating that constitutional rights have their repercussion on the interpretation of the general clauses of the Civil code which delimit and circumscribe in a somewhat vague way the extent of contractual liberty, of the testator's freedom, etc.[38] In extreme cases, violation of equality in a contract, or in a will, may therefore be contrary to good faith, or to public order and morals, but if the case is a more modest one, or less obvious, the principle of autonomy of private parties prevails.[39] It is to be noted that in this opinion equality holds exactly the same position as most other fundamental rights, like the freedoms of expression, of association etc.

From a comparative point of view, it is interesting to check in what form this same problem presents itself in other constitutional systems. Some further thinking may show us that this is a weird question: the problem could arise in Germany in a given constitutional setting, and in a certain legal tradition characterized by a good deal of influence of legal doctrine, which, in its turn, has always been marked by its systematic and somewhat dogmatic approach to legal phenomena. Our search for parallel developments should therefore make allowance for probable distortions of the analysis, occasioned by differences in general legal background.

Nevertheless, some statements can immediately be made. First of all, our problem could be scarcely recognized under Soviet law. The Soviet system of law is much more uniform than the Western legal systems in this sense that it does not admit the existence of any separate set of principles governing the relations between private persons.[40] In a way, it is entirely founded on the preponderance of public law, which at the same time embodies what a Western observer would call political control of private actions.[41] And this observation may lead us directly to a second remark: one could well sustain that British legal tradition presents the opposite feature, in its emphasis on the rule of law which is, in the last resort, the common law, that is, at least initially, private law.[42] Public law has grown, even in England, and British authors draw the consequences from it by admitting that something like 'public law' or 'administrative law' may begin to exist.[43] However, the starting point for any piece of legal reasoning is still some deep rooted feeling that the true law consists of the common law, and not of modern legislation with its administrative procedures, its delegation of powers and its institutional framework. Civil liberties form part of the common law tradition, not of any separate body of constitutional or public law.[44] For Canada, the British North America Act is true to this tradition by presupposing these liberties without making any express reference to them.[45] If, however, civil liberties find their roots in private law itself, the 'third-party effect' problem cannot occur for reasons of pure logic. And the somewhat obfuscated position fundamental rights occupy in Canada after the introduction of the 1960 Bill of Rights, does not yet give any indication as to the possible occurrence of the problem in the near future; at least, Canadian case law gives nothing to go by in this regard.

The French legal system offers a third variant of our problem. The separation between private law and public law is practically complete: public law can avail itself of its own jurisdictions, its own scientific methods and discipline, its own rules and principles.[46] Consequently, the boundary between public and private law is so strict and well-defined, that notions or principles developed in one of the two areas have difficulty in transgressing it. It would be hard, therefore, to find French case law on private law having recourse to the principle of equality or to any of the other rights recognized by the 1789 Declaration. The wording of some of the 'social and economic rights' in the preamble to the 1946 Constitution – to which the 1958 preamble refers – seems to indicate that these rights can be enforced against private persons: thus, for example, the provision that nobody can be disfavoured in his employment because of his origin, his opinions or his beliefs.[47] This provision constitutes, in German legal terminology, a specific equality clause with third-party effect; but its scope is fairly limited. At any rate, it did not find any significant echo in French case law. Cases on trade union freedom find their legal basis directly in applicable labour legislation and don't make even mention of the preamble.[48]

Recently, however, attempts have been made by French legal scholars to come to some rethinking of the problem of public liberties. In this current of thought, the idea that the scope of constitutional rights and liberties would be limited to the relations between individuals and the State, is rejected as erroneous. 'Liberties don't change their nature', writes Mr. Rivero, 'whether they are threatened by public authorities or by private persons; the freedom of expression may be endangered by conformism of employers as well as by that of the government'.[49] This opinion, which admits the third-party effect of all constitutional rights in principle, is not undisputed in France;[50] and it did not yet find its way into French case law. Traditions are tenacious, and it will be difficult to bridge the gap between practice of private and of public law as long as these two areas are so much moving in closed circuits.

The *Drittwirkung* problem did arise, albeit differently clothed, in American case law. We recall that initially the Supreme Court gave only limited effect to the XIVth amendment by means of the 'State action' doctrine, declaring that the amendment restricted only State action and was not applicable to discrimination by private persons.[51] The Court amended this doctrine in *Shelley* v. *Kraemer*[52] when it banned racially restrictive covenants between private sellers and buyers, holding that a court order enforcing such covenants was unconstitutional State action. In fact, this holding boils down to silent abandonment of the doctrine: if enforcement by the courts is State action, relations between private persons are fully covered by the XIVth amendment. Our review of American case law showed, however, that the consequences of the Court's revolutionary step were only gradually worked out, and that this elaboration did not always follow straight lines.[53]

As compared to French and German developments, the American scene offers two distinctive features. First, the Court took the lead, whereas in continental Europe legal doctrine discovered and elaborated the problem. Secondly, the State action doctrine concerned only the XIVth amendment and was in no way part of a general theory about the nature of constitutional rights and liberties. Maybe we are facing here one aspect of that famous pragmatic approach that is so often attributed to Americans. For the problem at hand, this approach might well be fruitful. Generalizing the equality concept, and expanding it to relations between private individuals, could justifiably be done in its own right, without having any recourse to the general nature of fundamental rights. Legal arguments for equal treatment of men and women in employment could certainly be framed in such a way that the nature of such rights as the freedom of expression is not necessarily at issue. Discussions on the nature of constitutional rights in general may be general to such a point, that it is a far cry from coming to the more specific moral and legal arguments that concern realization of equal treatment of individuals by non-public entities.

3. *Legal Structure*

a. Individual actions

It will already be clear from the foregoing paragraph that legal techniques for giving effect to claims for equal treatment are extremely various. Nevertheless, we shall briefly examine if it is possible to make some systematic arrangement. For that purpose, we shall first look into the question what kind of claims individuals can resort to if they feel equal treatment has been refused to them.

The most far-reaching method would consist of a general action for enforcement of equality rights through the courts. German law comes very close to it, because every individual may lodge a 'constitutional complaint' or '*Verfassungsbeschwerde*' when he pretends that public authorities have violated one of his constitutional rights. He should first have recourse to ordinary legal remedies, but if these are exhausted, or don't exist, he can address himself to the Federal Constitutional Court.[54] As the general equality clause of Art. 3 *Grundgesetz* is not only a guide-line to the legislator, but directly applicable and self-executing since 1953, the citizen is thus able to provoke a binding decision on the extent of his right to equal treatment. In German practice, the constitutional complaint is very important. It can also be filed against judgments of the ordinary courts or of the administrative courts, if no further appeal is open, so that it might in some ways be compared to a general final appeal in matters of constitutional rights.

In this latter respect, the constitutional complaint shows some resemblance to the petition for *certiorari* to the American Supreme Court. If a litigant considers that inferior courts – State or federal – have not, or not fully, allowed his claim for equal treatment, he can petition for a hearing of the case by the Supreme Court because of violation of the federal Constitution. However, review on *certiorari* is not a matter of right but of judicial discretion: the Court only 'takes' the case when there are special and important reasons for a hearing.[55] A system, one might say, which is only possible in a country where the judiciary, at least at its highest ranks, enjoys a large degree of public confidence. For the Court not only has discretion in taking or not taking the case, but it gives no explanation for its decision either: after receiving the petition and reading the papers, it simply announces whether it will hear the case or not. Peculiar American detail: this decision does not require a majority of the Court's members – if four of the nine judges think that the case should be heard, *certiorari* is granted. Most cases come to the Court now in this way.

The exercise of discretionary powers to grant *certiorari* tends to assimilate the American Supreme Court in one further aspect to the German Federal Constitutional Court. Initially, the American court was by no means a constitutional court or a court specialized in constitutional questions: it was just a supreme court, and in this regard quite comparable to the British House of Lords or the French *Cour de cassation*. But in the use it made of its discretion, it showed a tendency of taking cases that enabled it to decide constitutional issues.[56] From this point of view, the differences between the specialized constitutional powers of the court at Karlsruhe and the general competence of the court in Washington are certainly diminishing.

Apart from *Verfassungsbeschwerde* and *certiorari,* we met no general action to enforce the constitutional right to equality in the legal systems under consideration. Of course, this does not mean that no action is possible, only that the type of action that is available depends on the specific situation in which the equality issue arose. The entire scale of legal remedies is in principle available to any complainant, according to the procedures that are known to his legal system. Thus, statutes that are alleged to violate equality can be challenged before the courts in the United States and Germany, and to a certain degree in Canada.[57] The claimant should then have standing, which might possibly imply that he must contravene the law first, in order to provoke a prosecution which enables him to put the validity of the statute to the test. In case of administrative regulations, French law gives him a direct access to the administrative courts, if his 'interests' are at stake: he can then petition for annulment of the regulation on the ground of *'excès de pouvoir'*. Individual decisions of the administration which concern him may give rise to a claim for annulment under French as well as under German administrative law. The United States and Canada share the British tradition here: judicial review of administrative action may be obtained from the ordinary courts by means of tort actions against the administrative official concerned, or in certain cases by means of one of the 'prerogative writs' of older English law, like prohibition, *mandamus* or *habeas corpus.*[58]

We should add that the need for an action on the general ground of violation of equality diminishes to the degree that statutory provisions do more to give concrete shape to the principle of equality in different parts of the law. If equality of men and women in employment, or in education, has been minutely worked out in statutes, ordinary litigation can take care of its realization, in private law suits and in criminal proceedings alike. Soviet law, with its emphasis on precise regulation, may reflect such a situation.

b. Groups and class actions

The difficulty is that unequal treatment mostly does not concern individuals as such, but individuals as part of some disfavoured group or minority. Traditional legal approach, particularly in the field of procedural law, seems apt to assume that the law concerns only individuals, and those corporate entities which are legally assimilated to individuals, and that legal remedies are only available to these individuals and entities. The question that occurs to us is therefore to what extent legal action can be taken by groups, or by such associations which consider themselves as spokesmen and representatives of these groups, like consumers' associations, leagues for the rights of women, trade unions or 'associations for the advancement of coloured people', like the N.A.A.C.P. in the United States.[59] Under American law, N.A.A.C.P. could not ordinarily directly bring actions to defend the rights of the American Negro, but often it enabled Negroes to bring important cases before the Supreme Court by providing legal aid.[60] One should not underestimate the significance of this type of action: *Brown* v.*Board of Education*[61] had more important consequences for American Negroes in general than for Mr. Brown personally. By carefully choosing the cases it wished to carry on, the N.A.A.C.P. could thus contribute to the gradual development of the law of equality.

The general rule seems indeed that associations cannot bring law-suits for defending the interests of the groups they profess to represent; but there are some exceptions. First of all, trade unions occupy a special position: in Western countries, because of their power of collective bargaining and the ensuing faculty of litigating in the name of labour, and in socialist countries because of the official status they enjoy. Secondly, French administrative law seems somewhat milder towards associations representing collective interests than our general rule would indicate. If an administrative regulation or decision concerns the interests of a group, and if an association exists aiming at taking care of these interests, that association may file a petition for annulment of the regulation or decision on the ground of *'excès de pouvoir'*. It cannot substitute itself for its individual members by acting if the interests of one or some of them are involved, but it may act if the collective interests of the group are at stake.[62] However, this possibility only exists in case of actions for annulment, not in other administrative suits, like tort actions against public authorities, or, for that matter, in private law actions before the ordinary courts.

The interests of groups might also be taken care of by some official institution that could act in case of violation of these interests. Public prosecutors may have to adopt this function in certain instances, for example if criminal laws forbid certain forms of racial discrimination, or if penal sanctions have been attached to the rule on equal payment of men and women in employment. The Soviet procuracy, the *Prokuratura,* has another function which may be viewed in the same light: it has power to lodge protests against the legality of subordinate legislation and of the orders of officials, and it could thus act as spokesman for groups whose interests have been disregarded. This assumption is not entirely unfounded: some cases seem to indicate that the *Prokuratura,* in protesting the legality of certain measures, more or less takes care of collective interests of certain groups, like grant-aided students, or fishermen working in fisheries co-operatives.[63]

A certain analogy is present in the way German law has organized judicial review of legislation. If a federal statute should violate the equality principle, the government of a *Land* or one third of the members of the *Bundes-*

tag may refer the matter to the Federal Constitutional Court, under the system of *abstrakte Normenkontrolle,* form of judicial review without any 'case or controversy' requirement.[64] The petitioners may file their complaint because they consider the statute unconstitutional in a wholly abstract way, without any concrete motive to their action; but if the statute has given rise to protests by groups which claim the statute disfavours them, the petitioners may in fact be pleading the case of such groups. If the group in question is a large group, or regionally concentrated, electoral considerations could urge *Land* governments or members of Parliament to take the initiative.

c. Effect of judicial decisions

If gaining access to the courts is not always easy, some more difficulties face us when we come to think of the results that can be obtained by means of court decisions.

The first category of difficulties is of a legal nature: what can courts do to foster the application of equality principles? At first sight, their margin of operation appears fairly restricted. They can order direct enforcement of equality rules by sentencing offenders in case of penal sanctions, or by imposing civil liability on public authorities or on private persons if the applicable law of torts permits the court to do so. Neither of these two alternatives is apt to occur frequently. Penal sanctions are rare in this field, and they will only cover the most glaring breaches of equality, such as racist propaganda and similar offences. This is no wonder: the equality principle embodies a rule of conduct which yields different results in different factual situations, and criminal law is not an appropriate means of enforcing fluid rules. Tort liability is, under most legal systems, less rigid than criminal law, in so far as it may be used to uphold rules of social conduct and of common decency; but its actual application depends on numerous other elements (fault, the occurrence of damage etc.), which make it unwieldy for the purpose at hand.

Under these conditions, the most important contribution of the courts is perhaps their negative role, that of prohibiting public action which goes contrary to equality. The invalidity of a statute, and the annulment of administrative regulations or decisions, are the pronouncements of the courts that might keep the legislator and the executive within the boundaries set by the equality principle. But here, we are faced with a new problem: negative steps by the courts may be effective in realizing classical freedoms, like the freedom of expression, because these freedoms consist in principle of rules of non-interference; equality rules, however, are too complicated to be reduced to this category – particularly when they imply, as the German courts hold, a right to an equal share in State performance.[65] Negative steps may prevent unequal treatments from being lawful, they cannot bring about equal treatment. The German Federal Constitutional Court was confronted with this problem.[66] Notwithstanding the broad powers over legislation that are proper to the court, one is bound to draw the conclusion from German experience that in the last resort only the legislature is sufficiently equipped to do the positive steps. In invalidating statutes, the Court may indicate what kind of rules would, in its opinion, be compatible with the equality principle, but it is not able to proclaim such rules itself. Implicit in German constitutional law is the belief – or perhaps the faith – that, at least in the long run, parliaments will do no unconstitutional things and will therefore bring about the legal changes necessitated by the constitution as interpreted by the constitutional court. The question, whether such a belief is founded, cannot be answered in the abstract: the answer depends on political conditions, social climate and legal tradition in which constitutional law-making is embedded. Experience shows, however, that the same belief ended in disillusionment in some countries;[67] but this observation is not meant to imply that there would be any viable alternative.

A second category of difficulties concerning the effectiveness of court decisions is of a more sociological character: if access to the courts can be gained, and if the courts are able to give adequate decisions, what is then the importance of these decisions for the social problems that gave rise to the constitutional issue? We propose to come back to that question when we shall deal with the social impact of equality.[68]

d. The political process

In democratic countries, there is an obvious link between equality and the political process. Political democracy works under the general assumption that political opinions can have equal access to the citizens' minds and that citizens have equal opportunities to express their political opinions. Equal voting rights seem even the very prerequisite for any form of democratic government.

On the basis of this picture, one should expect to come across important laws, cases or assertions on political process in our review of equality in five legal systems; in fact, only the chapters on the United States and the Federal Republic of Germany provided materials in this respect. Even if we make an exception for the U.S.S.R., which does not recognise political democracy in the sense as here defined, the result may appear disappointing. But is it?

First, we have to admit that the American and German cases affect the very heart of the notion of democratic government as it is understood in those countries. This is true of the German cases on subventions to political parties and on the attribution of broadcasting and television time to them,[69] but also of the American cases on the implementation of the XVth amendment to the Constitution, relating to equal voting rights, and particularly of such famous reapportionment cases as *Baker* v. *Carr* and *Reynolds* v. *Sims*.[70] In their aim and in their effect, they involve the essential conditions for democratic government; but in doing so, they stress at the same time the intimate connection between the legal notion of equality and the democratic character of the political process.

French and Canadian law show nothing of the same kind: equality cases may concern important social issues, like the position of Indians and Chinese or access to the civil service, but they don't relate to central problems of political process. Perhaps, we might see an exception to this general statement in such French cases as the *Barel* case, in which equal access to examinations for admission to the *Ecole Nationale d'Administration* was deemed to imply that the competent Secretary of State could not exclude candidates on the sole ground of their communist opinions.[71] Even these cases, however, cannot be said to have the same political importance as *Baker* v. *Carr.*

The reasons for this distinction between the United States and Germany on the one hand, Canada and France on the other, are perfectly clear from a strictly legal point of view: the extent to which judicial review of legislation is possible makes all the difference, as measures which really strike at the heart of the political process will be taken in the form of Acts of Parliament or statutes. In France, the powers of the Constitutional Council – existing only since 1958 – are very limited (they can only be used before the promulgation of the statute and then exclusively at the request of the President, the Prime Minister or the speaker of either of the houses of Parliament);[72] in Canada, the powers of the courts traditionally concerned only the federal division of powers under the British North America Act, and it is not yet clear whether the Canadian Bill of Rights 1960 will bring a significant change in this tradition.[73] In both countries, judicial powers over legislation are slight if compared to those existing in American and German law.

Fundamental differences such as these, however, are not due to accident; they betray broad undercurrents of opinion, which are basic for any understanding of the political and legal system. The Canadian case is the simpler one: Canada shares very much the British tradition with its aversion to leaving political matters to the judiciary. It is built on the assumption that there is a legal sphere for the judiciary, and a political sphere for Parliament and cabinet, and that the wall separating these two spheres should be impenetrable. The question whether this wall actually is impenetrable is open to discussion, but the mere belief that it is, helps to make it so. Some British cases give a fair illustration of this thesis.[74] In France, underlying attitudes are not so easy to define. Initially, there was certainly some trace of Rousseauite thinking, in which any utterance of Parliament was seen as a manifestation of the 'general will', and thus unassailable.[75] This doctrine was joined by the general feeling, prevalent on the European continent for a long time, that political matters should not be left to judges, who have no special qualifications for handling them and who, moreover, do not bear any responsibility for the consequences of their rulings in this field.

And this brings us to the heart of the matter. For in this opinion, the more political the subject is, the less the courts are qualified to tackle it. Thus, it goes counter to a great deal of American thinking, according to which the basic rules of the political process form the very thing that one shouldn't leave to political institutions themselves. It was Mr. Justice Stone who, in a footnote to a 1938 case, seems to have launched the doctrine that a presumption of constitutionality of legislation – then normally adopted by the Supreme Court – should not apply if the legislation in question involved restriction or curtailment of the ordinary political processes.[76] The idea is then that legislation which prevents political processes from operating freely, should be subjected to the most exacting judicial scrutiny; for only if these processes are untrammeled, their products can be considered as embodying the majority will. And it looks as though this doctrine could be the only possible rationale of a so far-reaching political decision as *Baker* v. *Carr*. The judiciary is then more or less the guardian of the rules of the political game.

On this essential point, American attitudes are irreconcilable with those adopted in Britain and France. The gap is not caused by any difference of appreciation regarding the nature of political process, and the role of equality in it, but by a diverging assessment of, and confidence in, the role to be played by political and judicial institutions, respectively. This could be the subject of a separate book, as supporters of both schools of thought are able to mobilize solid arguments. The implementation of the Supreme Court's desegregation cases brought unrest and even civil riots to the United States that political institutions had to cope with – whether they were prepared for this task or not. But the same Supreme Court was able to invalidate legislation on unequal treatment of foreign nationals to a degree many European countries might be envious of. We shall resist the temptation to continue the discussion.

4. *Social Impact*

a. Law and social developments

In his essay on the Soviet law of equality, professor Osakwe made the observation that 'racial or, in fact, any other discrimination, is a state of the mind which is not totally amenable to State regulation'.[77] This statement was made in connection with a rule of Russian family law forbidding discriminatory practices, but its validity stretches far beyond this domain. In fact, it summarizes the problem we are faced with, when we focus attention on the social impact of legal rules and principles concerning equality.

The situation of the American Negro is illustrative in this regard. On the one hand, social practices of discrimination have by no means been banned by statutes or by Supreme Court decisions; on the other hand, the Court decisions constituted one of the mainsprings of comprehensive federal legislation on race relations in the sixties and the early seventies, which made an important contribution to the struggle against racial discrimination.[78]

Obviously, law is not an all-embracing technique of achieving social change; 19th century ideas on the effectiveness of law as an instrument to govern society[79] – still sometimes implicitly present, and occasionally nourished by lawyers and politicians alike – form a dangerous oversimplification. However, common experience seems also to refute the opposite view, according to which the law is only a reflection of social realities and adds nothing of its own. The truth must be found somewhere between those two extremes; it seems to be, as one sociologist put it, 'that law both reflects and in turn influences the course of social change'.[80] This proposition, which we could embellish by speaking of a 'dialectical' relationship between legal and social change, leaves all the options open as to the extent to which the law 'reflects' and in turn 'influences'; but it might well be that that proportion varies according to the social problem concerned, the kind of society giving rise to it, the legal system in question, etc.

Let us try to list some of the variables before embarking on our tour through the social problems that gave rise to equality issues.[81] Before any modification of the law directed at social change can materialize, at least two conditions must be met: there should be some kind of social activity aiming at the achievement of the change, and there should be a cultural climate, in the broadest sense of the term, that doesn't discourage the change or the use of legal tools for achieving it. New rules of law may then be introduced on a minimum basis, that is, without any broad consensus in society being available for supporting its introduction into social life. Even in that case, however, the new rule of law will in some way begin to make its influence felt: most people are, consciously or vaguely, law-abiding; since a rule of law is not only a rule of conduct, but also one that is clearly formulated, emanating from a State whose authority they normally recognize, and enforceable with the help of the State's powers, they begin to obey. This, however, does not tell us much about the actual influence of the rule on the people's behaviour; here, we should make a distinction. In the short run, open defiance of the rule will not be found, if we except the case of civil disobedience to recently introduced rules – which is a rare case. Even without accepting the correctness of legal change, people will tend to conform to it as they accept the authority of the law-giving institution. Thus, in case of legislation on race relations, open forms of discrimination, for instance in public transport or in schools, will disappear, although underlying attitudes or prejudices may subsist. Some rules have no other object than this: their effect is achieved when citizens submit their open behaviour to them, whether they like it or not. However, our example of rules on race relations shows that some laws have farther reaching objectives: they aim at changing people's attitudes, and this can only be achieved, if ever, in the long run. The legislator will not primarily be interested in changing people's attitudes for the moral value of such a change; but certain practices can only be banned if a great many people believe they should be banned. Courts may refuse to uphold racially restrictive covenants between sellers and buyers of houses; but no legal means are available if white owners of houses in a certain area simply refuse to sell to potential Negro buyers. Informally concerted practices form a difficult enemy for any legal system; but at the same time, they are often the most tenacious sustenance of unequal treatment. This is indeed, in a nutshell, the first problem of the effectiveness of legal rules on equality. Readers who are less familiar with racial discrimination could ponder a little while on relations between men and women.

A second difficulty tends to reinforce the importance of this first one. Some legal rules, like traffic regulations, are morally neutral; they have scarcely any emotional content. People's reactions to such rules are, in a way, rational: the observance of the rules is determined by the conduct of others, by traditional patterns of obedience to legal rules, by the chance to be caught by the police in case of contravention, by the amount of the fine to be expected in that case etc. Rules on equality, on the contrary, carry an ethical load and have a high emotional content; and this is particularly true when they have been issued as a reaction against current discriminatory practices. But people will then tend to respond in an emotional and not in a rational way; consequently, the chance to be caught and the sanction to be expected have hardly any influence on their willingness to conform to the rule.[82] In case of strong resistance, efforts to implement the rules will therefore meet with a stubbornness which is not amenable to being influenced by the use of ordinary legal instruments.

The two difficulties we sketched carry their full weight under present-day conditions, now that prevailing egalitarian ideologies make their influence felt in conscious efforts to give a concrete meaning to equality principles in different walks of life.[83] Social problems are bound to arise, because any appeal to equality principles as a means for achieving social change will at the same time question some privileged social position. As the appeal to equality is expressed in terms of justice, and may be supported by legal arguments, vested interests will have to couch their opposition to social change in ideas of a different kind: they will resort to economic arguments, as for example that equalization of incomes necessarily disfavours exertion and that inequality in this field is therefore to the benefit of everybody; or they will point out the risks for internal peace and public order, resulting from social upheavals; sometimes, they will simply be playing for time, in the hope that egalitarian tendencies will subside; and incidentally, they will try to mobilize irrational fears, in particular when racial or political minorities are involved.

For the moment, we may conclude that equality is one of the most explosive notions that a legal system may dispose of.

b. Man and woman

Discrimination on the basis of sex seems to belong to the common heritage of mankind's history. It is not surprising, therefore, that the five legal systems we considered had all to do with the problem in some way:

- in the United States, a proposed XXVIIth amendment to the Constitution, providing that equality of rights shall not be abridged on account of sex, is waiting for its ratification by the States;[84]
- the Canadian Bill of Rights forbids, in its general introduction, any discrimination by reason of sex;[85]
- in the German federal Constitution, the general clause on equality before the law is immediately followed by a specific provision on equality between man and woman,[86] and the Constitutional Court left little room for more flexible applications of this rule;[87]
- the French *Conseil d'Etat* holds since 1936 that man and woman ought to have equal access to public facilities and to public employment;[88]
- finally, the Soviet Fundamental Principles of Labour Legislation created working conditions and social arrangements intended to guarantee equal opportunities to women in production activities.[89]

Voting rights and legal capacity of women have been realized in the five States. Unequalities occasioned by marriage and the family situation have been recognized and are gradually abolished; we saw the evidence when we met such problems as nationality, the exercise of parental powers and maintenance after divorce, most clearly in German law.[90] The hard core of the problem is now situated in the socio-economic position of women, and efforts to realize equality by legal means in this sphere are not always successful.

In this regard, the Soviet Union occupies a special position. Soviet labour law draws the full consequences from biological differences – physical force, maternity etc. – by giving a preferential treatment to women workers as far as labour conditions, maternity leave, dismissal etc. are concerned.[91] A high percentage of women is engaged in productive activities, not only in unskilled work but also in skilled, administrative and academic functions. This situation might indicate that legal rules have the support of a pattern of values which respects preferential treatment as a method for achieving equality of opportunities.

In Western countries, the same arguments might apply: in order to lift traditional barriers to a female share in economic activities, it might be necessary to give some preferential treatment to women in order to compensate for certain attributes with which nature endowed them. We met this type of reasoning in German law on the position of illegitimate children.[92] However, in countries adhering to a system of private enterprise, preferential treatment from a legal point of view might well turn out to be a liability rather than an asset in actual social life: for employers, preferential treatment means higher costs, so that they prefer other applicants to the job; and they have liberty to do so, as the choice of their employees is theirs. Thus, the logic of the economic order traces the limits to law and ethics. Formal barriers can of course be abolished; sanctions may, for example, be attached to the rule on equal pay for men and women in employment.[93] More concealed forms of discrimination, however, can only be countered by the evolution of a pattern of values with a direct impact on social behaviour. For the moment, the assessment of professors Lusky and Botein of the American situation will be applicable to most Western countries: 'The grosser forms of sex discrimination . . . have . . . disappeared; but a heavy cultural residue persists'.[94]

c. Race

In its attitudes to racial problems, the law openly betrays its double-faced being: as the embodiment of sets of norms and values on the one hand, as an instrument for realizing political decisions on the other. Ideally, the two functions work towards the same end, but even a staunch optimist would have to admit that history has examples to the contrary at its disposal. Under the Hitler regime, the law was a mere servant to Nazi power, and legal rules were used as one of the tools to accomplish the extermination of European Jewry. The present non-discrimination clause of the German Constitution is primarily a reaction to this state of affairs.[95] And American law, that formalized the subordinate position of the Negro first, is now a repository of values that permit developments towards growing equality. The same ambiguity can be observed in Canadian case law: restrictive covenants to be used against Jewish buyers were held void, but in cases involving the tiny Negro minority freedom of contract was estimated at a higher worth than prohibition of the discriminatory effects of this same freedom;[96] and older Privy Council decisions on the situation of Asiatic minorities ('Chinamen' and Japanese) were, to say the least, not very clear in their philosophy.[97]

However, American experience in the field of racial relations certainly provides one of the most interesting areas for studying the interaction between legal developments and social realities. This interaction was present from the outset. Judicial decisions and legislative enactments were not made in a vacuum: the initial successes of the civil rights movement resulted from social pressure, exercised by groups of the population which were consciously aiming at social change and which could, for that purpose, appeal to the equality ethos that is so deeply rooted in American society. But in doing so, this protest movement also demonstrated its loyalty to American values and to the American constitutional system[98] – a loyalty which enabled the movement to find the legal channels for its struggle and to use the law as an agency for partially achieving its ends. At this point, however, the success created an impetus which was bound to follow its own course. Legally, because the notion of equality, once vivified, began to manifest its full impact on other social problems than race. And socially, because the very success of the (loyal) protest movement aroused a kind of 'revolution of rising expectations' among the black population, which, in its turn, could be conducive to the birth and growth of more radical protest movements, that were presently denouncing their loyalty to American society and its legal system.

The overriding question is here indeed whether the poor blacks, who were the principal supporters of the radical groups, were in a position to benefit from the achievements of the civil rights movement. Social research shows, for example, that New York City fair housing legislation was profitable to Negroes and Puertoricans of some prosperity, but didn't help the poor black.[99] It seems likely, therefore, that some social conditions should be fulfilled before any legislative scheme that tends to create equal opportunities can be fully effective. In the great American cities, racial problems are aggravated by the fact that the boundary between black and white is often identical with that between poor and rich – a situation which can hardly be ameliorated by legislation on equal opportunities.

A separate social problem subsisted in the American South, where State laws upholding discriminatory practices were backed by prevailing attitudes of the white population and of State and local authorities. Discrimination belonged, in a way, to the traditional Southern social pattern; the Civil War and its aftermath, and the agricultural and industrial crises after World War I seem to have reinforced that pattern – there is some good literature analyzing the causes of this development.[100] In that climate, Supreme Court decisions could not have any immediate social effect; but the indirect consequences were manifold. First, the decisions roused expectations among the black population and gave a new push to the civil rights movement. Secondly, the federal government was obliged to take sides in the ensuing conflict between the Court's authority and the conduct of Southern officials – and it did so without hesitation, resorting not only to legislation, as in the case of the 1964 Civil Rights Act, but if necessary to the use of federal troops, as in the famous case of school desegregation in Little Rock, Arkansas. Finally, the refusal of the Southern States to implement *Brown* v. *Board of Education*[101] caused the Supreme Court to be more and more specific in indicating the kind of policy it expected from the State authorities. It was case law that introduced 'bussing' of children to integrated schools as a method of making an end to segregation; a political issue was made of it during the 1972 presidential elections, but no action was taken afterwards.

Ultimately, desegregation seems to succeed, even in the South.[102] This result could only be achieved, however, because legal decisions were corroborated by social forces and by political action.

d. National minorities

In their approach to national minorities, constitutional systems vacillate between autonomy and assimilation. The latter course is that of the Soviet Union: legally, everybody has the right to education in his own language, but facilities for materializing these rights are often lacking.[103] Thus, the law tends to veil a social reality which is rather directed at russification. Most observers believe that the policy of assimilating non-Russian ethnic groups has been in considerable part successful;[104] recent troubles with the Jewish population may suggest that the success was not complete. The option for autonomy was made by Canada as far as its French-speaking minority was concerned; and this option was more or less imposed on it by its former colonial power, as Canadian independence was subordinated to the organization of a federal form of government which respected the special position of the province of Quebec.

It is an intriguing question why the *'problème québecuois'* did not give rise to legal issues resulting from an appeal to the notion of equality. For the problem – and in this, it resembles the Flemish problem in Belgium – does not concern the relations between a French-speaking Quebec and an English-speaking rest of Canada, but primarily the relation between the French-speaking majority of Quebec and its economically dominant 'Anglo-saxon' minority. The statement that social inequality exists between these two groups, is adamant.[105] Why, then, was the problem not discussed in terms of equality? Maybe our foregoing findings give us some materials that provide the beginning of a reply.

We saw that the American civil rights movement took to legal means and thereby adopted an attitude of loyalty to the American constitutional system. It is not unlikely that the *Québecuois* have no intention of professing their loyalty to Canada, because the option in favour of separation is a more realistic perpective for them than for the American Negroes. They are more concentrated geographically; they don't share only a common language and a disfavoured social position, but also – to a large degree – a common religion, and a way of life which distinguishes them from their English-speaking compatriots. In short, they have been able to maintain something of a culture of their own, and hand in hand with it a proper pattern of norms and beliefs. The American blacks, on the contrary, had no cultural identity to the same extent: they were largely sharing normative opinions and attitudes of the white population.[106] When we look at the two problems from this point of view, we can state that the *Québecuois* form much more a separate group with a separate identity in Canada than the American blacks do in the United States. Any move for legal change implies some loyalty to the constitutional and political system in question; separatism denounces loyalty and denies the legitimate character of the national State and its institutions as a 'fountain of justice' – to use the old English expression. Evolutions in Quebec have not gone that far, but far enough to discourage recourse to any legal change that confirms Quebec's belonging to the Canadian federation.

e. Other differentiations

Other differentiations than the ones we dealt with show similar social problems.

The relation between the rich and the poor is one of the favourite battlegrounds of politics in Western countries, particularly in Europe. Socialist parties and trade unionism form, in a sense, the response to the challenge of this problem; and they achieved, with or without the help of others, impressive results in the field of social security and welfare, better labour conditions and housing facilities, more justice in taxation and education etc. It is questionable, though, whether measures of this type are effective in alleviating the position of the very poor, who, moreover, often lack the power to organize themselves in order to exercise social pressure. Psychological barriers may prevent them from getting engaged in political or social activities.[107] *'Le problème reste entier'*, as the French would say.

Foreigners have to cope not only with a social but also with a legal disadvantage; traditionally, they are not in a legal position to invoke equality rules embodied in a national law which, in principle, is not applicable to them. Soviet law still sticks to this tradition;[108] a national treatment is only given on the basis of treaties that guarantee reciprocity. In the Western countries, however, there is some tendency to soften the effects of nationality and to consider national treatment as the most desirable situation. The United States Supreme Court went one step further, by considering the status of alien as a 'suspect' criterion liable to strict judicial scrutiny.[109] Therefore, aliens could not be disfavoured with regard to welfare benefits, admission to law practice and admission to the State civil service (but not the federal).[110] They are still excluded from the exercise of political rights and, more generally, from political participation, but in a country like Germany, with its huge number of foreign workers, even this exclusion is in discussion now.[111] Here again, however, social reality will require its toll: aliens will hardly be able to enjoy political rights if their residence permits can be withdrawn by the national administration at will.

Finally, we could draw the attention to problems of minors and infants. Reduction of the voting age seems to pass noiselessly, or at least without the emotional resistance that accompanied the introduction of woman suffrage. Equal treatment of legitimate and illegitimate children, recently realized in France and Germany, has been silently received and accepted by public opinion, although it might have been otherwise twenty or thirty years ago. For the situation of minors in employment, however, the same problems occur that we met in dealing with female labour: only the economic system of the U.S.S.R. is able to give full social significance to the equality of opportunities the legislator intends to achieve for minors. Recent experience in the Netherlands, where minimum youth wages occasioned unemployment among the young, appears to confirm this pessimistic conclusion.

f. Conclusion

The industrial society we live in requires a high degree of division of labour, which is accompanied, also in the U.S.S.R., by differences in the quality of performance and, concomitantly by differences of income. These differences may lead to differences of property, of education, of knowledge. Such differences form part and parcel of the economic system we seem to adhere to, in the East as well as in the West; they cannot be abolished by decree. The law may, nevertheless, neutralize the attendant circumstances. If the existence of privileged economic 'achievement groups'[112] is given, it should at least be put under guard. Legal instrumentalities may help to prevent that considerations derived from irrelevant qualities like origin, colour, sex, race, opinion etc. govern admission to privileged groups. They may also help to create equal opportunities in education and culture, which contribute to disappearance of social rigidity and caste building. They may finally help to enhance possibilities for non-industrial *élites*, in the field of the arts, literature, music, science etc., which, thank God, survived all world-wars, economic crises and industrial rages until now. As long as Mr. Salvador Dali can be an *élite* of his own, the world is one grade less unhappy.

Consequently, the tasks of the law are modest if compared to the social problems involved. That even these modest tasks are very hard to accomplish, may be clear from our foregoing observations.[113]

5. *Conceptual analysis*

a. Equality and generality

Initially, the notion of equality before the law only confirmed the decision that an end had been made to privileged or underprivileged positions, like the special situation of nobility and clergy in France, or slavery in the United States, and that this decision was irrevocable. The law should be the same for everyone, irrespective of status, race, religion or political conviction. It was this notion that was embodied in the 1789 Declaration of the Rights of Man and in the XIVth amendment to the American Constitution; we find it again in the Diceyan concept of 'formal equality' (as professor McWhinney labels it) which had a profound influence on Canadian legal thinking; and we found the same concept in a leading Soviet legal encyclopedia.[114]

The main charm of the equality problem is that this simple notion, limited though it was in its initial meaning, started a new life at a certain point in time. However, the patterns of this new life were so varied, that it is sometimes difficult to recognize the original concept. One is even tempted to speak of different lives, diverging from time to time and from place to place. Nevertheless, we shall make some attempts at discovering the basic features that the concept could retain in its waltzes through recent legal history; but we ask the reader's indulgence for the result.

b. Equality and non-discrimination

Equality before the law, in the sense just mentioned, seems closely akin to the idea of non-discrimination. It could therefore provide a basis for what American authors call 'the attack on caste barriers'.[115] It could, in the United States, be used for the victory over the 'separate but equal' doctrine and, more generally, for the struggle for Negro rights. And that use hardly implied any extension of the initial meaning of the concept; but from that point onwards, the problems begin to arise. Non-discrimination may be a clear-cut notion in some paradigmatic instances, its application is very uncertain in borderline cases.

The principal difficulties can be reduced to two categories. First, the law can impossibly be the same for everybody, it will necessarily have to draw some boundaries and to make some distinctions and classifications. The most obvious examples are the professional laws, like the Commercial code in France, promulgated only some years after the 1789 Declaration. However, when the law recognizes the existence of special regimes for particular groups, the non-discrimination principle gets a different and more complicated meaning: it then implies that the distinctions and differentiations made by the law must be justified by the nature of the matter to be dealt with. We saw that connotation of equality very clearly in the French case which refused to consider geographical origin as a reason for admitting students to faculties of medicine.[116] Non-discrimination then does not mean non-distinguishing; it means that only certain motives may justify the distinctions. The second category of difficulties makes for a further complication: in order to promote true equality in the social sense of the word, it may be necessary to give a privileged legal status to certain disfavoured groups. We encountered this problem in German legislation on illegitimate children, in Soviet laws on female workers, in Canadian legislation on Indians and in some other instances. As the law cannot turn a blind eye to social realities, its notion of non-discrimination has again to be reviewed: in defining equal treatment, it should take account of the social effects of legal rules and decisions.

Central to both categories of difficulties is the question: what is equal to what? If it is clear that identical situations have to be treated in an equal way, it is by no means clear at what moment situations stop being identical. And more specifically: is this judgment, on the identity of factual situations, primarily a political or a legal one? Probably, it is both; but then the real issue is how much discretion the judiciary will leave to political institutions. Our evidence from the United States, Germany and France shows that this is indeed the starting-point for judicial action: it is up to the discretion of the legislature, or of the administration, to draw the distinctions, but the courts trace certain limits to this discretionary power. From this point onwards, however, approaches are divergent. For the German Constitutional Court, discretion ends where the distinctions drawn by the legislator are 'arbitrary', that is unreasonable, not resting on objective grounds. And sometimes, this approach leads the court to a search for the reasons that the legislator may possibly have had, so that the 'reasonableness' of these reasons can be verified; the case of the Baden–Württemberg Fire Service Act provided a good example.[117] A distinction is, however, always unreasonable when it goes counter to one of the specific equality provisions of the German *Grundgesetz*, like that on the equal position of men and women. It is this latter idea, that distinctions on certain grounds ought to be subject to the most strict scrutiny, which seems basic to the American Supreme Court's attitude. Certain classifications are, in the eyes of the Court, 'suspect', which means that they 'bear a far heavier burden of justification'.[118] This justification may then be found in a 'compelling State interest' which is promoted by particular treatment of a specified group.[119] And that standard enabled the Court to condemn distinctions between residents and non-residents for welfare purposes, and discrimination against a hippie commune. Perhaps, the difference with the German approach is less important than it appears at first sight: the American examples suggest that the Court, in considering certain classifications as 'suspect', checks whether the object of the classification has to do something with the object of the legislation in question, that is, whether the distinction is 'arbitrary' or not.

Thus, non-discrimination has, in the hands of the courts, a legal and a political component. The legal one involves that no classification of legal subjects with a view to different treatment is allowed, unless that classification finds an objective basis in the applicable rules, and the matters they deal with, themselves. The political one implies that no discrimination can exist where overriding considerations of public interest necessitate unequal treatment: the American case law terms it as 'compelling State interest', but the *Conseil d'Etat* adopted the same idea when it held that the general interest may impose a separate treatment of certain groups without impinging on the notion of equality.[120] For French courts, the problem consisted particularly of the tendency of modern economic legislation, and of urban planning or industrialization schemes, to descend into a great many differentiations. The very importance of this kind of measures lies in its selective character; and the selection of the regions, enterprises or persons to be favoured is inherently political. The courts can only interfere if there is a manifest misuse of power, for example if the real purpose of selective measures is not to promote industry in a certain region, but the personal interests of a senator or a prefect (*détournement de pouvoir*).

Modern welfare State mechanisms add to the difficulties. If the arts are sponsored by the State, who is then eligible for State subventions? More specifically, does non-discrimination imply that anybody producing what he considers as 'art' himself, can claim his share? Obviously, a sound financial management suggests the contrary; but it doesn't help much in finding the guide-lines for making distinctions between artists and artists, or between artists and pseudo-artists. The law will withdraw here to its second line of defense: institutional safeguards should be found if the substantive questions are too ticklish. Non-discrimination means that the law should objectify, and if the subject matter defies objective standards, some form of objective treatment can be found in the ways of structuring the decision making process. Here again, the ultimate limit to the discretion of decision makers consists of the notion of 'arbitrariness' as the Federal Constitutional Court understands it; decisions may be arbitrary by their contents, but also by the way they have been brought about.

Non-discrimination is therefore a purely legal notion only in very clear cases; normally, its dimensions can only be established by an interplay of legal and political considerations.

c. Equality and liberty

Lincoln's famous word that 'the sheep and the wolf are not agreed upon a definition of liberty' suggests that the notions of liberty and equality are interdependent. An impressive body of political doctrine holds that in the last resort the two notions are incompatible.[121] Perhaps, one could reduce this apparent contradiction to one central question, viz. whether equality reinforces liberty or ultimately destroys it. This question is of course too complicated and too speculative to be resolved here; nevertheless, in our foregoing chapters we found some materials which may help to clarify things.

Equality reinforced liberty in different ways. First, in some case law, the non-discrimination principle was employed as a tool for protecting the freedom of opinion and of expression; the most notable example was the French *Barel* case.[122] Unequal treatment based on political or religious convictions is nearly always 'arbitrary' or 'suspect'; this way, application of the equality principle is apt to foster political and religious liberty. Secondly, the American Supreme Court made a conscious attempt at promoting equal treatment through extension of the general constitutional liberties.[123] Here, reinforcement worked the other way round: protection of constitutional liberties was used as a tool for achieving equal treatment, particularly of the black population. In the cases, one could therefore observe a mutual reinforcement of each other by liberty and equality.

At another level, we could also illustrate the intimate connection between the two. Liberty can be expressed in terms of equality: no political or religious liberty exists where the freedom of opinion and of expression is reserved to one confession or to some convictions. This is the very reason why that liberty can't be said to exist in the Soviet Union. But we could also express equality in terms of liberty: this was done by Arndt when he noticed that equality constituted one of the most fundamental freedoms, namely the freedom to be different without being disfavoured by the law for that reason.[124] This opinion is founded on a choice, in its appraisal of values; but it is an attractive choice: it goes back to the same humanist and libertarian tradition that stood at the cradle of the 1789 Declaration of the Rights of Man, and of the American Bill of Rights.

We did not find any direct evidence of a contradiction between equality and liberty in the reports on the five legal systems we examined. However, the development of German case law on equality led some German authors to questioning its positive value in the long run: they wondered whether socializing or collectivist tendencies would not, if politically strengthened, be destructive of liberal constitutionalism.[125] Would it? In politics, future developments are even more unpredictable than in other fields of human activities; but much seems to plead for Dr. Klein's assessment[126] that harmony between liberty and equality is not so much a question of political ends to be attained, but rather of methods to be used for it. The thesis of ultimate incompatibility is not founded on the intrinsic properties of the principles of equality and liberty, but in social and political consequences that would probably result from an 'overdose' of equality. The occurrence of such consequences is uncertain; we can therefore have different judgements, or creeds, as to its probability; we can also, whatever our judgments or creeds, help to promote developments which enable possible transitions to a more collectivist type of society to be made without colliding with equal exercise of traditional liberties.

d. Equality and justice

Finally, some words should be said on the relation between equality and justice. Earlier, we concluded already that equal treatment of similar cases is not only a general assumption underlying the lawyer's work, but is also a central element in the idea of justice.[127] This conclusion is not only shared by legal philosophers like Radburch and Hart, and by a leading Soviet scholar like professor Voevodin,[128] it can also be found back in recent literature on moral philosophy.[129]

The question, however, which case is similar to which other case, cannot be resolved by legal or moral philosophy. The thought that it could be resolved by positive law, or by lawyers' craftmanship, would perhaps be reassuring. Our research showed us, however, that such is not the case: the similarity of cases and situations depends on changing social realities and on variable moral judgments – legal arguments come into play, but so do political and purely moral arguments. We saw also that in this interplay the law played its double role: that of obedient servant to the political system it is part of on the one hand, that of body of values created by an international and historical evolution on the other. In its latter role, it assigns a place to political decisions and it traces the limits to their scope; in its former role, it duly translates political decisions in applicable legislation and case law. As part of the political system, it has to be flexible: 'some play must be allowed for the joints of the machine', as Mr. Justice Holmes put it.[130] But as a true embodiment of traditional values, it has to be tough, and therefore to look for reasons, for argument, for objectivity: only argued law is tough law.[131]

In some way, then, our research showed us the law in its poverty and in its wealth. The notion of equality before the law cannot be implemented by the law alone; but the law is instrumental in banning distinctions and classifications for which no rational justification can be found. Thus, it may contribute to realizing a situation in which equality is not only a central element in the idea of justice, but also in the administration of justice.

NOTES

1. Gerhard Leibholz, *Die Gleichheit vor dem Gesetz, eine Studie auf rechtsvergleichender und rechtsphilosophischer Grundlage* (Berlin, 1925; 2nd. ed., Munich-Berlin 1959), p. 24.

2. Author's translation.

3. See Saint Just, *L'esprit de la révolution,* seconde partie, chapitre III; Roussau, *Du contrat social,* livre II, chapitre 4; Montesquieu, *L'esprit des lois,* livre Ier chapitre 3. See also art. 6 Declaration of the Rights of Man and of the Citizen, 1789, and Böhtlingk-Logemann, *Het wetsbegrip in Nederland* (Alphen aan den Rijn, 1966; How to define a statute in the Netherlands), par. 1-11.

4. The expression was introduced in Burdeau's *Traité de science politique,* tome VI (Paris 1956) par. 8-13. See also George Burdeau, *La démocratie* (Brussels-Neuchâtel, 1956, new edition Paris 1966), chapitre 3.

5. See also Carl J. Friedrich, *La crise de l'égalitarisme,* in: Buch, Foriers, Perelman (editors), *L'égalité* (Brussels, 1971), p. 306.

6. *Supra,* chapter 5, particularly the Introduction.

7. See on this development, generally, Wolfgang Friedmann, *Law in a changing society* (1959, now in Penguin), chapter I.

8. *Supra,* chapter 2, particularly par. III.

9. *Supra,* chapter 3, particularly the concluding paragraphs.

10. Reference should in particular be made to Julius Stone, *Social dimensions of law and justice* (London, 1966).

11. Conseil d'Etat 26 June 1959, *Syndicat général des ingénieurs-conseils,* Dalloz 1959, 541. See also Maxime Mignon, *La valeur juridique du Préambule de la Constitution selon la doctrine et la jurisprudence,* Dalloz 1951 Chr. XXX.

12. *Supra,* chapter 5, note 76. See on this decision also James E. Beardsley, *The Constitutional Council and constitutional liberties in France,* 21 American Journal of Comparative Law 431 (1972).

13. See on this question W. B. Tarnopolsky, *The Canadian Bill of Rights* (Toronto, 1968), pp. 66-89; S. B. Ybema, *Constitutionalism and civil liberties* (Leyden, 1973), pp. 85-90 and 210-226.

14. *Supra,* chapter 3, note 18. See also Ybema, o.c., pp. 222 *et seq.*

15. See J. C. Smith, *Regina* v. *Drybones and equality before the law,* 49 Canadian Bar Review 163 (1971).

16. E.g. *Regina* v. *Gonzales* (1967), 32 D.L.R. (2nd) 290, as compared to *Drybones* (see note 14).

17. *Supra,* chapter 2, particularly the Introduction.

18. *Supra,* chapter 6, par. I.

19. *Supra,* chapter 4, par. I-1.

20. Art. 4 *Grondwet voor het Koninkrijk der Nederlanden.*

21. See Hoge Raad 12 febr. 1940, Nederlandse Jurisprudentie 1940 no. 622 (street walking case).

22. *Supra,* chapter 4, par. II-5 and 6.

23. *Supra,* chapter 2, par. III-B.

24. See, about the Acts, *supra,* chapter 2, par. IV-B.

25. See *supra,* chapter 4, par. III-1.

26. *Supra*, chapter 5, par. I.
27. *Baker* v. *Carr*, chapter 2, note 125.
28. *Numerus clausus,* chapter 4 note 186.
29. See note 11.
30. See on this problem H. W. R. Wade, *Administrative law* (3rd. ed., Oxford, 1971), ch. IX; Gordon J. Borrie, *Elements of public law* (London, 1967), ch. IX.
31. *Kruse* v. *Johnson* (1898) 2 Q.B.D. 91.
32. See Edward McWhinney, *Judicial review* (4th ed., Toronto, 1969), in particular p. 13-30, 49-60 and 115-120.
33. H. L. A. Hart, *The concept of law* (Oxford, 1961), p. 155.
34. Hart, *eodem.*
35. *Supra*, chapter 2, par. II.
36. See McWhinney, as quoted in note 32, p. 240-243.
37. See for example Theodor Maunz, *Deutsches Staatsrecht* (19th ed., Munich, 1973), par. 14-11.
38. *Supra*, chapter 4, par. II-8.
39. See the examples quoted in chapter 4, par. II-8.
40. See Leon Boim, *Party-State control in the Soviet Union,* in: Boim-Morgan-Rudzinsky, *Legal controls in the Soviet Union* (Leyden, 1966; Series Law in Eastern Europe no. 13), p. 11-101, especially the conclusions.
41. See also *supra*, chapter 6, particularly the Introduction.
42. The *locus classicus* is of course Dicey's famous work, *Introduction to the study of the law of the constitution* (London, 1885).
43. See the titles quoted in note 30.
44. See also Roscoe Pound, *The spirit of the common law* (Boston, 1921), ch. IV.
45. See Ybema, quoted in note 13, at p. 84-85.
46. See André de Laubadère, *Traité élémentaire de droit administratif,* vol. I (5th ed., Paris, 1970) no. 2-4, 26 and 29; Maurice Duverger, *Droit public* (5th ed., Paris, 1968), Introduction.
47. Section 5 of the preamble to the *Constitution du 27 octobre 1946*.
48. Example: Cour de cassation 20 Nov. 1959, *Compagnie industrielle des téléphones* v. *Dame Papaux,* Bulletin IV no. 1162.
49. Jean Rivero, *Les libertés publiques,* vol. I (Paris, 1973) p. 166. See also Jean Rivero, *La protection des droits de l'homme dans les rapports entre personnes privées,* in: *Liber amicorum discipulorumque R. Cassin,* vol. III (Paris, 1971), p. 311.
50. See P. Braud, *La notion de liberté publique en droit français* (Paris, 1968), p. 72. Also, implicity, Hauriou-Sfez, *Institutions politiques et droit constitutionnel* (Paris, 1972) ch. III-II par. 2.
51. *Supra*, chapter 2 par I.
52. Quoted chapter 2 note 23.
53. *Supra*, chapter 2 par. II.
54. *Supra*, chapter 4 par. VI-A; *Grundgesetz*, art. 19 par. IV; *Bundesverfassungsgerichtsgesetz* (Act on the Federal Constitutional Court) sec. 90 et seq.
55. See Marc A. Franklin, *The dynamics of American law* (Mineola N.Y., 1968) p. 157-159.

56. See Mauro Cappelletti, *The significance of judicial review of legislation in the contemporary world,* in: *Ius Privatum Gentium, Festschrift für Max Rheinstein* (1969) p. 161.
57. See par. 2-a.
58. See Wade, quoted in note 30, ch. III; Gellhorn and Byse, *Administrative law* (Brooklyn N.Y., 1960), ch. III-4.
59. See on this organization *supra* chapter 2 par. II.
60. *Supra,* chapter 2 par. III-A.
61. *Supra,* chapter 2 note 26.
62. See Letourneur, Bauchet and Méric, *Le Conseil d'Etat et les tribunaux administratifs* (Paris, 1970), p. 132; de Laubadère, quoted note 46, no. 862; Jacques Puisoye, *Le contentieux administratif* (Paris, 1969) no. 98.
63. Glenn B. Morgan, *The protests and representations lodged by the Soviet Procuracy against the legality of government enactments, 1937-1964,* in: Boim-Morgan-Rudzinski, quoted note 40, nos. 59 and 72.
64. See *supra,* chapter 4 par. VI-B-2a; Maunz, quoted note 37, par. 31-IV.
65. See *supra,* chapter 4 par. II-7.
66. *Supra,* chapter 4 par. VI-B-2b.
67. See, for South Africa, McWhinney, quoted note 32, ch. 10.
68. *Infra,* par. 4.
69. See *supra* chapter 4 notes 238-240.
70. *Supra* chapter 2 notes 125 and 127.
71. *Supra,* chapter 5 note 8. Compare also *Darmon, eodem* note 31.
72. Art. 61 Constitution 1958. Since 1974, 60 members of Parliament may also take the initiative.
73. See par. 2-b; McWhinney, quoted note 32, ch. 4.
74. See, e.g., *Mortensen* v. *Peters,* (1906) 8F (Justiciary Cases) 93 and *Blackburn* v. *Attorney General,* 9 Common Market Law Review 94 (1972).
75. See also Dorothy Pickles, *The government and politics of France,* vol. I (London, 1972), p. 5-17.
76. *United States* v. *Carolene Products Co.,* 304 U.S. 144 (1938), at 152.
77. *Supra,* chapter 6 note 58.
78. *Supra,* chapter 2 par. IV-B.
79. See par. 1-b.
80. Edwin M. Schur, *Law and society, a sociological view* (New York, 1968), p. 136.
81. We borrow some ideas from Schur, op. cit.
82. See also Karl-Dieter Opp, *Soziologie im Recht* (München, 1973), p. 193-207.
83. See par. 1-a.
84. *Supra,* chapter 2 par. III-B.
85. Act for the Recognition and Protection of Human Rights and Fundamental Freedoms, (1960) 8-9 Eliz. II ch. 44, section 1.
86. *Grundgesetz,* art. 3 s. II.
87. *Supra,* chapter 4 par. II-5a.
88. *Supra,* chapter 5 par. II-A and par. III-A.
89. *Supra,* chapter 6 par. II-B.

90. See note 87.
91. See note 89.
92. *Supra*, chapter 4 par. II-5c.
93. See, for France, chapter 5 par. I. Compare also art. 119 of the E.E.C.-Treaty, which is still the object of much discussion.
94. *Supra,* chapter 2 par. III-B.
95. *Supra,* chapter 4 par. II-5b.
96. *Supra,* chapter 3 notes 7 and 8.
97. *Eodem* notes 12 and 13.
98. See also C. J. M. Schuyt, *Recht, Orde en Burgerlijke Ongehoorzaamheid* (Rotterdam 1973), ch. 3 par. II (English edition forthcoming: *Social Order, Law and Civil Disobedience,* Rotterdam 1975).
99. See H. Goldblatt and F. Cromien, *The effective social reach of the fair housing practices law of the City of New York,* 9 Social Problems 365-370 (1962).
100. See particularly W. J. Cash, *The mind of the South* (New York, 1941).
101. *Supra*, chapter 2 note 26.
102. See the figures at chapter 2 par. II.
103. *Supra,* chapter 6 par. II-C.
104. E.g. Almond and Powell, *Comparative politics, a developmental approach* (Boston-Toronto, 1966) p. 275.
105. See the Royal Commission's Report, quoted chapter 3 notes 19-21.
106. From this point of view, it is interesting to read Eldridge Cleaver's *Soul on ice* (New York, 1968).
107. For a good sketch of the psychology of poverty, see Oscar Lewis, *The children of Sanchez* (Penguin, 1964).
108. *Supra*, chapter 6, par. I-C.
109. *Supra*, chapter 2 par. III-B.
110. Chapter 2 notes 115-117.
111. *Supra,* chapter 4 par. IV.
112. On the importance of economic achievement in modern society, see for example Harry M. Johnson, *Sociology, a systematic introduction* (London 1966), p. 241-247.
113. For the entire par. 4, the author relied heavily on research work done by Mr. J. F. Bruinsma, assistant to the Leyden Faculty of Law, to whom he is greatly indebted.
114. *Supra*, chapter 6 note 9.
115. *Supra*, chapter 2 par. II.
116. *Jourde et Malleville,* chapter V note 13.
117. *Supra,* chapter 4 note 31. It is interesting to note that the American Supreme Court followed a same type of reasoning in *Eisenstadt* v. *Baird,* 405 U.S. 438 (1972).
118. *McLaughlin* v. *Florida,* chapter 2 note 79.
119. *Shapiro* v. *Thompson,* chapter 2 note 82.
120. *Supra*, chapter 5 par. III-A-a.
121. See Tocqueville, quoted chapter 5 note 7. On Bodin, see John Plamenatz, *Man and society* vol. I (London, 1963) ch. 3. For a 20th century appraisal in the

same sense: Walter Rathenau, *Von kommenden Dingen* (in: Rathenau's Schriften und Reden, Frankfurt, 1964).

122. *Supra,* chapter 5 note 8.

123. *Supra*, chapter 2 par. III-A.

124. Quoted chapter 4 note 284.

125. See *supra,* chapter 4 par. V-4.

126. *Eodem.*

127. See par. 2-d.

128. Voevodin, as quoted chapter 6 note 4, at p. 283.

129. See John Rawls, *A theory of justice* (Cambridge Mass., 1971), particularly ch. 11, 13 and 17.

130. *Missouri, Kansas and Tennessee Railroad* v. *May,* 194 U.S. 267 (1904).

131. Thus Megarry, J., in *Cordell* v. *Second Clanfield Properties Ltd.,* (1968) 3 All E.R. 746, a British case.